SANTERÍA STORIES

LUIS MANUEL NÚÑEZ

SANTERÍA STORIES

SPRING PUBLICATIONS, INC.
PUTNAM, CONNECTICUT

Copyright © 2006 by Spring Publications, Inc.

Published by Spring Publications, Inc.
Putnam, Conn.
www.springpublications.com

Inquiries should be addressed to:
PO Box 230212
New York, N.Y. 10023
editor@springpublications.com

Distributed by The Continuum International Publishing Group
80 Maiden Lane, Suite 704
New York, N.Y. 10038
Tel: 212 953 5858
Fax: 212 953 5944
www.continuumbooks.com

First Edition 2006

Printed in Canada

Design: white.room productions, New York

Library of Congress Cataloging-in-Publication Data

Núñez, Luis Manuel.
    Santeria stories / Luis Manuel Núñez. — 1st ed.
        p. cm.
    Includes bibliographical references.
    ISBN-13: 978-0-88214-567-9 (pbk. : alk. paper)
    ISBN-10: 0-88214-567-3 (pbk. : alk. paper)
    1. Santeria. I. Title.

BL2532.S3N87 2006
299.6'7413—dc22
                                                    2006027607

∞ The paper used in this publication meets the minimum requirements of
the American National Standard for Information Sciences — Permanence of
Paper for Printed Library Materials.
ANSI Z39.48-1992.

CONTENTS

THE ORISHÁS

Representation of **Elegguá** or **Eshú**
Photo: Solar (shahmai.org)

INTRODUCTION

These are some of the stories told in Santería (Osha or La Regla, as it is formally known), a widely practiced religion resulting from the syncretism of African religion and Catholicism. Yorùbá elements predominate in Santería since a large number of Yorùbá slaves were brought to the Caribbean basin by the Spanish.

The Yorùbá are a people native to Nigeria. They have a very sophisticated culture. Their religion is intrinsically woven into the fabric of their lives. Yorùbá religion was, and is, intimately tied to a concept of family, those living and the dead. Control over natural forces is attributed to the ancestors. Those with ashé (power) were transformed into divine beings, Orishás. These Orishás, and the stories of their actions and conflicts, came to the new world with the slaves.

A peculiarity of Spanish culture allowed these stories to survive. By 1390 there existed in Seville organizations of slaves presided by their own majors know as cabildos. These cabildos were part of the cultural legacy left by over 800 years of Islamic occupation of Spain. The institution of the slave cabildo was taken to America during the Spanish conquest. It was not only introduced to Cuba, but also to all Spanish and Portuguese colonies with a large slave population. The first record of a cabildo in Cuba is in 1598.

Following the pattern established in Spain, the cabildos were mutual-help associations of native-born Africans and their

11

Cuban-born descendants. Most or all members of each cabildo came from the same tribe or cultural area and spoke the same language. Yorùbás associated with Yorùbás and became Lukumí, Congolese with Congolese, becoming Congo. Dahomians united with Dahomians, becoming Abakua.

Membership was not limited to slaves. Men and women who had bought or been given their freedom, as well as their descendants, were able to belong to a cabildo if they wished to do so.

Every Sunday, the members of the cabildos gathered to dance their secular and sacred dances, retell the myths and stories of their people and perform their sacred ceremonies. The cabildos also organized carnivals and festivals, during which, the slaves paraded images of their African Orishás. Scandalized, the Catholic authorities prohibited the images. The members of the cabildos then adopted the figures of the Catholic saints as representations of their Orishás.

The Catholic authorities finally realized that their images were being used in African religious ceremonies. They prohibited the presence of Catholic images in the cabildos. But it was too late. By the time the authorities acted, the slaves had accepted the old Orishás in their new guise as Catholic saints. For example, St. Lazarus became associated with Babalú-Ayé, Aggayú with St. Christopher, Shangó with St. Barbara, and Elegguá with the Holy Child of Atocha. The Orishás had a new look as well as a new home.

Towards the end of the 1800s, the Cuban cabildos were suppressed by the colonial authorities. They were seen to be centers of nationalistic revolt. The carnivals and festivals were also prohibited. After Cuba gained its independence, freedom (although with racial prejudice and police hostility) meant the decline of the cabildos as the centers of Afro-Cuban cultural life. But the cabildos had fulfilled their function. They protected the languages, stories, traditions, and beliefs of the ancestors.

THE BEGINNING

THE BEGINNING OF THE WORLD

This story tells how the primeval world was created by Olodumaré and how, in turn, the Orishás arose from Olodumaré's creation.

The world was founded on nothing. There was no one to witness its beginning. Nothing lived. There were no animals, not even the smallest insect. Nothing moved. Nothing grew. There were no plants.

Olodumaré, the Supreme Being, moved alone in this desolation. Huge flames roared up from lifeless rock. Fire and stone, that was all that was in the world.

The flames had been burning forever. Time and change were not in the world. Steam and smoke overhead, rocks beneath the layers of clouds, this was where Olodumaré lived. It must have been the way he wished to live, for that was the way it was.

Olodumaré grew tired of the flames and the loneliness. He looked around at the smoke and the rocks and thought of change.

He said, "Let it rain."

All those clouds that had been growing for so long, those clouds were so heavy that they could hardly stay up in the sky. Oceans came down when they opened up and let their water fall. An eternity of rain fell.

The torrent put out the flames that covered the world. Giant rivers broke up the solid rock. The stones ground and tumbled against each other. Boulders the size of houses became pebbles. The pebbles became dust.

Parts of the world had deep charred pits where the fires had burned hottest. The waters poured into these gouges until they became oceans. It was in these oceans that all the Yemayas were born, from Okute to Olokún.

Olodumaré grew as bored by an eternity of water as he had been by an eternity of flames.

He said, "Stop."

The rain stopped. Everything was dark and quiet. Olodumaré wished for a sun.

He said, "Let there be light."

Aggayú, the sun, was born. His light shone upon the earth. The sky was blue for the first time.

Another eternity went by. Ashes swirled around in the quiet waters. They clumped together and sank. The thick muddy mass grew higher, higher than the level of the seas.

Rot and pestilence bubbled up from the mud's depths. Disease and epidemics were released. They gave birth to Babalú-Ayé.

Aggayú's light dried the mud until it became fertile soil. This was where Orishá Okó was born.

The soil gave life to grasses and shrubs. It was from these that Osaín was born.

The very highest parts became hills. The hills became mountains and volcanoes. Oggué came from these.

The volcanoes poured out rivers of molten iron, the iron that Oggún uses. From Oggún come all the weapons used by the warrior Orishás.

That was the beginning of the world.

IROKO AND THE VULTURE

This story describes a great drought and the great flood that followed it. It tells how Iroko, the world tree (the baobab tree in Africa, the kapok tree in the Caribbean), sheltered the living beings of the earth.

It was the beginning of the world. The Sky and the Earth argued.

The Earth said to the Sky, "I am the most important, therefore you should bow to me in respect."

"You are wrong," said the Sky. "I surround you. It is you who should show me respect."

Neither would concede. Neither would bow to the other. They grew tired of the argument.

The Earth said, "Let us go to Obbá Olorún and let him judge who is the most important."

"I agree with that," said the Sky, "for he is sure to judge me superior to you."

When they stood before Obbá Olorún, the Earth said, "I am older and more powerful than the Sky. You created me first."

"That is true," said Obbá Olorún. "I did make you first."

The Earth argued her case, "I am the base of all that is. Without my support, the Sky would crumble and fall."

Obbá Olorún asked the Sky, "Is this true?"

"Yes, it is," the Sky had to admit, "but there are other things as important as a base."

Obbá Olorún frowned at the Sky, "We'll get to you later." He turned back to the Earth and said, "What else have you to say?"

"All living things come from me," said the Earth. "I provide their food. I provide their substance."

The Sky said, "I, too, have my function."

"Do not interrupt," said Obbá Olorún, and the Sky had to be quiet.

"You see?" said the Earth. "The Sky is only smoke. He is only air while all that is originates in me and returns to me."

"I have my powers too," said the Sky.

The Earth ignored him. "I am solid," she said. "The Sky is empty. How can his possessions be compared to mine?"

"My possessions are important too," said the Sky, but he could see that Obbá Olorún was not paying him any attention at all.

The Earth said to the Sky, "You don't have a body. What do you have other than clouds and smoke and light? They are things without substance." She bowed to Obbá Olorún and said, "I am more valuable than he. The Sky should praise me. The Sky should offer sacrifices to me, his foundation."

Obbá Olorún was silent. He thought about what the Earth had said and it made sense to him.

"Depart from my presence," he told the Sky. "The Earth has convinced me that she is right. Substance has more importance than emptiness."

The Sky was angry, for he had not even been given a chance to speak. "I am leaving you, Earth," said the Sky. "It will be a hard lesson for you. Your victory will be your punishment."

When the Sky left, a profound silence settled upon the Earth.

Iroko worried. The great baobab tree had her roots sunk deep into the Earth. Her branches reached high into the Sky. Iroko was afraid.

Iroko thought, "Harmony has left the world. A great calamity is on its way."

Indeed, harmony had graced the world. Before he left the Earth, the Sky had made sure that the seasons were not too hot and not too cold. There were no floods. There were no droughts. All creatures flourished and the Earth had been free to indulge its pride.

Ikú (death) came as a friend back then. There was no wailing at her coming. There were no tears or suffering. Illness was unknown in those happy days. Life was long for men and animals. Old age held no fears. It promised not pain, as it does now, but a drowsiness, a desire to lay down and rest.

A man who was ready to die laid down his tools and went home. He'd gather his friends and his family around him and say, "It is time for me to rest. It is time for me to close my eyes."

His family and friends rejoiced and made a feast, gathering around the dying man.

He'd say, "I feel peace approach my heart. I feel a dark happiness traveling through my body. Gather around me. I will tell you my thoughts."

His children and his children's children's children gathered around the dying man eagerly. The end was considered beautiful and dignified back then. They listened with respect.

The dying man gathered his thoughts and spoke, "Rejoice with me! I have eaten and I will now be food! Generations of worms and insects will feast on me and praise me!" He could say this because compassion had not yet left the world.

"Rejoice with me!" he said. " My body will dissolve into all bodies. I will be a bird. I will be a cow. I will be a yam that you will eat! I will make you strong! I will uphold the world!"

That was the way men died before the great silence came, before the Sky left the Earth.

The thoughts in people's hearts back then were:

"How can I help my neighbor? What will make everyone happy?"

Neither plants nor people had poison and thorns. There was no envy or enmity or evil spells. People are astonished when they hear of the world as it was.

"Who ruled such a world?" they ask. "Who was king? Who upheld the laws?"

There were no kings and there were no laws. Justice resided in men's hearts and there was no "yours" or "mine."

That was the way it was when the Earth and the Sky were united. That was the way of it before the Sky thundered vengeance upon the Earth.

Iroko, knowing that suffering and cruelty were on their way, began to cry, mourning what had been. Her tears took the form of white flowers that floated far and wide, carpeting the world. Her sadness spread with the flowers and entered the world's creatures.

That evening, the sun's blood red rays were a cry of pain. Iroko spread her branches, trying to protect the living and console the dead.

That night, nightmares came to the world for the first time. For the first time, sleep brought fear instead of bliss. Men and women tossed and turned tormented by images of burning, by images of thirst. Dead screaming children filled their dreams.

The next morning, husband spoke with wives. Neighbors visited neighbors.

"What happened last night?" they asked. "What were those things? What were those feelings?" There was no word for fear. There was no word for anguish. How can there be a word for a thing that does not exist?

A pitiless sun rose that morning, a glaring sun that blistered flesh and wilted crops. Rivers and lakes dried up. Fishes flopped on hard cracked mud. Cattle collapsed, their black tongues lolling out of their mouths.

Iroko called out, "Come children. Come to me and shelter under my branches before the sun eats you."

The people asked, "What is this thing that is happening? Why is the sun like fire? Why is there no water?"

"The Earth has offended the Sky," said Iroko. "He is angry. Let us pray to our mother, the Earth, and our father, the Sky, for these terrible things to end."

The people did not understand. "What is 'offend'?" they asked, confused. "What is 'angry'? What does 'terrible' mean?"

The water in the ocean dried up. People could drink from the sea back then. The Earth became parched and thirsty.

The Earth called out to the Sky. "My brother, my thirst is terrible. I am drying up. My children are dying. Please send me a little water."

The Sky laughed and said, "Sister, you said I was empty and had nothing to give. All I will send you is emptiness. I will give you nothing."

A howling wind swept across the earth. It was hot and burned like fire. Every last seed, every last grain and insect and leaf was burnt dead and buried in white hot sands.

Men fought each other to eat the eyeballs out of a child's skull. They drank each other's blood.

New words were invented:

"I'll kill you."

"Curse you and yours."

"You thief! That's mine!"

The old and the very young were torn to pieces by their relatives. The dead were dug up and eaten.

The Earth looked upon all this horror and cried out to the Sky, "Forgive me. I beg relief. It is not for me that I ask, but for our children. How can you bear to see our children suffer?"

"Our children?" said the Sky. "How can I have children? You are the foundation of all, or so you said. Who walks upon my bosom?"

Dust and sand blew against the mountains and wore them down. The bones of men and animals tumbled and mingled. Only a tiny island of green remained. It was Iroko.

She was the last and only tree. Walking skeletons, the last men and women, huddled around her, eating the last of the wilting grass. The spirits of the dead flocked to her branches for shelter.

Iroko sent her voice up to the Sky, "Dear father, I do not ask for myself, but for the sake of the few still alive under my protection. End this punishment of the Earth."

The Sky remained silent even though Iroko had been his favorite child.

To the few who were still able to move, Iroko said, "Dig into my roots. You shall find mysteries there."

The pathetic scarecrows scrabbled at her roots, tearing their fingernails. Many died. Those that survived found Iroko's secrets.

They said, "The Earth and the Earth's children have sinned against the sky. We must purify ourselves in blood. We must make a sacrifice in the Earth's name. May the Sky have pity on us."

These few made the first sacrifice at Iroko's base.

They said, "Who shall take the offerings up to the Sky? Who can take these proofs of our humbleness up to our Father?"

A small bird flew down from Iroko's branches. "I can take the offering to the Sky," it said.

Up went the little bird. It flew higher and higher. Harsh winds buffeted it. The sun threatened to set its feathers on fire. The Sky had gone so far away from the Earth!

Exhausted, the small ball of feathers fell back to Earth.

"I tried," it said before dying.

A hawk said, "I'll take the offering to the Sky. I am bigger. I can fly higher."

It soared up on the blistering currents of hot air that rose from the scorched rocks. Higher and higher it rose into the intense white glare until it was lost from sight.

The people sheltered by Iroko's shade looked up and said, "He will surely make it to the Sky. Our petition will be heard."

But the hawk's heart burst before it could reach the Sky. The forlorn bundle of bones and feathers came apart as it fell back to Earth. A single feather drifted down and gently landed in Iroko's branches.

Then Ara-Kole, the vulture said, "I will take your prayers to the Sky."

The people refused. "We cannot allow our prayers to be taken up by a repulsive bird," they said.

"But I'm the only one who has eaten well," said Ara-Kole. "I'm the only one who is strong enough."

The eagle spread its mighty wings and said. "I will take the offering. A noble bird can accomplish a noble purpose."

"It is so." said the people. "You are worthy."

The eagle flew for a day and a night. It's mighty wings grew tired. Hunger and thirst took their toll. Exhausted, it fell, unable to fly, unable to save itself. It came down on Iroko's roots.

The people looked at the broken body.

Someone said, "All hope is gone."

Another said, "Perhaps that stinking and ugly bird that feeds on corpses can do it."

"I can," said Ara-Kole, "if given the chance."

A woman said, "He may be disgusting, but he's our last hope. Give him the offering."

So it was that the ugly, the most despised, the loathsome Ara-Kole became the last hope of a dying Earth.

Ara-Kole was as strong as he was ugly. He flew for three days and three nights and passed the boundary that separates our world from the infinite.

Ara-Kole's perseverance was as great as his stink. He crossed over to the other side of existence and flew farther still until he reached the Sky.

The Sky was very surprised. He thought that he was beyond the reach of anything that belonged to the Earth.

"Who are you?" he asked.

The vulture replied, "I am Ara-Kole. I have brought you an offering so that you may hear the plight of your children on the Earth."

"I will listen to your prayers," said the Sky. "You may be the ugliest of my children, but you have gone through much to deliver your message."

The vulture gathered itself up and in its most formal croak said, "Father Sky! The Earth and the children of the Earth have sent me to beg you to have pity. We beg for your forgiveness. Have compassion! We throw ourselves at your feet. Father, the Earth is dying down there. Have compassion. The animals, the birds, the people, we all implore you. We are dying. For-give us!"

The Sky was moved by Ara-Kole's words. For the first time in a long while the Sky looked down. He saw death and desolation. His heart changed.

"I have caused too much suffering," said the Sky. "I accept the offering. I forgive the Earth."

When the Sky said these words, clouds began to gather.

The people sheltered by Iroko's branches let out a great shout, "Ara-Kole has reached the Sky!"

The first rain drops fell on the dead dust. The drops became a shower. The shower became a rainstorm. The rainstorm be-came a torrent of water that roared over the bare Earth and began to fill the oceans.

Ara-Kole said to the Sky, "I and your other children thank you. I think it time I returned."

The vulture flew down through the emptiness that defines the infinite. Three days and three nights it flew back to the Earth. But that was too long. That was too far. Ara-Kole was too weak to fly against the deluge. The water swept it away. It swept him to the Earth, who opened up to receive her son. A great lake was born to receive the body of Ara-Kole.

The survivors of the drought had to survive the flood, but Iroko sheltered them with her branches. The Earth drank her fill. Trees and grasses sprang up and she was no longer naked. People and animals multiplied and she was no longer alone. She praised the Sky and she was no longer prideful.

The harmony that was the world's at the beginning never returned. That happiness was lost. The Sky never reunited with the Earth. He never gave her much care or affection. We have known the pain of that separation since that time long ago.

THE FLOOD

This is another story of a flood at the beginning of the world. It tells of Olokún's anger against humanity and how Obatalá saved the world from destruction.

Olokún of the dark ocean depths where the glowing hair of the drowned is a playground for eyeless fish. Olokún of the tidal wave that rips mother from child and leaves beaches where houses stood. Olokún that crushes ships in his embrace. Olokún was angry.

The race of men had forgotten the mystery of the masked dances. The drummers had forgotten his song. No one made the terrible sacrifices to appease the waves.

Olokún said, "If no one remembers me, there will be no one to remember. If no one stands by me, there will be no place to stand."

Dark green water stirred, swirled and boiled. First a swell, then a wave, then a terrible wall of water rolled across the ocean and clawed at the homes of men.

Thousands, then millions died. Those that still lived struggled to reach higher ground, but the water rose hungrily and made ready to wash away what was left of humanity.

Men, women and children huddled cold and hungry on mountaintops that were now islands rising from a sea carpeted by corpses. They had no food. There was no sweet water. Cries and prayers were drowned by the roar of water against rock.

Obatalá came down a spider web thread. He came to rejoice in the world. He came to look at the people he had created. He found chaos, death and destruction.

Obatalá went deep into the ocean, where there is no light. He went to Olokún's palace.

Obatalá said, "It is not your place to destroy Olofín's creation. It is not your right to kill the people that I cherish."

Olokún roared, "I will have no part of a creation that does not honor and respect me. I care nothing for men that do not sacrifice to me," and sent a black wall of water hurtling towards Obatalá.

Obatalá raised his opá, his white scepter, and the waters parted to either side, leaving him unhurt.

"You forget who is your lord," said Obatalá and struck Olokún with his opá.

Olokún fell. There, in Olokún's own palace, Obatalá bound him with seven silver chains.

Olokún came to. He roared and shouted and struggled, but Obatalá's chains held him powerless.

"You will remain bound until you learn to give as well as to take," Obatalá told him.

Up in the world of men, the water began to retreat, revealing mud, death and ruins.

Obatalá came out of the ocean. He took his iruké, his white horsetail whisk, and swept the land clean. Trees, grasses and crops sprang up from the mud. Dead animals stood up and walked.

When the survivors came down from the mountains, they marveled to see their houses restored and their relatives and friends waiting for them.

They made great praise and sacrifices to Obatalá who told them, "As you praise me, let some of you and some of your children and some of your children's children praise Olokún. It was your forgetfulness and your heedlessness that brought disaster on you."

"We will obey," said the people, and they did.

Obatalá left Olokún chained in his palace for many generations of men. When he thought the time was right, Obatalá returned and released him.

"You see that the people have not forgotten you," said Obatalá.

"They have not," said Olokún. "I receive my due and they shall receive theirs from me."

So it is to this day that Olokún is not forgotten. The ocean's wrath is respected.

YEMAYÁ AND ORUNGÁN

■ ■ n the previous story, Yemayá, in her Olokún aspect, tried to destroy the world. In this one, she is the seed from which all Orishás spring.

Back in the beginning, before there were things or the thought of things, there was the Couple Who Created. They were Odduduá and Obatalá.

They were large, larger than can be imagined because size did not exist. They were beautiful beyond compare. There was nothing to compare them to. They lived forever because time was not. They were in love.

They made love and their love became Yemayá and Aggayú. Odduduá and Obatalá loved their children with a love that was all and filled all. A mother feels this love as it echoes through the ages. A father feels this strength.

Yemayá and Aggayú grew and from two there were now four. There was change, so time began.

Obatalá went to her children and said, "It is time for you to marry." There was ceremony where there had been none. There were things that had to be.

"We must have a place to live," said Yemayá, and there were houses.

"I must have something to do," said Aggayú, and there was work.

Yemayá and Aggayú made love in their house and Orungán was born of the union.

Time that passed was. Things became.

When Orungán was grown, he said, "It is time for me to marry, for that is now the custom."

"There is no one for you to marry," said Yemayá.

"I can marry you," said Orungán.

Aggayú was angry at this and said, "You cannot marry your mother. That is not the custom."

"You have a wife," shouted Orungán. "Odduduá has a wife. What about me? Why should I be the one to be alone?"

Among the things that were, there was now anger between father and son, a bitterness.

Orungán kept quiet. Orungán kept his anger. The anger became this thought, "I will have Yemayá."

He waited, for he had time to wait in. He behaved himself, for there were customs to follow. He envied Aggayú. There was now envy.

Aggayú went to work. He left Orungán and Yemayá alone in the house.

Orungán waited. When he was sure Aggayú was not coming back, he embraced Yemayá and lifted her apron.

"You are mine," cried Orungán. "Not Aggayú's."

Yemayá fought against her own son. "Don't touch me!" she screamed. "Do not do this thing!"

Orungán did not listen. He ran his hands over her body. He kissed her breasts.

Yemayá hit Orungán in that part where men hurt the most. She ran out of the house terrified.

Orungán hobbled after her. "You will be mine," he gasped. "You will be mine."

One whole day Yemayá ran with Orungán close behind. One whole night they ran. They ran through forests and mountains. They ran through deserts. They ran until they reached the coast. There, Yemayá fell, dead from exhaustion. Sea foam washed her hair.

Orungán fled, afraid of Aggayú's punishment.

Yemayá's body lay on the sand. It turned black and began to swell. Her breasts grew huge. Her belly bloated.

Suddenly, two streams of water began to flow out of her breasts; unending streams that joined together to form a vast lake of silver water.

The skin of her belly split open. Instead of worms and corruption, Shangó stepped forth holding his double-headed ax. Thunderstorms circled his brow.

Then, with a mighty roaring of waves, Olokún stepped out of Yemayá's belly. The terrible Orishá of the angry ocean walked into the sea and sank from sight.

Oggún came forth next. The god of iron was resplendent in his tiger skin. He slashed the air with his machete and strode off into the forest.

Orishá Okó came out of Yemayá's belly. He had his hoe and his plow. He sought the most fertile fields and began to raise the crops that feed men.

Oshosi sprang out of the gaping wound. His bow was ready. His arrow was nocked. Off he went into the forest, to hunt.

Aye Saluga came next. He had baskets of cowry shells and precious parrot feather fans and all things that are used for money, for he is the Orishá of wealth and prosperity.

Orishás poured out of Yemayá's body. Olosa went to the lake. Oke went to the mountain. Orun went to the sun while Oshún went to claim the moon. With Oshún came Oyá and Obbá. They took the rivers that bear their name.

And this was the birth of the Orishás. This is the secret of their coming into the world.

IRON

This story tells how the Orishás made their paths on the earth and how they declared Oggún their king. In all other accounts, Obatalá rules the Orishás.

A very long time ago, when Olodumaré created the world, there were no mountains. There were no trees. There was no dry land. Everything everywhere was mud. It was nasty, sticky deep mud that went down forever quivering and bubbling and making nasty wet noises.

Even though it was a very unpleasant place, Oggún and the other Orishás came from heaven to visit the world.

They traveled down a long, long spider web. Back then, this was the only path between heaven and the world.

Why did they come? They came to hunt. They came to amuse themselves. There was nothing to do in heaven.

Down on earth, the Orishás had fun. They chased the giant leeches that played in the mud. They hunted the big dumb beasts that honked and growled at each other on the mud plains.

Thousands of years went by. The solid parts of the world were formed.

Olodumaré called the Orishás together and said, "You have played long enough. It is time for you to have responsibilities."

He gave each of the Orishás duties and tasks to perform. For the first time, the Orishás came down to the world to do the Supreme Being's bidding.

They came to a place where their way was blocked by large trees. Heavy brambles and thorn bushes made it impossible for them to go around or through the trees.

Obatalá said, "Move to one side. I will clear a path for us." But his blade was made of lead. It bent when it struck wood.

Shangó stepped forward. "Move aside," he said. "I will clear a path for us."

Shangó took a deep breath and blew. A long tongue of fire came out of his mouth. It licked the trees and the bushes. But the living wood was too wet. His fire smoked and went out.

Oshosi was the next Orishá to try to find a way out of their difficulty. "Follow me," he said. "I will find a way around this obstacle." But every path Oshosi found just led them back to their starting point, frustrated and scratched.

Oggún stepped forward and addressed the other Orishás, "What will you give me if I clear the path?"

The Orishás laughed. "If you can clear our path in this world," they told him, "We will make you a king."

They didn't really mean it. After all, wisdom, strength and guile had failed. What could Oggún do?

Oggún lifted his machete. "The sky is my witness," he said. "In exchange for a kingdom I will make us a path through this world. Move to one side."

His blade was made of iron. It cut through the brambles' tough wood. His machete cut into the hard wood of the trees. His arm chopped up and down without stopping, without rest. At the end of the day, the Orishá's way was clear.

The Orishás were astonished. They said, "It is because of Oggún that we can make our way through this world. We will pay our debt to him."

When they reached Ilé-Ifé, the Orishás gathered around Oggún.

"We will now honor the maker of paths," they said. They brought out the only crown that they had brought with them. "With this crown we name you Osin Imale, King of the Orishás."

Thus, with Oggún as their chief, the Orishás settled in Ilé-Ifé. They built a beautiful town full of large rich houses. There was plenty to eat and the crops never failed. The Orishás prospered in this world.

Oggún did not like his new sedentary life.

He grumbled and complained to everyone. "I love wars and conquests," he said. "I love to hunt. What do I care for court life and honors?"

The other Orishás were stern with him. "You are our king and our leader," they said. "It is your duty to stay here and rule us."

Oggún became angry. "Having to do what I hate is no honor," he said.

"It doesn't matter what you want to do," said the Orishás. "You must stay."

That night Oggún waited until everyone was asleep. He took his iron blade and ran off into a jungle called Ori Oke.

He was happy there for many years, leading the life of a wild and solitary hunter.

One day Oggún was walking through the jungle searching for prey. He heard himself say, "I am tired of being alone." This was a strange thing for him to say and it surprised him.

The next day, as he was drinking from a stream, Oggún heard his voice say, "I want some company." This was even stranger. He had never even thought of such a thing before.

Oggún spent the next day thinking about the things his mouth had said.

"I will return to Ilé-Ifé," he decided. This he did.

When Oggún came out of the jungle of Ori Oke, a great wall of fire surrounded him. A torrent of blood drenched him and put out the fire.

"I can't let people see me like this," he said. "It would frighten them too much."

Oggún made himself clothing out guano, palm frond sheaths.

Wearing his new clothes, he arrived in Ilé-Ifé and said, "Rejoice, for your king has returned."

YEMAYÁ IN THE BEGINNING

In this Caribbean story, Yemayá shows a much milder destructive aspect. She also demonstrates her wit.

It was the beginning of the world, when only the Orishás walked upon the earth.

Obbáloke lived upon his mountain. Every day the sea crashed and washed against Obbáloke's home, taking a little bit away each day, then a little bit more.

"At this rate, my house will tumble down into the sea," said Obbáloke. "Who does Yemayá think she is to destroy my home in this way?"

Oggún worked his forge, making tools and weapons. Every day, the sea's salt air rusted and spoiled what he had made.

"All my work is ruined," grumbled Oggún. "Who does Yemayá think she is to rust my iron and make it worthless?"

Orishá Okó worked hard in his fields, plowing the ground and caring for his crops. Every day, the tide came in and crumbled his rows. The salt water killed his plants and made his fertile fields sterile.

"How will people eat?" said Orishá Okó. "Who does Yemayá think she is to gobble up the crops in my field?"

All the Orishás were in an uproar. They went to petition Olorún, the Supreme Being, for relief.

"Yemayá can take over the land when and where she pleases," complained the Orishás.

"Why don't you do something about it?" asked Olorún. "You are many. She is one."

The Orishás hemmed and hawed and finally admitted, "We don't want to make Yemayá angry. When she becomes furious, she raises her waves and destroys everything."

Olorún summoned Obatalá and told him, "Go down to the world and see what is going on. See if Yemayá is abusing her powers."

Elegguá, as always, was hiding behind the door and heard everything. Being a mischievous trickster, he decided to help

Yemayá. He went down to the earth and took the path that led to the ocean.

"Yemayá, Yemayá!" Elegguá shouted. "Obatalá's coming. Your power's in danger!"

The waves rose and formed themselves into the body of a beautiful woman whose feet barely touched the waves.

"Is this one of your tricks, Elegguá?" she asked him.

"It's no trick," said Elegguá. "All the Orishás are angry with you. Olorún has sent Obatalá to see if you are behaving yourself."

A huge wave smashed a rock to pieces. "Oh, dear," said Yemayá. "You see? It is my nature to be what I am and to do what I do. Obatalá is sure to give a bad report about me."

"This is what you should do," said Elegguá, for he already had a plan. "Go visit Orunlá. He can look at his Ifá board and tell you how to avoid trouble."

Yemayá went to Orunlá's house. "My nature has brought me trouble," she told him. "What can I do?"

Orunlá consulted his oracles and said, "Your nature will also save you. Make ebó (a sacrificial offering) with a lamb."

"How should this sacrifice be carried out?" asked Yemayá.

"Place the lamb on your bosom," said Orunlá. "This will confound your enemies and all will be well."

Yemayá did as Orunlá advised. She sacrificed a lamb and placed it on the bosom of the waves.

Obatalá came down. He came down in the land of the Orishás, which is Ilé-Ifé. With him came all the Orishás who were angry with Yemayá.

"Now you will see what we are talking about," said the Orishás. "You will see what outrages Yemayá has done against us."

"Yemayá!" Obatalá called out over the waves. "Yemayá, come to us!"

The sea answered in a soft murmur. A gentle swell brought a lamb's head out of the depths of the sea and softly deposited at Obatalá's feet.

The foam gathered around it and Yemayá appeared, offering Obatalá the head. "If I had known you were coming, I would have made better preparations," said Yemayá. "But please accept this small gift."

Obatalá turned on the Orishás and said, "Where is her bad behavior? I see no outrages. Yemayá's head is well placed. She knows how to treat a guest. Who among you has brought a gift? No one!"

"She is destroying my house!" said Obbáloke.

"She is rusting my iron!" said Oggún.

"Yemayá has ruined my crops!" said Orishá Okó.

"All you bring is gossip and complaints," said Obatalá. "I find no fault with Yemayá."

This is the way that Yemayá won out over her accusers. This is the way Yemayá kept her nature and her powers.

THE POWERS

THE DOVES

This story explains how Obatalá came to be the owner of peoples' eledás, their heads.

Every day, the Orishás gathered in a palace in the sky. It belonged to Olofín, the Supreme Being. Every day, Olofín listened to their petitions. The Orishás wanted many things done and many favors granted. What they all wanted most of all was to own the eledás, the heads of the human beings living in the world.

It was during one of these meetings that Shangó brandished his double-headed ax. "Make me the owner of the heads, Olofín," he shouted. "All the people will be as great in battle as I am."

Oggún laughed at Shangó, "You, a brave warrior?" He pounded his chest. "I am the only one fit to own the heads. After all, the tools they use are mine."

Oshún wrapped her arms around Olofín's neck and purred, "Now you're not going to listen to those two, are you? You know that it's love that human beings need. Make me the owner of their heads and my oñi, my sweetness, will be part of them forever."

Now, it so happened that Olofín needed doves for a ceremony. He did not need ordinary doves, like the ones that fly around the park. The ones he wanted had a great deal of ashé, power. Great and powerful spells could be worked with them.

Olofín was very old. Creating the universe had made him very tired. The doves were far away and difficult to catch. He did not want to go through the trouble of getting them himself. The Orishá's bickering gave him an idea.

Aggayú and Obatalá were arguing with each other.

Aggayú said, "I am strong enough to protect the humans. I deserve to own their heads."

Obatalá answered him calmly, "Strength is nothing. Human beings need to be pure. They need to be ready for what life has in store for them. Only my dreams can give them that." She turned to Olofín. "Isn't that right?" she asked. "Don't I deserve to be the owner of the heads?"

Olofín cleared his throat. "I have come to a decision about who is to own the heads of the human beings," he told the Orishás.

All arguments stopped. An expectant silence fell over the gathering.

Olofín said, "I have decided that the Orishá who brings me the doves I need will rule over people's eledá."

There was a mad rush for the door. The Supreme Being was left alone in his palace. He chuckled to himself, "Well, I guess it's time for a nap. Then we'll see what happens."

The Orishás raced across the world searching for the doves. Both Aggayú and Obatalá had an advantage over the others. Aggayú had seen the tree where the doves nested. Obatalá knew where the doves lived. White doves were one of the animals that 'belonged' to her.

Aggayú arrived at the tree early the next morning. He got there first because he takes such big steps. Since it was daylight, the doves were not in their nests.

Aggayú thought, "I can wait until night, when the doves come to roost, but the other Orishás will get here by nightfall."

The astute Aggayú had an idea. He went through the forest with a large basket. He gathered all the snakes he could find. Aggayú took the basket of snakes back to the tree. He shook the snakes out of the basket along the path that led to the tree. There was no way anyone could get to the doves now!

Aggayú grunted with satisfaction. "Let them try to get through that," he said.

He climbed the tree, settled himself comfortably on a branch and waited for night, when the doves would return to roost.

Obatalá arrived that afternoon. She saw the tree and started walking down the path. Then she saw the snakes.

She screamed, "Aaah, snakes!" Terrified, she ran away.

She fled down the path until she ran headlong into Shangó.

Shangó rubbed his nose. "Why can't you watch where you are going?" he asked crossly.

Obatalá , panting, said, "Oh, Shangó, I'm so glad to see you. I need your help to get the doves."

Shangó was confused. "You can't ask for my help," he said. "This is a contest."

Obatalá said, very sweetly, "Do you know where they are? Do you?"

Shangó scratched his head. "Well, no," he said. "But they're around here somewhere."

Obatalá said, "You probably will not find them before some-one else gets them. I'll tell you where they are if you help me."

Shangó was suspicious. "Why don't you get them yourself?" he asked.

"The path is full of snakes," confessed Obatalá. "I'm afraid of snakes."

Shangó waved his ax over his head. "Ha! Snakes? Snakes are nothing to a strong warrior like me," he bragged.

"Good," said Obatalá eagerly. "I'll tell you where the doves roost. You take care of the snakes and we'll share the ownership of the eledás."

Obatalá told Shangó how to get to the tree. Confident of his strength, Shangó started off down the path.

He saw a couple of snakes and killed them with his ax. "This is easy," he thought. "The snakes are no problem at all."

He cut off the heads of a few more snakes. The doves were as good as his.

Shangó was thinking, "I'll own the heads and won't have to share anything with Obatalá."

That's when he saw a snake as big around as his waist. It's mouth opened so wide that a cow could have walked inside. This was too much, even for a mighty warrior. Besides, Oyá was not with him to help him fight. Shangó turned around and ran away from the snake as fast as he could.

He sat on a rock wondering what to do next. Elegguá came walking down the path.

Shangó called out to Elegguá, "Elegguá, I need your help!"

Elegguá sat down next to him. "I thought you were out looking for the doves," he said.

Shangó told Elegguá about meeting Obatalá. He told him about the snakes.

Shangó said, "You are the smartest of us all. If you can figure out how to get at the doves, we'll share the ownership of the heads with you."

Elegguá said, "I don't want anything. I'd just rather keep on doing what I want when I want."

Shangó looked so upset that Elegguá said, "Don't worry. This sounds like fun. I'll help you."

Elegguá disguised himself as an old man. He filled a large sack with smoked fish, corn, jutia, and the other things that snakes love to eat. He walked down the path towards the tree, feeding all the snakes he met. As he fed each snake, it fell asleep and let him pass.

Elegguá got to the base of the tree. He looked up and saw Aggayú sitting in the branches.

Elegguá reached into his sack and brought out a large bottle of aguardiente ("burning water," an extremely strong drink distilled from sugar cane juice). He waved to Aggayú and called out, "My dear friend, wouldn't you like a little drink?"

Aggayú had been in the tree all day and he had worked up a terrible thirst.

He peered down and saw an old man. "You're not here to get Olofín his doves, are you?" he asked, not knowing it was Elegguá.

Elegguá lied. "I have no interest in doves." He patted the bottle. "I'm interested in what's inside this bottle."

The bottle seduced Aggayú's thirst. Besides, the old man looked too frail to be a threat to him.

Aggayú reached down with a massive arm. "Come up here with me," he said. "I have to wait for the doves to come back to roost." He easily lifted Elegguá up and sat him on the branch next to him.

The bottle passed back and forth. Aggayú took mighty gulps. Elegguá only pretended to drink. Soon, the bottle was empty and Aggayú was very drunk. Night fell, so did Aggayú. He lay at the base of the tree snoring loudly as the doves came to roost.

Elegguá stuffed his sack full of doves. He came down from the tree and called out to Shangó.

As they walked away from the tree, Elegguá asked, "What are you going to do now?"

Shangó said, "I'm going to give these doves to Olofín."

"What about Obatalá?" asked Elegguá.

Shangó shrugged. "I'm going to own all the heads," he said. "I don't care about Obatalá and I don't care what you say."

Elegguá said, "Well, you did get the doves."

"That's right," said Shangó.

Elegguá said, "And you have all that spare time that you spend drumming and partying."

"That's right," said Shangó.

Elegguá said, "Yes, Olofín will probably make you spend all that spare time taking care of people's heads."

"What?" shouted Shangó. "Spend my time running around taking care of people's heads instead of drumming?"

"That's right," said Elegguá. "That's probably what you'll have to do."

Shangó hurried to where Obatalá waited for him. He thrust the sack full of doves into her hands.

"Here, take this," he told her. "I have my drums. The eledá will just be too much trouble."

The next morning, all the Orishás, except Aggayú, who was still sleeping it off under the tree, met in Olofín's palace.

Olofín stood up and announced, "Obatalá has brought me ashé (power). I give her the eledá. From now own she will rule over the heads of all the human beings in the world."

Some Orishás cheered. Some muttered that they could have done better but were too busy to bother with a stupid contest.

After Obatalá and Shangó told Olofín the whole story, he gave Elegguá the paths.

OSHOSI

Oshosi became an Orishá. But by doing so, he also became responsible for his mother's death.

Oshosi supported himself and his mother by hunting in the forest. He was a very skillful hunter. Oshosi knew the forest like the back of his hand. He knew everything there was to know about the animals he hunted.

One day Oshosi was hunting in the forest when Orunmilá appeared to him. Oshosi fell to the ground and trembled before the Orishá.

Orunmilá gently laid his hands on Oshosi's head and said, "Have no fear, Oshosi. I am here to ask for your help."

Oshosi said, "How can I help an Orishá?"

Orunmilá said, "Olodumaré, the Supreme Being, has a craving for the delicious quail that can only be found in this forest. He sent me out to get one. I have been hunting for days, but I haven't caught one yet."

Oshosi said, "Those quail are easy to catch. I can get as many as you want."

Orunmilá sighed with relief. "Do so and you will have my blessing as well as Olodumaré's," he said. "Every wish that you have will come true."

Oshosi was delighted. Imagine, being able to help an Orishá! "Come to my house tomorrow," he said. "I will have a sack full of fat quail ready for you."

As soon as the words were out of Oshosi's mouth, Orunmilá disappeared.

Oshosi went into the forest. By the end of the day, his sack was full of plump quail. He took the birds home and put them in a cage.

Oshosi shouldered the empty sack and went back into the forest. He still had to provide for his mother and himself. He hunted until the moon went down. Oshosi was too tired to return home. He made a comfortable bed under a tree. He fell asleep imagining all the wonderful things he was going to wish for: a new house for his mother, clothes, chests full of ornaments. He was so happy!

Oshosi awoke with the sun and hurried home.

Orunmilá was waiting for him. The Orishá said, "A good day to you, hunter. Did you get my quail?"

Oshosi said, "I have a cage full of fat delicious quail. Wait here and I'll get them for you."

Oshosi went into his house and came back with the cage. It was empty!

"I see the cage," said Orunmilá. "Where are the quail?"

Oshosi trembled before the Orishá. "I filled this cage last evening," he said. "I swear I did."

Orunmilá became angry. "I don't like jokes," he said. "It's not wise to break a promise to an Orishá."

Oshosi stammered, "I would not dare do such a thing. Perhaps my mother knows what happened to the birds." He called out, "Mother!"

Oshosi's mother hobbled out of the house. She bowed to Orunmilá. "Good morning, Lord," she said.

Oshosi asked her, "Mother, what happened to the quail I left in this cage yesterday?"

"Quail?" said his mother. "I didn't see any quail yesterday."

She wasn't telling the truth. She had eaten the quail. She thought her son had brought her the tasty birds for her evening meal. But how could she tell the Orishá such a thing? She was too afraid.

Orunmilá glowered at Oshosi. Oshosi cringed and said, "There's no problem. I can go into the forest now and return with another sack full of quail in an hour."

Oshosi was as good as his word. He was back in an hour, the sack full of delicious quail.

He opened the sack and showed Orunmilá the beautiful birds. "Here they are," he said. "Just as I promised."

Orunmilá smiled. "These are wonderful," said the Orishá. "Come with me to Olodumaré. You can present the birds with your own hands."

"To Olodumaré?" gasped Oshosi.

"Yes," said Orunmilá. "It was your skill that made this gift possible. You should have all the credit for it."

Orunmilá took Oshosi to Olodumaré's castle in the sky.

Olodumaré was delighted with the quail. "You have gladdened my heart," he told Oshosi.

Oshosi bowed and said, "It is an honor."

Olodumaré said, "I wish to honor your skill, Oshosi. I will make you an Orishá. You will be the first among hunters; a king!"

Olodumaré, Orunmilá and the other Orishás heaped praise and wealth on Oshosi. They were impressed by his humility and his simple manners.

The ceremonies were over when Oshosi bowed to Olodumaré. "Lord," he said. "Please grant me one more thing."

"What would you like, Oshosi?" asked Olodumaré.

"My mind keeps going back to the thief who stole the quail from my house," said Oshosi. "Grant that, with one arrow, I can find that thief's heart."

Olodumaré sighed sadly. "I must grant your wish," he said. "But you will never forgive yourself for it."

Oshosi lifted his bow and shot an arrow high into the air. His keen eyes followed the arrow's flight. Horrified, he saw it plunge into his mother's heart.

Oshosi wailed. Tears ran down his cheeks. He rolled in dung and covered his head with ashes.

Oshosi buried his mother and observed the proper period of mourning. Then he returned to Olodumaré's presence.

"I will no longer be a hunter," he told Olodumaré. "I will fulfill my duties. I will help all hunters. But I will not forget that it was my desire to kill that caused my mother's death."

THE ILLNESS

Both Cuban and African stories agree that Babalú-Ayé's body is covered with disgusting suppurating sores. This is the story of how he got them.

Olodumaré is the Supreme Being. He created all the Orishás. When he decided that it was time for them to leave childish things behind, he summoned them to his palace in the sky.

Olodumaré waited for the rustling and the talking to settle down. Then he addressed his children, "The time of your childhood is past. You must now fulfill your duties and responsibilities. I will share my ashé, my spiritual power, with you."

The Orishás were thrilled. "Who's going to get what?" they wanted to know.

Olodumaré held up his hand. "Quiet," he said. "Each one of you will receive gifts in accordance with your temperament and capacity. Then it will be up to you to make your own way in the world."

The Orishás lined up before Olodumaré, who began to assign the responsibilities they would have in the world.

"Oshún," said Olodumaré. "To you, I give the rivers."

"Thank you, Father," said Oshún.

"Shangó," said Olodumaré. "To you, I give thunder."

"Thank you, Father," said Shangó.

"Oyá," said Olodumaré. "To you, I give the wind. I will also give you the shooting star."

"Oggún," said Olodumaré. "To you, I give the metals in the earth."

He went on, "Orunmilá, to you, I give the power of divination so that you can guide mankind.

"Elegguá," said Olodumaré. "Elegguá? Where is Elegguá?"

· The Orishás found the mischievous Elegguá laying a trip wire across the front door. When they brought him before Olodumaré, Elegguá muttered something about not having any fun.

"Elegguá, settle down and listen," said Olodumaré. "To you I entrust all paths and all doors. You will open the way for men and the Orishás."

When Babalú-Ayé's turn came, Olodumaré was getting a little tired. He couldn't think what to give the handsome Orishá. Yes, Babalú-Ayé was young and very handsome back then.

"What would you like your gift to be?" he asked Babalú-Ayé.

Being young, Babalú-Ayé's main preoccupation was women. He loved to make love. He said, "I want to make love to every woman in the world."

Olodumaré did not like this at all. "I am assigning duties and responsibilities. Be serious," he said.

"You asked me what I wanted," said Babalú-Ayé. "I want pleasure to be my duty and love my responsibility."

Olodumaré sighed. He was too tired to argue. "Very well," he said. "You get your wish, but I will put a condition on it."

Babalú-Ayé was thrilled. "I will do anything you say," he said.

Olodumaré said, "I forbid you to be with a woman on Thursdays during Easter week."

Babalú-Ayé was careful to obey Olodumaré's order. Every year, when Easter came around, he stayed home. He worked in his garden. He fixed up his house. He stayed away from temptation.

One Easter week, on a Monday, Babalú-Ayé was working on his garden. He heard a woman's voice say, "What beautiful flowers!"

He looked up. There, leaning on his fence, was the most beautiful woman he had ever seen.

He gave her a flower. "Their beauty is nothing compared to yours," he told her.

On Tuesday, Babalú-Ayé held her hand.

On Wednesday, they kissed.

Thursday, the woman came back. Babalú-Ayé took her to bed.

He woke up the next morning to find his body covered with gaping sores.

The woman jumped out of bed when she saw them. "What are those disgusting things?" she cried out.

Too late Babalú-Ayé remembered Olodumaré's words. "Olodumaré has punished me," he said. "I have broken my promise."

The smell of rotting flesh was too much for the woman. She gagged and ran outside.

Babalú-Ayé tried everything he could think of to cure his sores. He took herbal baths. He prayed. He made sacrifices. The sores grew larger. They were eating him alive.

Babalú-Ayé dragged his rotting body to Olodumaré's palace. He knocked on the door with a stump.

Olodumaré opened the door. "Has someone left a dead animal at my door?" he said, covering his nose.

Babalú-Ayé croaked, "I need your help."

Olodumaré looked at the thing on his doorstep. "This sounds like someone I knew who can't keep a promise," he said.
"Please help me," begged Babalú-Ayé.

"I don't speak with those who don't keep their word," said Olodumaré. He slammed the door in Babalú-Ayé's face.

Babalú-Ayé died in horrible torments there, on Olodumaré's doorstep.

All the women in the world wailed and mourned when they learned of his fate.

"Bring Babalú-Ayé back to life," they prayed to the Orishás. "How can you let one who loved us so, die?"

Their prayers and petitions reached Oshún.

She was moved. "It is cruel to make so many women suffer," she said. "I will go to Olodumaré and make him change his mind."

Oshún went to Olodumaré's palace. She found an open door and sneaked in. She sprinkled her oñi, her power to awaken love and passion, all over the palace. Soon, her oñi had its effect on Olodumaré.

He was resting on a pile of cushions when He began to think about old loves and conquests.

Olodumaré stood up and went to a mirror. "I haven't changed that much," he thought, smoothing back what was left of his hair.

He felt great, full of energy and vigor. He put on a splendid robe and went back to stand before the mirror.

"Not bad," said Olodumaré. Then he surprised himself by adding, "I bet I can still set a few hearts fluttering." He had not thought about sex in ages.

He laughed. Olodumaré is wise. He knew the effects of Oshún's oñi. He called out, "Oshún, come out. I know you are in here."

Oshún came out of hiding, sexy and irresistible as always. "I wanted to give you a present," she said.

"I feel great," said Olodumaré. "What a wonderful gift you have."

Oshún said, "You punished Babalú-Ayé for feeling as you do now."

"Never mind Babalú-Ayé," said Olodumaré. "Spread a little more oñi on me. It makes me feel so young."

Oshún laughed and shook her head. "Not until you forgive Babalú-Ayé," she said. "Bring him back to the world and I'll give you more oñi."

"Babalú-Ayé will live again," said Olodumaré.

Oshún gave her oñi to Olodumaré and Olodumaré gave life to Babalú-Ayé. He did not bring him back as an Orishá of love and desire, though. Babalú-Ayé came back into the world as the Orishá of illness and suffering. His sores are a constant reminder of that.

OLOFÍN'S DISTRIBUTION

Obatalá showed the Orishás the way to Olofín and he convinced the Supreme Being to share his power with them.

The world was going through a terrible time. Rain did not fall. Drought punished the earth. The crops did not grow. Desperate, the people watched their animals die of thirst.

Their hungry children cried, "Way, way, way."

Their hungry goats bleated, "Beh, beh, beh."

If the king said, "Do this," the men said, "Why should we? We are busy with our own affairs." There was no order in the land.

Hunger brought hate. Men became enemies. "May death enter your house and pass mine by," was a curse often heard in the streets. Husbands and wives stole bones from graves to work black spells on each other.

The Orishás were as desperate as the people.

"No one is performing the ceremonies," cried Shangó angrily. "The people have forgotten us."

"How can you be angry?" said Yemayá. "They don't even have food for their children."

"Their love has dried up," said Oshún, "and there is nothing I can do."

"If we knew the way," said Elegguá, "we could go ask Olofín to make everything better again." This was in the time when the Orishás did not know the difficult path that led to Olofín's home.

"We must go to Obatalá," said Osaín. "He is our king and knows the way back to Olofín."

Obatalá had been appointed by Olofín to be his representative on earth. He was the only one who could take messages to heaven.

The Orishás went to petition Obatalá. "Ibikeji Edumare," they said. "You are Olofín's representative. You must take us to him."

Obatalá shook his head and said, "The world is your responsibility. Olofín is no longer concerned with it. Why do you want to disturb him?"

"The world is in a terrible state," said the Orishás. "The people have forgotten the sacrifices and are busy killing each other for a bite to eat. We don't understand why this should be so. What good does it do to talk of responsibilities if the world ends?"

Obatalá considered these words. Then he said, "You are right. I will take you to Olofín."

He led them on the journey back to heaven. They went by way of Osankiriyan, the long and hard climb. After many days, they arrived at the peak of the craggy mountain and entered Olofín's house.

Obatalá and the other Orishás bowed low before Olofín. They said, "Mighty Olofín, we seek your help."

Olofín sighed and shook his head. "I am tired," he said. "I cannot do anything."

The Orishás bowed. They tried again, "Mighty Olofín, the world is dying. We need your help."

"I am tired," repeated Olofín. "I cannot do anything."

Obatalá went to the throne and implored Olofín, "Babami, dear father, we come because the world's needs are great." Before Olofín could refuse him again, he said, "Please divide and share your power with us."

Olofín shook his head.

Obatalá insisted, "Father, we need your help to keep on living."

Olofín said in a very soft, tired voice, "Obatalá, line up my children in front of me."

When all the Orishás were gathered around his throne, he told them, "I must think about what Obatalá has said. You have traveled long and hard to come to me. Please eat and refresh yourselves. I will give you my decision this afternoon."

A great banquet was laid out for the Orishás. They had forgotten that such delicious food existed. They ate like famished wolves until there was not a scrap of bread left on the table. When Olofín sent for them, they eagerly gathered around the throne.

Obatalá asked, "Father, what is your decision?"

Olofín said, "I agree to your idea, Obatalá. To each of you I will give what is suitable to your capacity. To each I will give of my ashé."

He addressed Yemayá. "Yemayá, you wish to nurture humanity in your bosom. At the same time, your anger is like a storm. I give you the sea."

He pointed to Shangó. "Shangó, your temper flares up sudden and violent. Your passion, too, is strong. I give your thunder and fire."

He looked at Oyá. "Oyá, you have compassion for dying children, their lives are brief but brilliant. I give you the shooting star."

When it was Oshún's turn, he said, "Oshún, your curves and oñi, sweetness, flow to the delight of all. I give you the rivers."

One by one, the Orishás filed past Olofín. He granted his ashé to each one. "Elegguá, it was your idea to make the long journey to my house. To you, I give the roads. Osaín, you like the deep, hidden places of the forest. To you I give all the healing plants."

Finally, it was Obatalá's turn. Olofín said, "Obatalá, because of your trustworthiness and concern for humanity, I make you the olori, the owner of all the heads."

That is the way that Obatalá brought the Orishás to Olofín. That is the way the Orishás received their ashé.

Another version of this story goes like this:

In the beginning, Olodumaré, the Supreme Being, created the Orishás without all the powers that they have today. If they needed anything done, they had to ask Olodumaré for the power to do it. Since Obatalá was the only Orishá that knew where Olodumaré lived, all the other Orishás had to depend on him to get anything done. The knowledge gave Obatalá a lot of power and prestige, but it also gave him a lot of trouble.

Every day it was something. For instance, the Orishás came running to Obatalá's house and said, "Obatalá! Obatalá! Shangó and Oggún are fighting again. Go to Olodumaré and have him settle it."

Obatalá had to stop eating dinner, and make the long trip to Olodumaré's house.

When he arrived, he asked, "Father, please settle the dispute between Oggún and Shangó."

Olodumaré said, "Very well. Have them do such and such."

Obatalá then had to turn around, and make the long trip back to his house and tell the Orishás, "Olodumaré said to do such and such."

When he returned to his dinner, his food cold and full of flies.

He never had a moment's rest. If he wanted to take a nap, Oshún might show up and demand, "Obatalá! Obatalá! There is a person that needs the healing power of love. Run to Olodumaré's house and ask him to give me enough ashé so that I can heal."

Or, it might be Oshosi calling at his front door, "Obatalá! Obatalá! The hunters come home empty handed. Have Olodumaré show me where the game is."

Poor Obatalá. He spent his days trudging back and forth from his house to heaven and back again.

"I am like a parrot," he sighed. "All I do is repeat messages all day long."

What was worse, the other Orishás began to resent the favors he granted. They muttered and grumbled among themselves.

"Obatalá is giving himself airs," some said. "He struts around acting like a king just because he knows where Olodumaré lives."

"We have to go to him like children begging for treats," others complained. "He sits and nods his head looking important while we are the ones that do all the work."

Of course, this made Obatalá feel bad. He didn't care about power and prestige. He didn't mind hard work. But he didn't want abuse.

One day, Obatalá had enough. "You think it's so easy running back and forth?" he told the Orishás. "Well, today you are coming with me." He led all the Orishás to Olodumaré's house.

Olodumaré was surprised to see all his children gathered in front of him. "Welcome, Obatalá," he said. "Welcome my children. What can I do for you?"

"With all respect, Father," said Obatalá, bowing low. "Could you not share some of your power with your children? That way, I would not need to come and ask for ashé every time something needs to be done."

Olodumaré looked uncomfortable. "That is a very big request, Obatalá," he said. "Do you think that is necessary? After all, power is a very dangerous thing."

"Great lord," said Obatalá, "you are very old and very tired. Imagine how nice it would be if you could rest all day and not be bothered by our constant requests."

Olodumaré really was tired. Creating the universe had been a big job. He didn't have the energy to deal with the everyday problems of the world.

"You are right, Obatalá," he said. "I am weary. I will do as you suggest."

Olodumaré went to each of the Orishás and gave them ashé according to their natures. They were his children, after all, and deserved his gifts.

When he had finished with the others, he turned to Obatalá and said, "You are wise and responsible, Obatalá. You had a hard job and you did it well. To you, I grant control over the heads of all human beings."

The head of a person, his or her eledá, is what makes them good or evil. It is what makes them live a good life or live in jail. It makes them a good son or daughter or one that doesn't care for their parents. Olodumaré had made Obatalá the Orishá with the most power over human beings, setting him above all the others.

When they saw what Olodumaré did, the other Orishás were very jealous. "We knew that he wanted to be king," they said. "He brought us up here just so that he could get more power than anyone else."

It just goes to show that you can't please everyone.

HOW ORUNMILÁ RECEIVED THE ORACLES

In this story, Orunmilá, with Elegguá's help, convinces Olofín that he has the perception to use the oracles wisely.

Olofín, the Supreme Being, sat on his throne. At his feet lay an Ifá board, the ekuele, and a pile of cowry shells.

"I want to give these things to Orunmilá," thought Olofín, "He's trustworthy and mankind will benefit from using the oracles. But how do I know that Orunmilá has the perception needed to use them wisely?"

He decided to test Orunmilá. He summoned Shangó and told him, "Go and bring Orunmilá before me." Olofín waited until Shangó was well on his way. Then he opened the large trunk next to his throne and took out two small bags.

Olofín walked out of his palace and went to a field that had been made ready for planting. From one of the bags, he took out toasted corn and planted it in the half of the field that lay to his left. He took out fresh corn from the other bag and planted it in the half of the field that lay to his right.

Olofín dusted his hands, satisfied. "Now, let's see if Orunmilá has the perception to tell which side of the field will grow. If he does, I'll give him the oracles."

Elegguá is everywhere and he sees everything. He'd watched Olofín planting the corn.

"Oho," said Elegguá, "Olofín is planning to trick Orunmilá? I'm going to trick Olofín," and he ran off to find Orunmilá.

Elegguá caught up with Orunmilá on the steep road that leads to Olofín's palace.

"Orunmilá, Orunmilá," shouted Elegguá. "I have news for you."

"I have no time for your tricks now," said Orunmilá. "Olofín has summoned me to his palace."

"That's what I want to talk to you about," said Elegguá, trotting to keep up with Orunmilá. "Olofín has prepared a test for you."

Orunmilá stopped. "What kind of test?"

Elegguá told Orunmilá how Olofín had planted half of a field with toasted corn and half with fresh corn. "And, if you guess which is which," added Elegguá, "He will make you the owner of the oracles."

Orunmilá arrived at the palace. When he was led to Olofín, he bowed before the throne and said, "My respects to you, Supreme Being. I am grateful that you are considering bestowing the oracles upon me."

"Very perceptive," thought Olofín. Aloud, he said, "Before I do so, Orunmilá, I must test your capacities."

"I am ready to go to the field," said Orunmilá.

"Er, yes," said Olofín, "Please come with me to be tested."

"Orunmilá is very perceptive, indeed," he thought.

Orunmilá and Olofín went to the field. Olofín stretched out his arm and, in a very important tone of voice said, "In this field . . ."

Orunmilá did not let him finish the sentence. "Dear father," he said. "The corn to our left is not going to grow. You planted toasted corn. The corn that you planted to our right will produce a crop. That is where you planted fresh grain."

Olofín was amazed. "You have convinced me of your perception and your wisdom," he told Orunmilá. "Come with me back to the palace and I will grant you ownership of the instruments of divination."

That is how Orunmilá became the greatest of soothsayers.

THE PEOPLE

OBATALÁ IN THE BEGINNING

Oodumare created the world and sent Obatalá to make a solid place to stand on.

Olodumaré created the world, but he didn't make it the way it is now. What the Supreme Being created was nothing but a huge swamp. It was no place for people. The place was full of thorn bushes and fierce animals.

One day, the Orishás gathered in Olodumaré's palace for an audience. They waited a long time for Olodumaré to arrive.

"We're bored," they said. "Let's go down to the world until Olodumaré returns." They climbed down a huge spider web to explore the wasteland.

Shangó raced through the mud chasing and killing the wild beasts. Osaín spent his time studying the thorn bushes and boiling their leaves and roots. Oggún cleared the way for the others with his iron machete. All the Orishás had a wonderful time.

When the Orishás returned to Olodumaré's palace, they made a mess. There were muddy footprints on his floor. Bits of branches and leaves were everywhere. A pile of hairy animal skins was thrown in a corner of the throne room. Olodumaré came in and saw what his children had done.

He threw a fit. "I leave you alone and you destroy my house," he shouted at them.

"We went down to the world to see what it was like," said the Orishás. "It was fun."

"Fun!" exclaimed Olodumaré. "You ruin my house and you call it fun?"

"We couldn't help it," they said. "The world is muddy. There is no place to stand."

Olodumaré told them, "Clean all this up and get out of my sight."

Olodumaré sat on his throne and thought about what the Orishás had said. "A place to stand would be a good thing," he said. "It would be something new that would keep my children from bickering all the time."

The next day, he called Obatalá to his presence. "Obatalá, you are the most responsible of my children," said Olodumaré. "I entrust you with the creation of a new thing."

"What is that, father?" asked Obatalá.

"Earth," said the Supreme Being, handing him a fistful of dry earth inside a snail shell. "Take this earth, this chicken with five toes and this dove. Go down to the world and create a place to stand."

Obatalá went down the spider web and began to search all over the world for the right place where he could create the new thing Olodumaré wanted.

"A place to stand is an important thing," he thought. "Not just anywhere will do."

Some places were too hot. Others were too cold. Some were too high and some were too low.

Finally, he came to a place that was not too hot or too cold and not too high or too low. "This is the place to stand on," said Obatalá.

The place was called Ifé. Obatalá carefully poured the dry earth inside the snail shell on the mud. Then he stood the five-toed chicken upon the small patch of dry ground. The chicken began to scratch and peck, spreading the dry earth with her feet. Obatalá then released the dove. It flew above the chicken, sending clouds of dust rolling up into the air. For four days and four nights the chicken scratched and the dove beat its wings. By the fifth day, the dry earth was scattered in all directions. Most of the mud that made up the world became firm dry land. This is why the fifth day is set aside for rest and the worship of the Supreme Being.

When Obatalá returned to Olodumaré's palace, the Supreme Being was pleased.

"You have done well, Obatalá," he said. "It is a good thing that there is a place to stand on in the world. Come with me, I have something to show you."

Olodumaré took Obatalá to a garden. "What are these, my father?" asked Obatalá when he saw the plants.

Olodumaré said, "Now that there is a place on which to stand, it is time to make it beautiful." He showed Obatalá the plants. "These are royal palms. These are baobab. These are kapok trees."

They kept walking in the garden. Olodumaré showed Obatalá every good and beautiful thing that grew there. Finally, they arrived at a place where a group of people were sitting.

"What are these, my father?" asked Obatalá.

"These are human beings," said Olodumaré. "I made them so they can stand upon the new place in the world. Their chief is named Orelueré."

He called out to Orunmilá, the Orishá of wisdom, who was talking with Orelueré. He said, "Orunmilá, Obatalá. It is my wish that you take these people down to the world. You are to give them these trees and all good things in this garden."

Obatalá and Orunmilá followed the Supreme Being's orders. And, that is the way that people came into the world.

Another version of the story goes like this:

This story is a variation of the previous one. In this one, Obatalá proves untrustworthy and his elder aspect, Oddoduá, is sent to create dry land upon the world.

One day, Olodumaré summoned Obatalá to him and said, "Go down to the world and create dry land, for there is no place to stand on."

Obatalá took the things Olodumaré gave him, a handful of dry earth, a chicken with five toes, and a dove and went down into the world.

The way was long and it was hot. Soon, Obatalá grew thirsty. "That sun is hot and this mud is no fun to walk in," he said. "I wish I had something to drink."

He came across a gourd and looked inside. "This looks like palm wine," said Obatalá. He sniffed. "It is palm wine, just what I need."

He took a sip. "Hmmm, that tastes good," he said.

He took another drink. "Yes, just the thing to take a thirst away," he said.

Obatalá drank the whole gourd of palm wine.

"I feel very sleepy," he said. He put his head on the chicken. "I'll take a nap and then go about my business." Obatalá fell asleep.

Up in heaven, Olodumaré paced back and forth in his palace. "Where is Obatalá?" he asked. "I sent him days ago to make a place to stand on and he hasn't returned."

Another day went by. Olodumaré grew more and more worried. Then he called out, "Oddudúa!"

Oddudúa came into Olodumaré's throne room and said, "Here I am father."

"I want you to go down to the world," said Olodumaré, "and find out what has happened to Obatalá."

Oddudúa went to the giant spider's web that led to the world and climbed down. He followed Obatalá's tracks through the mud until he found him, still fast asleep.

He saw the gourd and said, "It's no use trying to wake Obatalá after all that palm wine."

He lifted Obatalá's head and took the chicken. He put it in a sack along with the handful of dry earth and the dove.

"Olodumaré wants a good place to stand on," said Odduduá. "I better start looking."

He walked until he came to a place called Ilé-Ifé.

"This looks like a good place," said Odduduá, putting down his sack.

He took out the handful of dry earth and spread it on the mud. He took the chicken out of the sack and put it on the small patch of earth. The chicken started to scratch and spread the dirt. Odduduá took the dove out of the sack. The dove tried to fly away and the wind from his wings spread the dirt far and wide.

When Odduduá returned to heaven, Olodumaré was very pleased with him.

"Odduduá," he said, "From now on you will be known as the creator of dry land."

THE SACRIFICE

Human beings bickered among themselves until Olofín made them separate into groups and settle new lands.

Sacrifices are important. Ebós are one of the most important things you can do because they feed the Orishás.

This is a story of something that happened a long time ago, when the world was still young. Back then, there were hardly any people living in the world. They all lived together in peace. Their chief was a very old man, a saint. His name was Baba Ndum.

When Baba Ndum said, "Plant the yams today," everyone said, "Yes, Baba."

They took their digging sticks and machetes out to the fields. They were happy and ready to work. They knew the crop would be good if they followed Baba's advice.

When Baba Ndum said, "Winter is coming. These roofs won't keep away the rain. They need to be fixed," everyone said, "Yes, Baba."

The people went out to the fields and cut down fresh palm fronds to put new roofs on their houses.

The world was so new that Olofín, the Supreme Being, still took an interest in it. He came down to see what people were doing with the world he had made. He liked talking with Baba Ndum.

Every time he visited, Olofín asked Baba Ndum, "Is everything all right with your people?"

Baba Ndum always answered, "My people are happy, my Lord."

This pleased Olofín very much. He likes peace and quiet. He doesn't like problems.

One day, the peace and quiet came to an end. This is what happened:

The old women in Baba Ndum's village were tired and worn out. Age made their joints creak, so they didn't move very fast.

Age dimmed their eyes so they couldn't do fine work. Age ate away at their strength so they couldn't pound grain into flour or lift the heavy cooking pots. Since the old women couldn't do any of these things, they asked the young women to do the chores for them.

When an old women asked nicely and said, "Daughter, please go to the market for me. It's a long way and my knees hurt,"

The young woman did not mind. She said, "Yes Auntie. I'll run your errand for you."

When an old women said, "Daughter, this pestle is too heavy for me. Take it and grind the grain," the young women took up the pestle and ground the flour saying, "Here, Auntie. I'll do the grinding for you."

Well, this went on for a while and anybody, even strong young women, will get tired. They went to talk with Baba Ndum.

"We're unhappy," said the young women. "The old women sit around all day smoking cigars and giving orders. We are the ones that have to do all the work."

Baba Ndum thought for a moment. Then he told them, "The old women gave birth to you. They have grown old taking care of you. It is only right that you should use your strength to help them now that they are weak and can't do things for themselves."

The young women said, "But what about us? It is not fair that we should work all day and not have rest."

Baba Ndum said, "You too will grow old. Someday young women will be doing the work you can no longer do."

"We do not agree with you, Baba," said the young women. "We want to enjoy some of our life now."

"I have spoken," said Baba Ndum. "Now go take care of your responsibilities." That was that, or so he thought.

It was the custom in Baba Ndum's village for the woman to walk to the spring at dawn. When the rooster crowed, every woman placed a large pot on her head and went to the spring to get the water she needed for her household. It wasn't a long walk. The spring flowed from the side of a hill right outside the village. But even though it was near, the old women walked slower than the young women. They were always the last to arrive.

By the time the old women got to the spring, all the young women had filled their pots. Being young, they splashed and played in the water. Their games stirred up mud and dirtied the spring.

The old women complained, "Look at what you are doing. We can't get clean water."

The young women replied, "It's the only time we get to have fun. We need to cool off."

Every day, it was the same.

The old women asked, "Why don't you wait until we get our water? Then you can play all you want."

"It takes you forever to get here," said the young women. "We have chores to do."

The young women never listened to the old women's complaints. Nothing the old women said made them be more considerate. That's usually the way it is when a person wants to get even with another.

The old women returned to their houses and complained to their husbands, "I go for water and I get mud. You must do something. The young women don't respect us."

Heaven help the husband who complained. His wife shrieked, "You say that the water is dirty? You go to the spring in the morning and see if you can do better."

The arguments and bad feelings went on for a long time. Then, one morning at the spring, an old woman said, "Daughters, we've asked you and asked you to keep the spring clean. Look at it. We can't take this dirty water home."

"It's good enough for a bag of bones like you," shouted a young woman.

The old woman threw her pot and hit the young woman on the head. She, in turn, threw a rock, missing the old woman that had thrown the pot, but hitting another on the ear.

Pots and rocks began flying through the air. It was a free for all. Hair was pulled. Arms were bitten. There were shouts, shrieks and yells. The fight lasted an hour. In the end, the old women got the worst of it. The young women were stronger and faster and able to do more damage. The old women hobbled back to their homes.

"What happened to you?" asked their husbands. "You're black and blue. Where's your pot? Where's the water?"

Most of them got a piece of firewood thrown at them for an answer.

There was another fight at the spring the next day, and the next and the day after that.

Baba Ndum called together all the men in the village. He said, "Something must be done. The women can't keep fighting every day. The village is in an uproar."

"Yes, do something," said the men.

An old man said, "At least make my wife stop hitting me on the head with a piece of firewood."

One man said, "Maybe we should go and get the water ourselves."

"That's women's work," said another man.

A third man said, "But the women aren't doing any work at all. They're just fighting."

The first man said, "If we went to the spring with them, we could make sure that they got the water and didn't fight."

"Then who is going to do our work?" asked another. "Who's going to take care of the animals and the fields while we make sure the women don't hit each other?"

A man way in the back of the crowd said, "Let the old women and the young women take turns fetching the water. They can't fight if they're not in the same place at the same time."

Baba Ndum said, "That sounds like a wise idea. The women will take turns going to the spring."

Someone asked, "Who's going to go first?"

Baba Ndum said, "Tomorrow, the old women will go to the spring first."

Baba went around the village, telling the women of his decision. The next day, there was no one at the spring.

Baba Ndum gathered the men together again and asked, "What happened? All the women stayed home."

A man said, "I asked my wife if she was going to the spring. She hit me on the head for calling her old."

That's what happened. No woman would admit to being old. None of the women wanted to go to the spring.

Baba Ndum said, "Let's see if we can solve the problem. Tomorrow, the young women will go to the spring first."

He went around the village and told the women what he had decided. The next morning, all the women went to the spring at the same time. There was a fierce fight.

Baba Ndum gathered the men together for the third time.

"What are you going to do now?" they asked.

Baba Ndum said, "I must go talk with Olofín and get his advice."

Baba Ndum walked until he came to the highest mountain. He climbed to the highest peak.

When he reached the top, he lifted his arms and spoke to the heavens, "Olofín, my father. I need your advice. Please come. I pray to you."

Olofín appeared. He looked like a very old, very tired old man. He said, "What do you want of me, Baba Ndum? I am tired. I need my rest."

Baba Ndum said, "The women won't obey me. I don't know what to do."

Olofín asked, "Why is that? Why don't you talk to them?"

"I have tried, Father," said Baba Ndum. "Olofín, you created men and that is good. But you also created women and that is not so good. You can reason with men. With women, it's something very different. Nobody understands them."

"Tell me what has been going on," said Olofín.

Baba Ndum told him about the spring and about the fights between the old women and the young women.

Olofín said, "Tomorrow, I will go and see what can be done."

The next morning, Olofín went to the spring and hid behind a large rock. He made sure that no one saw him.

The women came to the spring. Olofín saw the shouting and the thrown pots and stones. He watched the whole fight. He waited until the last woman had staggered home holding her head.

Then Olofín went to the village and had Baba Ndum gather together all of his people.

Olofín told them, "I have come down to impose order among my children. Today, I saw fights and arguments. There is no longer peace among your people, Baba Ndum."

The men said, "It isn't our fault. The women were the ones that fought."

Olofín raised his hand and said, "It is no one's fault. There are too many people living together here. That is what has led to all this trouble."

Baba Ndum asked, "What are we to do? How can the fights be stopped?"

"Men are men and women are women. Nothing can change that," said Olofín. "I command that you take your families and move away from here."

"Where will we go?" asked Baba Ndum. "This is the only place we know."

Olofín said, "Some of you walk that way. Some of you walk the other way. Some of you walk to the right and some of you go to the left."

A man asked, "And the animals? What shall we do with the animals?"

Olofín said, "Each head of a family will take a male and a female animal, one of each kind. Release the rest of the animals to run free into the jungle."

It was done as Olofín ordered. The women packed up their households. The men went off to divide the animals. It did not go smoothly.

There were fights. "The fat cows are not yours," said some. "Yours are the skinny brown ones."

Others said, "You're taking all the best chickens. Leave some for me."

Each man wanted to take the best animals. They did not follow Olofín's advice. Neighbor fought against neighbor. Fathers and sons argued. Brothers hit each other.

The whole village was in an uproar until Olofín came back and shouted, "What is going on here?" Everyone stopped fighting. "I leave you alone for an afternoon and you're ready to kill each other?" asked Olofín.

Everyone hung their heads in shame.

Baba Ndum said, "It is not their fault. They just got carried away."

"Not their fault?" said Olofín. "I suppose you're right. It's my fault. I can fix it right away."

Olofín raised his arms. Huge thunderclouds appeared over the village. Bolts of lightning sizzled down frying chickens and making houses explode. The terrified people ran under whatever cover they could find.

Baba Ndum fell to his knees before Olofín and pleaded, "Olofín, destroy me if you must, but spare my people. I'm supposed to be the wise one. I'm their leader. I'm responsible for what they do. They are normal people. They act as normal people do."

Olofín lowered his arms and the clouds rolled back. The lightning stopped.

"I will pardon your people only if you do what I command," said Olofín.

"We will obey," said Baba Ndum.

Olofín said, "Kill all the animals. Sacrifice them to me. I will take them all. That way, there will be no more arguments.

The men took out their knives and killed all the animals. Cows, chickens, goats, all the animals were killed.

The men gathered around Olofín. Their bodies were covered with blood.

They asked, "How will we eat now? What will we do to live?"

Olofín said, "Go gather your pots. Fill them with the sacrifice's blood and go. When you reach your new home, the places where you will build your new villages, sprinkle the blood in the forest."

Baba Ndum said, "And then, what will we do?"

"Wait for the fruits of your sacrifice," said Olofín.

The blood was gathered as Olofín commanded. The people left Baba Ndum's village. Some went one way. Some went the other. Some traveled to the right and others to the left.

They all found new places to settle. The first thing they did was to sprinkle the blood from their sacrifice around their new homes. Then all they could do was trust and wait.

On the dawn of the fourth day, a rooster crowed in each one of the new villages. When the people rushed to the sound, they found the rooster surrounded by every kind of animal needed for a good life. There were cows. There were chickens. There were goats. There were pigs. The people were happy again, even though they now were spread out all over the world.

Since that day, people everywhere sacrifice to the Orishás. The sacrifice is to give thanks for what they have received. The sacrifice is also to beg Olofín's pardon and avoid his anger towards the people on this earth. We pray that he will spare us even though we still fight among ourselves.

ELEGGUÁ AND OBI

Obi means "coconut." This story tells of how Olodumaré's praise turned Obi's head and of how Elegguá arranged Obi's downfall.

Back in the beginning of the world, there was a man called Obi. Obi had a pure heart. He lived very simply and shared the few things that he had with those that had nothing. Whenever there was a fight, Obi stepped in and ended it. He always made sure that both sides were happy and that justice was done.

There were very few men in the world like Obi. There are very few of them now. God was pleased with him.

Olodumaré summoned Obi to heaven and told him, "You are a good man, Obi. I am going to reward you."

Obi bowed his head. "I am yours to command, Lord," he said.

Olodumaré made his skin white as milk. He made his heart and his entrails white. As a sign of his special favor, Olodumaré took Obi, now shining white, and sat him in a place of honor atop a palm tree.

Once Obi was seated on his beautiful palm throne, Olodumaré summoned Elegguá and told him, "This is Obi. He is the best of the human beings and I have rewarded his goodness."

Elegguá looked at Obi and said, "Kind of pale, isn't he?"

"None of your smart talk, Elegguá," ordered Olodumaré. "You are to be Obi's servant. I so command it."

Had Olodumaré forgotten that Elegguá took no orders? That he only did what he wanted when he willed?

Elegguá thought, "I might as well play along and see where this leads."

To Olodumaré, Elegguá said, "If you command it, so it must be." Under his breath, he added, "That way I can keep an eye on this prince among men."

The next day, Elegguá went to Obi and said, "Your friends are here to congratulate you."

Obi waved him away. "Tell them I am too busy," he said. "I am the best person in the world, so I should only talk to kings."

"Hmm," said Elegguá, and went to send Obi's old friends away.

A couple of weeks passed. Obi's pride and vanity grew.

Elegguá went to Obi and said, "Oh, Mighty Obi," that's what Obi wanted to be called now, "Two men want you to settle a land dispute."

"What?" cried Obi. "You dare to interrupt me? Can't you see how busy I am?" He wasn't busy at all. He spent all of his time sitting on his palm throne and thinking about how wonderful he was.

Elegguá insisted, "Mighty Obi, these men have come a long way to see you."

Obi shooed Elegguá away. "I am far too important to concern myself with peasants," he said, "Send them away."

Elegguá said to himself, "This gink really thinks I'm his servant. Let's see what happens if I give him enough rope." He sent the two men away.

A month came and went. Obi summoned Elegguá.

He said, "I wish to throw a giant feast so that all the world may come and worship me."

Elegguá gritted his teeth and said, "As you wish, Mighty Obi."

Obi adjusted the crown he had made for himself. "Invite all my new friends," he went on. "I want all the kings, the counselors and the wise men to come. They must realize that Olodumaré has made a very wise decision in naming me the best among human beings. Of course, he had no choice. I am the greatest."

Obi's arrogance and pride had changed his very soul. Unless Elegguá did something, Obi would become a monster, a tyrant.

Elegguá went to the ends of the earth and invited all the most important persons in the world to Obi's feast.

He went to the Akbobko, "Obi requests the pleasure of your presence," he said.

Eleggúa went to the Oloroso, "Your presence will adorn the feast," he told him.

He went to the Tobi Tobi and announced, "You will honor us by your attendance."

Eleggúa went to the Imisonse, "All our wealth and pageants would be as nothing if you do not come," he said.

He went to all the beautiful, the wealthy and the wise, "Come and be praised," he told them.

However, Eleggúa did not stop there. "I shall invite all of Obi's old friends too," he said to himself and smiled wickedly, because he had a plan. "Everybody is Mighty Obi's friend."

He went to the deformed and invited them, "Please come. Obi does not forget his old friends."

He went to the sick and invited them, "Come, Obi will heal you."

He went to all the poor and miserable people in the world. "Come. Obi will shower you with riches. Is he not the most just of men?"

The night of the feast arrived. Multitudes of kings and princes came dressed in their finest silks and jewels. Their courts and honor guards accompanied them resplendent in gold and silver. Even the chariots and harnesses were made of precious metals. They were all eager to honor Obi. Hadn't Olodumaré named him the best among men?

Obi outshone them all. On his head was the crown he had made. He considered himself the king of the world and wanted to look the part.

He made a grand announcement, "I am now ready to receive my guests."

The servants rushed to open the palace doors.

The palace guards shouted, "Announcing the Akbobko!" The Akbobko entered, went to Obi's throne and kissed his hand.

Obi nodded his head and said, "Welcome to my glorious presence."

The palace guards shouted, "Announcing the Oloroso!" The Oloroso went to Obi and kneeled before him.

Obi waved him away saying, "You show wisdom in recogniz-ing my magnificence."

The next guest entered and the guards goggled at him. "Announcing the Leper!" they croaked.

The crowd drew back from a hideous apparition wrapped in stinking rags.

The leper hobbled towards the throne and bowed to Obi.

Obi cried out, "What? What's this?"

The guards kept announcing the guests. "Announcing the Blind!" "Announcing the Crippled!" "Announcing the Starving!" Each shout was more desperate than the last.

Obi yelled, "Who are these people. Who asked these people to come here!"

Horrified, he saw a crowd of ragged, unwashed men and women making their way to the throne.

The Mighty Obi stood up on his throne to get away from them. "Who are you?" he yelled. "Who said you could come to my feast?"

"Elegguá invited us in your name," they answered. "Long live Mighty Obi! We knew that you would not forget your old friends."

Obi began to jump up and down on his throne. "Friends? You call yourselves my friends? You scum!" he ranted. "My friends are kings. My friends are the mighty."

The palace guards surrounded the hopeless of the world. They pointed their sharp spears at them.

A little child cried, "But we were invited."

"I would not invite you to empty my garbage," hissed Obi. "Get them out of here!"

The lost and defeated of this world were driven out of Obi's palace. They covered their faces to hide their tears of fury and shame. A rain of sticks and stones fell on their heads. The rich and powerful laughed and called out insults.

Obi kept on ranting and raving. "Where is Elegguá? Find me that idiot and I'll break his shepherd's crook over his head!"

Meanwhile, Elegguá was visiting Olodumaré.

Olodumaré said, "What are you doing here, Elegguá? I thought Obi was having a party."

Elegguá had thought it safer to keep out of sight while Obi's guests arrived, but he said, "Oh, you know that I don't like big crowds."

Olodumaré looked at him puzzled. He didn't like crowds? After all, Elegguá is the first to be called to a ceremony and the first to be fed.

He shrugged and said, "Well, I'm glad you dropped by. Obi invited me to the party and, as you know, I don't like to visit the earth. I'm tired. Please thank him and give him my regards."

Elegguá shook his head and said, "I will not do so. It is time for this foolishness to end. I do as I please. You said so yourself. I refuse to play at being Obi's servant any longer."

"I don't understand," said Olodumaré. "I thought it would be an honor for you to serve the most virtuous human being on earth."

"Obi has changed," said Elegguá. "Your honors have gone to his head. He is proud, vain and full of arrogance. He is no longer the friend of all men. Obi spits on the poor and the sick."

Olodumaré said, "I will go down to see for myself."

Elegguá was very surprised. "You'll go down?" he exclaimed.

Olodumaré said, "I am the Supreme Being! You may do as you will, but I, too, can do that as well."

Olodumaré disguised himself as a beggar and walked into Obi's palace. The guards tried to grab him, but he slipped past them. He made his way through the resplendent guests until he stood before Obi's throne.

Olodumaré disguised his voice. "I need food and shelter," he begged.

Obi screamed, "Another one?" He shouted at his guards, "I thought I ordered all this rabble to be removed."

Olodumaré addressed Obi again. This time he did not disguise his voice. "Obi, Obi, how you have changed," he said sadly.

Surprised, Obi peered at the beggar, "Who are you?" he asked.

Olodumaré said, "I am the one that placed you on that throne. Now, I'm sorry that I did."

Obi was terrified. He ran to kneel before Olodumaré. "Please forgive me," he blubbered. "I did not know it was you."

Olodumaré sighed. "That is what makes me sad," he said. "Obi, you used to be good and just."

Obi stammered, "I am good. I am just. I am the best. You said so."

"You are full of arrogance," said Olodumaré. "I made your heart white and made your body match your goodness. Now I'm sorry that I did. It's my fault that you have changed."

Obi asked in a tiny voice, "Are you going to punish me?"

Olodumaré loomed over Obi. "I will make you think about how you have changed," he said.

He raised his arms and power filled the palace. Obi scuttled away and hid behind the throne.

The terrified guests covered their ears as Olodumaré's voice boomed out, "From now on, you will remain white inside, but you will fall from your palm tree throne. You will roll through the mud and the dirt until you are black outside. You will be humble and you will serve all men and honor all Orishás."

That is the way that the lowly coconut became a food for men and animals and the most popular of all the oracles.

THE SON OF THE BABALAWÓ

The high priests of Santería, the babalawós, are Orunmilá's "children." They guard their secrets jealously. Their power derives, in part, from the belief that Orunmilá can, from time to time, control death.

A babalawó's son and the son of Ikú were good friends. They played together every day. Like all boys, they liked to argue with each other.

One evening, they were in the middle of a game. The boys had built a miniature village out of mud and sticks. They pretended that colored stones were herds of valuable cattle.

"I have more cattle than you," shouted the babalawó's son. "That makes me the chief."

"Those are just goats," sniffed Ikú's son. "Goats don't count."

Suddenly, the babalawó's son jumped to his feet and brushed the dirt from his knees. "I have to go home," he said.

"Don't get mad," said Ikú's son. "We'll count the goats."

"No, I really have to go home," said the babalawó's son. "My father told me to be home before the moon came out tonight."

"You are really stupid," laughed Ikú's son. "Don't you know that there's no moon tonight?"

The babalawó's son got red in the face. "Don't you call me ignorant, you jerk. I'm a babalawó's son. I know when the moon is coming out."

"You don't know anything," said Ikú's son. "You just pretend that your dad teaches you things."

"Oh, yeah?" shouted the babalawó' son. "Watch this!" He began moving his arms over his head. Then he drew lines in the dirt.

"What are you doing?" asked Ikú's son. "Are you crazy as well as stupid?"

"I'm making a spell that will stop the moon from rising for three days," lied the babalawó's son.

"You can't do that," said Ikú's son. "Besides, I was only kidding. There is going to be a moon tonight."

"There's not," said the babalawó's son. "My father taught me this mighty spell. He's a great babalawó and knows more that Ikú."

"Death knows more than anyone," shouted Ikú's son.

"All Ikú knows about is bones," sneered the babalawó's son.

"I bet you my father knows more than your father," said Ikú's son.

"A babalawó knows more than Ikú," said the babalawó's son. "I bet you he does."

"I bet you my life that there will be a moon tonight," said Ikú's son. "I bet you it will come out tomorrow and the day after, too."

"I bet you it won't," said the babalawó's son. "If it does, Ikú can come for me."

"It's a bet," said Ikú's son. They cut their fingers and mixed the blood to seal the bet.

When the babalawó's son got home, he told his father, "I've just played a great trick on Ikú's son."

"You didn't hurt him, did you?" asked his father. "Ikú is very powerful."

The son laughed. "No, but I told him I'd made a mighty spell that will keep the moon from rising for three days. He didn't believe me, so I bet him that Ikú could come for me if the moon rose."

His father was horrified. "My son, how could you do such a thing? Don't you know that the moon will rise tonight?"

"I know," answered his son. "But that dummy can't win the bet. After all, I am the son of a mighty babalawó."

"You have put your life in serious danger," said the babalawó. "Ask your mother for something to eat. I have to think."

"There is no danger, father," said the son. "You are a great babalawó."

The babalawó lit candles and prayed. While praying, it came to him that he should make an ebó on top of a hill.

He called to his son. "Come with me. If we make a sacrifice on the hill, you may yet be saved."

The babalawó gave his son a large jar of corojo oil. He rolled a cowhide and lifted it onto his shoulders. The two of them set off for the top of the hill.

"Hurry," said the babalawó. We must make ebó before the moon comes up."

When they arrived, the babalawó sewed the hide shut and told his son. "Pour the corojo oil inside." When the hide was full, the babalawó placed it on the ground, making sure that none of the oil spilled.

"Let us return home," the babalawó told his son. "Do not look back."

After they left, a stray dog came up the other side of the hill and began to sniff the big bag of oil. He licked it. Then he tore it open with his teeth, spilling the corojo oil down the hillside.

The moon began to rise. Slowly it rose to the top of the hill. Just as the moon began to show its face, it touched the corojo oil. It was awful. Oil and dirt smeared the moon's shining surface. Twigs stuck to its face.

"I can't show my face like this," said the moon. Ashamed, it hid and did not come out that night.

The next night, the moon began to rise above the hill. Again, the corojo oil left ugly smears on its face.

"I can't be see like this," said the moon. That night, too, it hid its face in shame.

It wasn't until the fourth night, when the corojo oil had dried and was no longer sticky, that the moon was able to rise over the top of the hill without dirtying its face.

On that fourth night, the babalawó looked up at the moon's shining face, knowing that he had saved his son's life.

"Maferefun Orunmilá," he said. "May what is prayed for be granted forever."

OSHÚN GBÓ

This story tells how Oshún first came to be worshipped. There was once a king named Laro. He led his people through the jungle looking for a good place to settle. The people were weary. They had walked through the jungle for months.

Every day they asked their king, "Is this the place where we will settle?"

Then King Laro looked at the signs and omens and said, "No, this is not the right place."

One day, King Laro, followed by all his subjects, arrived at a river named Oshún.

"Is this the place?" asked his subjects.

"I do not know yet," said the king. "I must consult the oracles. But it is a good place to rest."

The people made camp and sent out hunters to kill the evening's meal.

King Laro's daughters came to him and asked, "Father, we are hot and dusty. May we bathe in this beautiful river?"

"Yes, you may," said the king. "Be careful and do not go too far from the shore."

"We will be careful, father," said the daughters, and they ran to the river. Giggling at the strong warriors that followed them to protect them from danger, they took off their clothes and dove in.

King Laro was preparing the board and necklaces needed to consult the oracle when his warriors rushed into the camp.

"Oh king," said the warriors. "Your daughters dove into the river and they have not come up!"

King Laro and all his people ran to the river bank. His daughters were gone. They searched the shore looking for the girl's bodies. There was no trace of them. The king and his people began to cry and smear ashes on their heads.

Suddenly, one of the warriors pointed and shouted, "Look, over there! The waters are opening."

King Laro's daughters walked out of the bosom of the river. When they were closer all the people could see that their hair and bodies were dry. "It is a miracle," they shouted.

The king hugged and kissed his daughters. His eyes were filled with tears. "What happened to you?" he asked them. "We thought the river had taken you."

"Oshún, the river Orishá took us to her home," said the girls. "She gave us presents and said we were very beautiful."

"Oh, my people," said the grateful king. "We must make a fitting sacrifice to this powerful Orishá."

The women cooked big pots of oshin-oshin, spinach with dried shrimp. The men went into the jungle to look for honey. When everything was ready, they all gathered on the riverbank.

The king addressed the river, "Great Orishá, great Oshún, we are grateful for the return of my daughters. Please accept our offering to you."

All the food was carefully placed in the water. It was not thrown in, for that would have been disrespectful. The fish came and ate the food.

"Oshún's messengers have accepted the offering," said the king.

Then, a very large fish, the largest fish any of these people had ever seen, swam to the king. It held a pumpkin in its mouth, which it laid on the river's edge, right at the king's feet.

"A marvel!" cried the people.

Very gravely, the king picked up the pumpkin and said to his subjects, "This is proof that the Orishá wishes to make a treaty with me. To honor this moment, I change my name to Ataoja."

The people cheered. When they had all quieted down, King Ataoja continued, "Oshún Gbó, Oshún is mature, her abundant waters will never fail us. I name this place Oshogbó. Here we will settle."

And so it was that, in that place protected by Oshún, the city of Oshogbó was founded.

THE ORACLES

HOW ELEGGUÁ TAUGHT IFÁ

This story tells how Elegguá taught Ifá the secret of the oracle.

In the beginning, in the first days of the world, the earth was almost empty. There were very few people; a little handful here, a little handful there. Since there were so few people, the sacrifices to the Orishás were few and far between; a small chicken here, a plate of cornmeal there. The Orishás found themselves with nothing to eat. The Orishás began to go hungry.

Ifá became so hungry that he decided to go fishing. He sat on the river bank all day. He pulled up weeds. He pulled up sticks. He pulled up three little bony fishes.

"This is no way to live," said Ifá.

Elegguá came walking down the river road.

"A good day to you, Ifá," he said. "How is this new world treating you?"

"Terrible," replied Ifá. "Little piddly sacrifices don't fill me up. I've spent the day sweating in the sun to get three bony fishes. You're smart, Elegguá. What do you think I should do?"

Elegguá sat down next to Ifá. He put his chin on his knees and looked at the river. He thought very hard. After a long time, he turned to Ifá and said, "You should go visit Orungán."

"I'll go visit Orungán," said Ifá full of enthusiasm. Then he frowned and added, "Why?"

"He is the head of all the human beings," said Elegguá. "He's a most important man."

"So?" said Ifá crossly. "Is he going to feed me?"

"Don't interrupt," said Elegguá. "Orungán owns two palm trees. Go and ask him for sixteen nuts from those trees."

"I can't eat palm nuts," Ifá exclaimed.

"They're not to eat," explained Elegguá patiently. "Bring the nuts back to me and I will show you how to divine the future with them."

Ifá shrugged. "Then I'll know exactly how long it's going to take me to starve?"

"Knowing what the future has in store would be of great value to humanity," said Elegguá patiently. "People will stop neglecting us and feed us as is our due."

Ifá looked at him suspiciously. "And what's in this for you?"

"As your teacher and as your savior, I expect the best of the sacrifices to go to me," said Elegguá.

Ifá grumbled and tried to get a better deal from Elegguá, but he finally gave up. "I agree," he said. "It's better to give you part of something than to keep all of nothing."

Ifá asked Orungán for the nuts.

"I will give you these things that you ask," said Orungán. "But in exchange, you will teach me what you learn."

"I agree," said Ifá, and took the nuts to Elegguá, who taught him how to divine the future.

Ifá returned to Orungán's house and taught him, making him the first babalawó.

ORUNMILÁ AND THE EKUELE

This story tells how Shangó turned over the oracles to Orunmilá. It also tells how Elegguá forced Orunmilá to give him his due.

The ekuele and the Ifá board used to belong to Shangó. People came daily to ask for his help and advice.
Every time he wanted to go hunting, someone came and said, "Shangó, I need your help."

Every time he wanted to visit a beautiful woman, someone came and said, "Shangó, I need your help."

Every time he wanted to go to war, someone came and said, "Shangó, I need your help."

The time came when Shangó had enough of sitting at home reading oracles. "I don't get to do anything," he shouted. "I never get to have fun. I'm going to give the ekuele and the board to someone else."

Shangó knew of a very wise and holy old man named Orunmilá. "He does nothing all day," thought Shangó. "I might as well give the oracle to him." He set off for Orunmilá's house, the ekuele and the Ifá board under his arm.

Orunmilá greeted him graciously, "Welcome to my home, Shangó. How may I serve you?"

Shangó sprawled on a bench and tossed Orunmilá the collars and the board. "I'm bored with the life of a soothsayer," he said. "You keep the ekuele and the board. Give people advice and help them with their problems, just like I've been doing."

Orunmilá was astounded. "Thank you. Thank you," he stammered. "This is such an honor. I don't know what to say."

"There is one condition that you must abide by," warned Shangó.

"Anything," said Orunmilá. "I will do anything that you say."

"I want you to divide your earnings equally with my friend, Elegguá," said Shangó.

"I swear I will do it," said Orunmilá solemnly.

"See that you do," said Shangó. "Well, that's that. I'm off to a party in the next village."

Orunmilá practiced and studied until he learned to throw the ekuele. He became a very prestigious babalawó. Word of his knowledge spread all over the world.

If a man had difficulties, he was told, "Go see Orunmilá."

If a woman thought her husband was running around on her, she was told, "Go see Orunmilá."

Anyone who was sick was told, "Go see Orunmilá. He will divine the cause of your ailment."

Each passing day brought him more clients. Each client made him richer and more powerful. Wealth and power increased his pride.

He said to himself, "Why should I share my riches with Elegguá? After all, I do all the work." He decided to ignore the promise he had made to Shangó.

Every night Elegguá stood at Orunmilá's door and demanded, "Give me what is mine."

Every night Orunmilá dismissed him saying, "Don't bother me now with such trifles. I will figure out what I owe you on another day. Now, go away."

Elegguá was furious. He was out on the street, cold and hungry. He had been betrayed.

"That lying old man is going to pay every bit that he owes me," vowed Elegguá. "He will pay for all the harm and injustice he is heaping on my head."

Early the next morning, Elegguá stood at the crossroads and stopped all the travelers. "Where are you going?" he asked.

If they said, "To Orunmilá's house," Elegguá said, "Don't bother, he is sick today."

People became very upset, saying, "What? I've been traveling for days. I must consult Orunmilá."

"No, it's impossible," Elegguá told them. "The babalawó is very sick and very tired. Go back home."

"That old fraud," they shouted. "Everyone said that he could help me."

"No, no. Go back home," Elegguá told them. "He is very old. He is not working today."

Day after day Elegguá stood at the crossroads, turning people away from Orunmilá's house. As the word spread that Orunmilá was no longer giving consultations, there were fewer and fewer people for Elegguá to turn away.

Meanwhile, Orunmilá found himself in a desperate situation.

"Where is everyone?" he cried out. "Where are my clients?"

No clients came, but the merchants did. "Where is the money you owe us for your robes?" they demanded. "Where is the money you owe us for your food? Where is our money?"

Orunmilá told them, "Things are not so good right now. But things will get better."

The merchants took everything away and said, "Come see us when they do."

During all of this, Elegguá still visited Orunmilá every night and demanded, "Give me my due."

One night, Orunmilá confessed, "I have nothing left. The merchants took everything. I no longer have any clients. I have no money. I have nothing."

"Maybe you should call Shangó," Elegguá suggested. "He could throw the ekuele and find out the cause of your misfortune."

Orunmilá said, "Yes, that's a great idea, a wonderful idea. He will know." Right away, he sent for a runner to find Shangó.

When Shangó arrived, the first thing he said was, "Where are your servants? Where are your clothes? Where is your furniture? You don't even have a gourd of beer for a guest."

"I am ruined," wailed Orunmilá. "I sent for you so that you could divine the reason for my misfortune."

"Have you forgotten how to consult the oracle?" asked Shangó.

"I've lost my ashé. I've lost my power," said Orunmilá.

"He doesn't have a single client left," said Elegguá with a smile.

Shangó looked at Elegguá. He looked at Orunmilá. He knew what was happening without the help of any oracle.

"Orunmilá, pay Elegguá what you owe him and don't bother me any more with all this foolishness," said Shangó and he stalked off in a foul mood.

The moment that Orunmilá gave Elegguá his due, the flood of clients returned. His fame returned. His wealth returned. And, every night when Elegguá came to his door and said, "I have come for what is mine," Orunmilá paid him gladly.

Remember that the first Orishá that has to be given his due is Elegguá.

THE COCONUT ORACLE (BIAGUE)

The coconut oracle, the "Biague," requires ritual and prayers, but essentially it involves the splitting of an unhusked coconut, selecting four pieces, throwing them and interpreting the result.

The four possible results are:

ALAFIA: Affirmative. It is possible.

All four pieces land white (meat) side up.

It promises happiness and health

Alafia must be confirmed by Otawe or Eyife. Throw again.

EYIFE: Yes.

Three pieces white side up. One dark side up.

The answer is definitely affirmative.

If the previous throw was Alafia, the answer is yes. No need to throw again.

OTAWE: Maybe. There are doubts.

Two pieces land white side up. Two land dark (shell) side up.

There is hope, but no certainty. The question is subject to conditions.

Throw again. This time, make your question more specific. The next throw will give the answer.

If Otawe comes up again, the answer is no.

With Otawe, or if the previous throw was Alafia it might be necessary to make ebó (a sacrificial offering). By consulting the oracle, the type of sacrifice can be pinpointed.

OCANASODE: No.

One piece white side up. The other three pieces are dark side up.

The answer warns of tragedy. Be alert in order to avoid misfortune. Grave difficulties are in store.

Consult the oracle again and ask if Ocanasode just means "No," or if there are further difficulties and complications present.

OYEKUN: Death.

All four pieces are dark side up.

The answer is a definite no. An announcement of death and suffering.

A babalawó must be consulted immediately. You need to be ritually cleansed by a despojo, the brushing and washing away of evil influences.

Light a candle for the souls of the dead.

The babalawó and you must keep asking the oracle if the message of death comes from the Orishás who speak or from the spirits of the dead. That will give the babalawó or yalorishá an idea of the forces he or she must deal with.

BIAGUE AND ADOTO

The coconut oracle is known as the biague. That's because the first man to learn the secret of its use was named Biague. This is what happened:

A long time ago, so long ago that the Creator still took an interest in His creation. Olofín came down to the world to see how the different beings he had made were getting along and to give them his blessing.

He walked in the mountains and blessed the birds. He walked in the forest and blessed the animals. He walked in the plain and he saw a beautiful tree.

"What do you do?" Olofín asked the tree.

"I let the wind caress and bend me," said the tree.

"Is that all?" asked Olofín.

"That is all," said the tree.

"It is a pity that one so tall and beautiful as you should have no other purpose," said Olofín.

"What could be my purpose?" asked the tree.

"You should be of service," said Olofín. "What would you like to do?"

The tree thought. The wind made it sway one way and it thought one thing. The wind made it sway the other way and it thought something else.

Finally, it spoke. "I don't know," said the tree. "I would like to be of service, but it seems to me that the other trees already give enough food, wood and shade. The beings of this earth are happy as things are. What could I give?"

"I think I can think of a service that you can give," said Olofín.

"That would make me happy," said the tree.

"Each Orishá has power over a fruit or a food," said Olofín.

The tree sadly said, "But no Orishá owns me and I give no fruit."

Olofín said, "I will give you a fruit. I will make it into one that belongs to all the Orishás. That way it will be useful to all the people on the earth."

"That would be wonderful," sighed the tree. "What will my fruit be called?"

"Your fruit will be called Obi Gui Gui," said Olofín. And so it was.

The palm tree waved happily in the wind. "Thank you Olofi for this honor and privilege," it said.

The next day, Olofín summoned the Orishás to the palm tree. When they had all arrived, he showed them a coconut.

"This is Obi Gui Gui," said Olofín, "the child of your King, Olofín, and the palm tree. I have created this fruit so that all of you may make use of it."

The Orishás asked, "How can one fruit belong to all?"

Olofín told them, "The pieces of this fruit will have a meaning that I will teach you how to read."

Olofín taught the Orishás how to read the coconut oracle.

Then Olofín thought, "Now that the Orishás know how to understand the meaning of the coconut, I must find a wise and pure man and teach him too. That way the people of the world can gain wisdom."

Olofín searched the world for a worthy man. He found a man named Biague.

Olofín appeared before Biague and said to him, "Biague, I have a task for you."

Biague fell to the ground in wonder. He said, "I will do any thing you say, Olofín."

"Pay attention and study," said Olofín. He taught Biague the secrets of the oracle.

Biague became a famous babalawó. He married and had a son, Adoto.

When Adoto came of age, Biague said to him, "My son, God has taught me the secret of how to speak with the Orishás. You are my only son, so I will teach you in turn." He taught Adoto how to read the coconut.

Now, it so happened that Biague had two adopted sons who hated and envied Adoto. When Biague died, they took every-thing, leaving nothing for Adoto.

"Where is my portion of the lands?" asked Adoto. "Where are the animals that belong to me?"

"You have nothing," said the brothers. "Go away before we beat you."

"But this is my house," said Adoto. "You are wearing my clothes."

"You are a fool and crazy," said the brothers. "We don't know what you are talking about. Biague, our father, left us all these things when he died."

"That is not true," said Adoto. Before he could say anything more, his step brothers seized him and gave him a severe beating.

The village chief saw everything, but said nothing. He was a man who only listened to wealth. Adoto had to hobble to the outskirts of the village and sleep in an abandoned house.

The people of the village were scandalized. They had loved Biague and they loved his son. They knew Adoto to be wise and kind. The village elders went to see the chief.

They said to him, "You know that Adoto is Biague's true son."

"I have not seen any proof," said the chief.

The elders were angry. They told the chief, "You know that those two thieves don't have a right to Adoto's property."

The chief smiled a nasty smile and shrugged. "I have not seen any proof," he said.

The village elders said, "If Adoto shows you proof, will you return his property to him?"

Knowing that there was no proof, the chief said, "If Adoto shows proof that he was chosen by his father as heir, I will give him his property."

That afternoon, the chief summoned Adoto and his step brothers before the village council.

The chief said to them, "I have summoned you here so that you may show proof of your right to Biague's property."

The step brothers made a big show of protesting. "We live in his house," they said. "We wear his ornaments. Is that not proof of Biague's favor?"

The chief said, "That sounds reasonable to me." He turned to Adoto. "What have you to say for yourself?"

"I will let the Orishás speak," said Adoto and took out a coconut from under his robe.

"What kind of nonsense is this?" said the chief.

Adoto paid him no attention. He began his moyubá, his prayer. He broke the coconut and picked the four pieces.

"My father had a ring that he always wore," said Adoto. "Is that not so?"

"That is so," said the people.

The chief said, "So what? That is no proof."

The brothers shouted, "Beware, he is playing a trick."

Adoto calmly went on, "So, whoever can come up with that ring is the true heir of my father's property. Is that not so?"

"That is so," said the council. "Biague would have given the ring to his heir."

The step brothers laughed and said, "The ring is lost. We don't have it and we know you don't have it either."

Adoto said, "I will ask the Orishás where it is." He threw the pieces of coconut.

"Is it in the house?" asked Adoto.

"No," said the coconut.

"Is it on the ground?" asked Adoto.

"No," said the coconut.

"Is it in the water?" asked Adoto.

"No," said the coconut.

"Is it in the air?" asked Adoto.

"Alafia, yes," said the coconut.

Adoto said to the gathering, "Come with me. I know where the ring is."

The elders and all the people in the village followed Adoto. The chief and the brothers grumbled, but they came along too. Adoto led them to Biague's house.

The stepbrothers said, "This is our house. We told you the ring wasn't here."

Adoto paid no attention. He went to the big baobab tree that grew next to the house and began to climb it.

The chief said, "He's crazy. How can a ring be in a tree?"

The brothers were worried. What if Adoto could come up with Biague's ring? They would lose everything. "You must stop him," they said to the chief.

But it was too late to stop Adoto. He climbed until he reached a parrot's nest. He reached in and then climbed down again.

When he got to the ground, the people and the council of elders crowded around him. He opened his hand and showed them Biague's ring.

The step brothers blustered, "You hid that ring in the tree yourself."

The chief puffed himself up and said, "Yes, you could have hidden the ring yourself."

Adoto said, "My father loved that parrot. He fed it every day. After he died, I'm sure that my brothers did not feed it."

"Why should we?" said the step brothers. "It's just a noisy bird."

Adoto went on, "It must have been hungry. It flew into the house looking for food. When the parrot saw the ring, it took it because the bird had seen it on my father's hand every day."

The chief said, "You may have found the ring, but your father did not give it to you."

"He gave me the skill to find it," said Adoto.

The council said, "Adoto is right. If Biague had not passed on his skills to him, he would not have found the ring. That proves that he is the true heir."

So, thanks to the oracle Biague had taught him how to read, Adoto became the sole inheritor of Biague's goods. Not only that, the people of the village were so impressed by his wisdom that they named him chief.

Adoto taught his children how to read the coconut oracle and, ever since those times, the coconut has been a means through which men have communicated with the Orishás.

ELEGGUÁ, ESHÚ

OLD AGE

This is an old African story. Elegguá is an unknown urchin, more of a forest sprite than an Orishá. He uses his knowledge of medicinal herbs to cure Olofín. Olofín then rewards him, granting him the attributes by which Elegguá is known today.

Olofín felt old. Every step made his knees hurt. His neck was so stiff that he had to turn his whole body when he wanted to turn his head. His back hurt so much that he couldn't lift up a hoe. He couldn't work his land. Weeds grew in his fields and wild pigs dug up the few yams that were left.

His eyesight was terrible. Each breath sent shooting pains through his chest. He had to face it. He was old and he was sick. He became scared.

Olofín called all the Orishás together. He told them, "I feel strange. My chest hurts. I have pains in my back."

The Orishás asked, "What would you have us do?"

Olofín shouted, "I want you to cure me." Then, in a quieter voice, he said, "I need your help."

The next day, Yemayá came to Olofín and said, "I have prepared a seaweed plaster and linden tea."

Olofín allowed her to put the plaster on his chest and he drank the tea. But it didn't help.

Then Oshún came and said, "I have brought you fresh orange juice and wild lettuce tea."

Olofín drank the orange juice and fell asleep after drinking the wild lettuce tea. When he woke up, he felt as terrible as ever.

Shangó came to visit and said, "Eat this bran so you can get regular again."

Before Olofín could say that that was not one of his problems, his mouth was full of bran.

Shangó then poured a bowl of soup into Olofín's mouth. "Wash it down with this good leek soup. That will give you energy." The bran and the leeks did not help.

One by one, all the Orishás returned and offered Olofín an herb, a food, a bath, a plaster or a tea.

Olofín cried out, "None of this is helping me. All your medicines are doing is upsetting my stomach."

It was more serious than that. Olofín was now so weak that he could not get out of bed.

He propped himself up on his pillows and grumbled, "What good is to have lots of powerful children if not a one of them can cure me or help me?"

In those days, in the days of Olofín's illness, Elegguá was not doing well. He was not respected and famous like he is today. In fact, he wasn't even getting enough to eat. He was very poor, living in doorways and eating out of garbage cans. Since he was just a poor mischievous child, no one had bothered to summon him before Olofín. Elegguá found out about Olofín's illness when he overheard Oyá and Yemayá walking down the street talking.

"Olofín is getting worse and worse every day," said Oyá. "The plantain foo foo I gave him did not help. I even put camphor balls in his armpits and he's still the same."

Yemayá said, "I'm very worried. We have all given him every medicine we can think of and he doesn't improve."

When he heard this, Elegguá went running to his mother.

"Mother, take me to Taita Olofín," said Elegguá.

"Take you to the palace?" said his mother, shocked. "We can't go to the palace dressed in rags."

"I am sure that my medicines can cure Olofín," said Elegguá. "If I can do that, we won't be dressed in rags for long."

The woman took Elegguá to the palace.

Olofín saw the ragged pair at his bedside and asked, "What is it that you want here? Today is not the day that I give charity to the poor."

Elegguá said very seriously, "I have come to cure you."

Olofín was taken aback. "You? You think you can cure me? All my children have tried to cure me and none has been able to make me feel even the slightest bit better."

Elegguá was very sure of himself. "They did not have my medicines," he said.

"Very well," said Olofín. "What do I have to lose? Let's see if you have the skill and knowledge to cure me."

Elegguá spent an hour examining Olofín. He looked into his nose. He looked into his ears. He had him stick out his tongue and roll his eyes. He had him cough.

When he finished the examination, he said to Olofín, "I must now go into the forest to get the ingredients for my medicines," and, off he went.

Before entering the forest, Elegguá kneeled on the path, raised his hands and said, "O forest, O plants, O sticks and roots, O leaves, O creepers and vines, I come in need of you. I ask your permission. I ask your blessing. I come just to gather what I need and no more."

With that, he got to his feet and entered the forest.

Every time Elegguá plucked a leaf off a plant he said, "With your permission."

Every time he dug a root, he said, "Please pardon me."

He went through the forest politely asking, "Do you mind if I take a bit of this?"

When he took what he needed, never more, he said, "Thank you for your blessing. I have need of your help and your power."

All day long he wandered though the forest gathering plants and roots. He took everything back to the palace, where he spent the night preparing a very strong and powerful medicinal brew. He drummed the proper rhythms. He sang the proper songs. As the sun came up, he was finished.

Elegguá walked into Olofín's bedchamber with a big bowl of medicine and handed it to him.

Olofín looked inside the bowl. The medicine looked like what his servants cleaned out of the animal's stalls. It smelled like it, too.

"Are you sure this will cure me?" he asked.

Elegguá laughed. "What doesn't kill you fattens you," he said.

Slowly, Olofín began to drink the brew.

"Ugh," he said, and, "Waugh," and "Bleaugh," shivering with every sip. The taste was just as disgusting as the look and the smell.

Olofín gagged and shook for a few minutes.

Then he said, "You know, my back doesn't feel so bad," and he sat up in bed.

Another minute passed. Olofín took a deep breath. "My chest doesn't hurt any more," he said.

He felt well enough to swing his feet out of bed and sit up. This was the first time in two weeks that he'd been able to do that.

"Your medicine is working," exclaimed Olofín.

Elegguá said, "Give it a little more time."

Within the hour, Olofín was up on his feet. The bags under his eyes disappeared. His skin shone with health.

He shouted, "Look, I can move my fingers again."

Before, he'd barely been able to whisper.

Olofín took a few steps. "The arthritis is gone. I can walk without a stick." Then he ordered, "I'm starving. Bring me some food."

For the first time in months, Olofín had a good meal.

As he was munching on a chicken leg, Olofín said, "Come closer, Elegguá." Elegguá perched on the edge of the chair. Olofín threw an arm around him and said, "I want to thank you. Ask me for whatever you want."

"First of all," said Elegguá, "I want half of that chicken."

"It's yours," said Olofín.

Elegguá happily began to munch on the chicken. With his mouth full and his lips smeared with grease he said, "I want you to give me the right to eat before anyone else does."

This may not sound like much, but Elegguá knew what poverty was like. He knew what true misery was. Happiness is impossible if you have an empty stomach.

Olofín stood up and put both his hands over Elegguá's head. He said, "From now on, you will be the first to eat from any sacrifice. No one will be able to eat before you."

Elegguá added, "I also want to be shown respect before anyone else gets it."

Olofín said, "You will be placed behind every door. That way, you will be the first to be greeted upon arrival and the last upon departure."

Olofín reached into his robe and took out a tremendous key. He said, "Take this key. I make you the owner of all the roads and paths on the earth. No one will be able to talk to my children before first paying you respect."

That is what happened to Elegguá, the child with the face of an old man.

THE MICE

In this story, Elegguá saves Olodumaré from his children's treachery. Olodumaré rewards him by giving total freedom of action.

The Orishás were jealous of Olodumaré's power.

They gathered together and complained, "Why should he be king? What does he do for us?"

"He is too old," they said. "He doesn't know what he is doing anymore. If he did, he would share his power and knowledge with us."

The more they talked about it, the angrier they got.

"He has us trailing behind him like dogs," said the Orishás. "We don't need that anymore. We don't need him anymore."

For once, all the Orishás agreed, "We don't need Olodumaré any more. We're going to take away Olodumaré's powers."

They schemed and they plotted. However, none of the Orishás could come up with a plan to get rid of Olodumaré.

They talked of throwing him down a deep well, "He's too strong. We could never get him down the well."

They talked of drowning him, "He controls the waters. We can't drown him."

Someone suggested burning down his house, "He controls fire. We can't burn him."

They even talked about throwing him off the mountain where he lived, "He controls the air. He will just fly away and come back to punish us."

Every time they came up with an idea to get rid of Olodumaré, the Orishás found that they didn't have the power to carry it out.

Finally, someone, no one knows who, said, "We all know that Olodumaré is afraid of mice."

The other Orishás laughed. "So what?" they said. "Mice are too small. They can't do anything to him."

The Orishá insisted, "The mice may be small, but his fear is very big. His fear might kill him. If we fill his house with mice, he may be frightened to death."

The more they talked about the idea, the more they liked it.

"Even if the mice don't frighten him to death," they said, "they may frighten him so much that he will decide to go away and we'll be able to share his power among us."

Of course, each Orishá thought, "I'll have Olodumaré's power all to myself."

No one noticed Elegguá, the owner of the paths. As always, he was standing by the door. He heard all the Orishá's plans. He didn't care one way or the other about Olodumaré and his powers, but he liked to see things stirred up. Elegguá decided to do so.

The trickster ran out the door. He did not make a sound. Elegguá ran until he reached Olodumaré's house.

Olodumaré was not home. Elegguá sat by the door. Elegguá is the sentinel, the guardian. There, by the door, he waited.

Soon, the Orishás arrived. Each carried a large basket full of mice. They found an open window and went into Olodumaré's house.

They emptied the baskets into the kitchen. They emptied the baskets into the halls. They filled the cupboards with mice. They packed mice into the chests. They stuffed them into the rafters. They carpeted the floor with scurrying mice.

They whispered to each other, "Hurry, hurry. We must be finished before Olodumaré gets back."

Elegguá sat quietly by the door and watched. He was so still and quiet that not one Orishá noticed him. The trickster can make himself disappear.

One of the Orishás looked out the window. "Quick, hide," he said. "Here comes Olodumaré now."

The Orishás jumped out the window. They jammed all the windows shut and ran to hide in the bushes.

Olodumaré opened his front door. Something didn't seem right. His house smelled musty.

He called out, "Hello? Is anyone here?"

Three Orishás sneaked up behind Olodumaré. They pushed him into the house and barred the front door. Olodumaré was trapped!

Olodumaré saw the mice. "Mice!" he screamed.

Mice fell from the rafters into his hair. Olodumaré ran around screaming. He tried to hide in a large chest. Mice poured out of the chest.

"Mice!" yelled Olodumaré.

He dove into a cupboard. Thousands of mice ran over his body and under his clothes.

"Mice!" he cried.

Olodumaré scrambled out of the cupboard and fell to the floor, thrashing about hysterically.

"Mice! Mice! Mice!" he screamed.

A mouse ran into his mouth and Olodumaré's eyes bugged out in panic.

Elegguá thought this was the time to make his move. He said, "Do not be afraid. Olodumaré, I will save you from the mice."

Elegguá opened his mouth wide and began to eat handfuls of mice. He opened his mouth wider and gobbled up the mice in the cupboard. He shook the walls of the house. He opened his mouth like a huge snake and sucked up all the mice that fell from the rafters. He ate and he ate until there wasn't a single mouse left in Olodumaré's house.

Elegguá gave a discrete burp and helped Olodumaré to his feet.

He said, "You are safe now, my lord," munching on a couple of mice that had gotten caught in Olodumaré's hair. "I have taken care of all the mice."

Olodumaré roared, "Who did this to me? Who has dared to pollute my house?"

Elegguá said, "I'm not one to bear tales, but if you look outside in the bushes you will find your sons and daughters. They have done this thing to you."

Olodumaré ran outside and caught all the Orishás. He punished each one in the most terribly painful way he could think of. Then he went back inside his house. Eleggúa was waiting for him by the door.

Olodumaré asked him, "My dear Eleggúa, how can I repay you for saving me from those horrible mice?"

Eleggúa shrugged, "It is nothing, my lord," he said modestly. "Anyone could have done what I did."

Olodumaré insisted, a little testily, "Still, you must want some reward."

"My service is reward enough, my lord," said Eleggúa.

"Name your reward or else," shouted Olodumaré. "When I say I'm going to give a reward I give it."

Eleggúa, always the sly one, asked, "Can it be anything at all?"

Olodumaré was getting really annoyed. "Anything!" he said. "Name it and it is yours, but be quick about it."

Eleggúa smiled and said, "I want to have the right to do whatever I want."

Olodumaré was stunned. "What?" he said.

"I want the right to do as I wish whenever I wish," repeated Eleggúa. "That will be my reward."

Olodumaré did not like it, but he had to do as he had promised. That is why Eleggúa is the only Orishá that gets to do as he wills.

THE MAN WITH TWO WIVES

shú is Eleggua's malevolent aspect. He brings nothing but trouble, as this story shows.

A long time ago, in Africa, there was a man who had two wives. There was no jealousy between the two women. They knew that their husband loved them both. He did not play favorites. If he kissed one, he kissed the other. If he bought one a present, the other wife received one just as nice. The two wives shared equally in the house work and took joy in each other's children.

When the man and his wives went out to enjoy the evening breeze, everyone they passed said, "There goes a happy marriage." Other wives said to their husbands, "Why don't you treat us as nice?"

Eshú was sitting on an overturned basket, leaning his chin on his stick and contemplating what deviltry he could get into next.

When the man and his two wives walked by with their arms around each other, Eshú heard a father say to his son, "There is an example of married bliss. May you be as happy when you marry."

Eshú thought, "Ridiculous, everyone knows that there is no such thing as a happy marriage." He clamped his cigar between his teeth and muttered, "And I'll prove it, too."

Eshú went and made dozens of hats. He worked from midnight to dawn. Some hats had parrot feathers. Some were covered in cowry shells. All were magnificent.

As the sun came up, Eshú stood on one foot and twirled around. His body and his clothes changed as he twirled until he looked just like a market peddler. Then he packed all the hats in a big basket and took them to the market.

When he got to the market, Eshú set up a stall, laid out his hats and waited.

One of the wives came walking by, her shopping basket on her head.

Eshú called out to her, "Such a beautiful woman must be married to a man worthy of my hats."

The woman stopped. Eshú showed her a hat with a brim made out of peacock feathers.

"If your husband wore this hat," he told the woman, "he would look like a king."

She took the hat and looked at it. She had never seen such a magnificent hat.

"What a beautiful hat!" she exclaimed.

Eshú smiled and said, "It will make a wonderful gift for your husband."

"Yes," said the woman. "I know he'll like this hat. I'll buy it. He loves surprises and gifts."

She put Eshú's hat in her basket and hurried home singing a little song. The woman couldn't wait to surprise her husband with her gift.

Once home, she hid the hat behind her back and went to where her husband sat playing a small drum, waiting for the second wife to finish preparing lunch.

With a big, happy smile on her face, she said to her husband, "I have a surprise for you."

The husband exclaimed, "You found the first mangoes of the season in the market?" He loved mangoes.

"No, it's not that," she said.

The second wife asked, "The merchant had the cloth we ordered for his shirt?"

"No, it's this!" she said, taking the hat out from behind her back and giving it to her husband.

The husband put on the hat. He looked at himself in the mirror. It was splendid! He was thrilled. "This is the best gift I have received in my life!" he said.

Of course, the second wife was hurt by those words.

She thought, "I've given him many gifts and he's never said any of them was the best."

The man hugged his first wife. "Come here," he said. "Let me give you a big kiss."

The second wife felt a pang of jealousy. She thought, "Here I am cooking lunch for the both of them. Do I get a hug? Do I get a kiss? No!"

There was much kissing and laughing between the husband and his first wife while they ate lunch. They did not notice the second wife's angry silence.

Early the next morning, the second wife took the shopping basket and put it on her head.

The first wife asked, "Where are you going? I went to the market yesterday."

The second wife said coldly, "I want fresh greens for dinner tonight, not wilted seconds." She turned and walked away.

The first wife was puzzled. "I wonder what that was about?" she said to herself.

Eshú was sitting in his market stall, waiting. A wicked smile spread across his face when he saw the second wife striding straight towards him.

He called out to her, "Such a beautiful woman must be married to a man worthy of my hats."

"I want the best hat you have," said the second wife. "I don't care how much it costs."

He reached behind him and brought out a hat made of cowry shells sewn with golden thread.

Eshú showed it to the woman. "I think this is what you are looking for," he said.

The hat was even more beautiful than the one her co-wife had given her husband!

She snatched the hat out of Eshú's hands. "I'll take it," she cried.

The second wife hurried home. Eshú sat in his market stall, humming a little song to himself.

When the second wife presented her husband with the hat, he was overcome with wonder. He hugged and kissed his second wife. "This hat is even more beautiful than the one I was given yesterday!" he said in between kisses.

He took off the hat that his first wife had given him and threw it on the floor. He put on the new hat and paraded in front of the mirror.

"I truly look like a king!" he said.

His second wife cooed and hovered over him. "Here, let me fix it for you," she said.

Over her husband's shoulder, she gave the first wife a look that said, "See? I really know how to please our husband."

The first wife picked up her hat from the floor. She held her gift to her husband on her lap and cried.

Early the next morning, the first wife picked up the shopping basket and headed out the door.

The second wife asked, "Where are you going?"

The first wife looked at her down her nose and sniffed, "I know how to pick what my husband likes. I'm going to get it for him." She turned her back on the second wife and walked away.

Eshú waited in the market.

When the first wife approached his stall, he began his speech, "Such a beautiful woman must be married . . ."

The first wife slammed her basket down on the counter. "I want a hat that makes the one with the cowry shells you sold yesterday look like a cow flop," she said, breathing hard.

Eshú said, "I think I have what you want."

Of course, when the first wife presented the new hat to her husband, he loved it.

"This hat is the most beautiful," he said. "It makes that other one look like a cow flop."

The second wife was furious.

The next morning, the second wife stomped out of the house.

The first wife began to ask, "Where are you . . . ?"

The second wife didn't let her finish. "To get something my husband likes, if it's any of your business," she yelled.

Eshú still waited in the market. He saw the second wife and started to say, "Such a beautiful . . ."

The second wife shouted, "Give me a hat such as has never been seen in this world!"

On and on it went. First one wife and then the other would rush off to the market to buy a hat from Eshú. Every day, one woman or the other would return with a hat for their husband. Each hat was more sublime than the last. The hat war went on until one morning, when it was the first wife's turn to rush off to the market for a hat.

She elbowed her way past the second wife and hissed, "Get out of my way, you hag."

The second wife threw a wooden spoon after her and screeched, "Cow, watch your fat ass!"

The first wife raced to the market. "I'll show her," she panted. "I'll show her if I can please my husband or not!"

The hat stall was not there. Eshú was gone. She looked in disbelief at the place where his stall had always been. A tomato seller looked back at her.

Cheerfully, he started his sales pitch. "A woman with such fine tomatoes can certainly appreciate mine," he said.

"Where are the hats?" she screamed at him.

The tomato seller was take aback. "Do I look like a hat seller?" he asked.

The first wife dug through the piles and baskets of tomatoes. The man tried to stop her. She knocked him down.

"I know the hats are here!" she yelled. "They have always been here!"

"Help, mad woman!" shouted the tomato seller.

The other merchants ran to his aid. They jumped on the frantic woman and held her down.

The first wife struggled and yelled, "I know he has hats. He always has hats!"

A big burly market guard said, "Sure, lady. He has hats. They just look like tomatoes. Let's go."

The commotion was over. The first wife found herself unceremoniously escorted out of the marketplace.

The guard said, "Tell your husband to send his other wife to do the shopping."

The woman sobbed, "All I want is a hat."

Clothes torn, hair dusty, the first wife made her way home.

Her husband's eyes popped out when he saw her. "What's happened to you?" he asked his sobbing wife.

The first wife wailed, "I went to get you a gift and . . ."

The second wife pointed her finger and laughed. "You see? She doesn't even care how she looks!"

The first wife bared her teeth and spat out, "You stay out of this, you crow. This is between my husband and me!"

"Your husband?" snarled the second wife.

"Yes, my husband." yelled the first wife.

"Did you bring me a present? Maybe a hat?" asked the husband hopefully.

"You shut up!" the first wife screamed at her husband. "All you do is eat."

"I do all the cooking," yelled the second wife. "What are you complaining about?"

The first wife took a handful of boiled plantains from the pot and mashed them into the second wife's face. "Is this what you call cooking?" she screamed.

The yelling and screaming carried over the fields. It could even be heard at the crossroads where Eshú sat on a stone, his chin resting on his stick.

He shook his head and smiled. "There is no such thing as a happy marriage." he said.

THE ABSENT KING

In this story, Eshú again takes advantage of people's deepest desires in a most cruel way.

There was once a King who had no time for his wife.

The Queen took the time and trouble to cook his favorite dishes for him with her own hands.

Every day, the Queen brought the King his dinner and said, "I've made you a delicious plantain foo-foo," or "a delicious congri," or "yucca fritters." It was always his favorite food.

Every day, he pushed her away. "I have no time to eat now," he said. "I have to check the spears the blacksmith is making. I'll eat later."

If it was not the spears, he had to check the plows. He had to talk with the elders. He had to talk with the merchants. There was always an excuse. The King never ate with his Queen or even thanked her.

Every time there was a festival, the Queen dressed in her finest robe. She made her hair shine with coconut oil. She put on her most precious ornaments.

She tracked the King down and said, "I'm ready to go to the güemilere. The drums have started to play."

The King always rushed out of the palace shouting, "I can't waste my time with that foolishness, I have to go to the fields and make sure the yams have been weeded."

If he did not rush out to check the fields, it was the animals. He had to check the barns. He had to check the cisterns. The King never seemed to find the time to go to festivals or to dance with his Queen.

Every night, his wife put perfumed oils on her body and laid on the bed to wait for him. The King always came home very late.

When the King got into bed, the Queen always opened her arms and whispered, "I've been waiting for you."

The King always said, "I'm too tired." Every night, the King rolled over and started to snore. He never made love to his Queen. But she knew that he made love to others.

One day, after the King rushed out of the palace to do something or other, the Queen sat crying by the door.

"I'm so lonely," she sighed. "I'd give anything not to have to suffer so!"

A voice said, "Maybe you don't need to."

She looked up. Standing before her was a very old man with a cigar between his teeth and a disreputable straw hat on his head. He leaned on a crooked walking stick.

The Queen sniffed, "What do you mean?"

The old man said, "I know ways and secrets that will give you what you want." What he didn't say was that he was really Eshú in disguise, wandering the world, looking for an opportunity to make trouble.

The Queen sighed. "All I want is my husband," she said. "If I could get back his love, I would give you everything I have."

Eshú smiled a strange smile around his cigar. "Doing what I do is its own reward," he said. "What you must do is to get me a lock of your husband's hair."

The Queen was disappointed. "What good will that do?" she asked. "I've tried love spells like that. They never work."

"I hold the keys to all spells," said Eshú. "If you do as I say, I will make a magic so strong that the King will only live to please you."

The Queen's heart beat faster in her breast. Here, at last, was a shred of hope. She would no longer be unwanted and abandoned.

She grasped Eshú's arm. "I will get you some of his hair," she said.

Eshú gave the Queen a large knife. "Take this knife," he said, "and wait until the King comes home. When he falls asleep, cut off a lock of his hair and bring it to me."

The Queen was very excited. "And then you will do your work?" she asked.

"And then I will do my work," promised Eshú.

The King and the Queen had a son. He was a strong and proud Prince who led an army of fierce warriors. Even though he was the heir to the kingdom, he was on good terms with his father. He lived in his own palace close to the royal palace.

That afternoon, the Prince was lying on a pile of cushions under a mango tree, sipping a sherbet.

A voice said, "Your highness, if you will pardon me."

He turned his head and saw an old man dressed in a councilor's robe and leaning on a crooked stick.

The Prince asked, "What do you want?" He wasn't rude, that's the way Princes talk.

The old man bowed low. "This unworthy person is here to say that your father, the King, is going to war tomorrow."

"To war?" cried the Prince. "He has said nothing to me of these matters."

Eshú, for it was he disguised as a counselor, bowed. "Deep are the ways of Kings, your highness," he said, bowing again. "Your father, the King wishes you to gather your warriors and take them to the palace tonight so that he may review their fitness for battle."

The Prince was puzzled, but he agreed to the matter. "Yes, yes, of course," he said. "Tell my father that I hear and obey his commands. My warriors will be at his palace tonight."

Eshú bowed once more and walked away.

That same afternoon, the King was walking through his yam fields. He was headed towards a small house almost hidden by rose bushes.

A voice said, "Sire."

Startled, the King turned around and saw an old man smoking a cigar, wearing a ragged straw hat and leaning on a crooked stick.

The King thought he was a peddler. "Who are you? What do you want?" He was very abrupt. "I'm busy with affairs of state."

The old man, of course, was Eshú. He took off his hat and pretended to be frightened. "Sire," he said. "I have to tell you something very important."

A woman's voice called out from the little house, "Poopsie? Poopsie is that you?"

"I'll be there in a minute," shouted the King. He growled at Eshú, "This better be important."

A beautiful woman leaned out the front window of the little house. "If Poopsie-Woopsie doesn't hurry, he's not going to get any sugar."

The King was flustered. "That's my secretary," he mumbled. "We're going over the sugar crop." He regained his composure and blustered, "So what is it that you want?"

Eshú gasped and shook and quivered and finally blurted out, "Sire, the Queen wants to kill you."

"What?" yelled the King. "The Queen wants to kill me? Tell me everything, man."

Eshú leaned close to the King and whispered, "I was at the palace delivering the order of turnips that the cook had ordered. You know the cook, the big fat one? Not the little one with no teeth. I don't like her."

The King grabbed Eshú's shoulders and shook him. "Get on with it!"

"Well, like I said," Eshú continued, "I was leaving the turnips off and I was alone in the kitchen when she comes in."

"When who comes in?" asked the King.

"The Queen," said Eshú. "The Queen comes in and goes to the wall where all the knives are hanging. She's got a crazy look in her eyes. They're big and white all around and she gets this big kitchen knife and waves it all around laughing and giggling. 'Going around to other women?' she says. Then she stabs at this sack of flour and starts screaming, 'Let's see him chasing around after tonight!' That's what she said."

They were interrupted by a pouting voice, "Poopsie, are you coming?"

The King whirled around. "Shut up," he shouted. He turned back to Eshú and put his nose up to his. "The Queen said this?" he asked.

"That's what she said," said Eshú, pretending to tremble. "She's going to kill you tonight!"

That night, the King got home early.

The Queen was excited. She thought that the King's was early because of the old man's love magic. And she hadn't even given him any of the King's hair!

She tiptoed up to the King and put her arms around him. "It's so nice that you're home for dinner," she cooed.

The King jumped up into the air and spun to face his wife. "What do you mean by that?" he demanded.

The Queen shrugged and smiled. "It's just nice, that's all," she said.

She went into the kitchen humming and brought back a plate of rice and okra.

"I've made you your favorite," she said.

Thoughts of poison ran around the King's head. He peered at the food. "What did you put in it?" he said, pushing the plate away.

"You're acting so strange," said the Queen. "It's the little dried shrimps you like."

"I'm not hungry," said the nervous King. "I'm tired. I'm going to bed."

He took off his clothes and his crown and rolled himself up in the quilts. The King began to snore loudly, pretending to be asleep.

The Queen crept into the bedroom. "Are you sure you don't want anything?" she whispered.

The King kept on snoring.

She reached under the mattress and brought out Eshú's knife. Just as she was reaching for the King's hair, he sat up and grabbed her wrist.

The King roared, "It's true! You want to kill me." He grabbed her throat. "Give me the knife!"

At that moment, the Prince and his warriors entered the palace. They heard the commotion and ran into the King's bedroom. Horrified, they saw the King strangling the Queen.

The Prince shouted, "Take your hands off of my mother!"

The King thought he was under attack. "So, you're in this too? Guards!" he yelled. "Guards! Murder! Murder!"

The palace guards rushed in. They saw the Prince's warriors and thought their King was in danger. Spears and clubs flew through the air. Screams and blood filled the royal palace.

An old man wearing a straw hat stood outside. Eshú heard the shouts of warriors and the Queen's screams. He leaned on his crooked stick, lit his cigar and got ready to enjoy the massacre.

THE COCONUT

Elegguá is often represented by a coconut. This story tells how that came to be.

A long time ago, in Africa, there was a powerful King named Oba Okuboro. His Queen, Eshú Añagu, gave birth to a son. He was named Elegguá. He grew up to be a spoiled and willful Prince.

If he said, "Stand," everyone in the court had to stand.

If he said, "Sit," they had to sit. All except the King and Queen, of course. Pampered and selfish, nothing of note happened to him until he turned fourteen.

Elegguá went outside the palace one beautiful morning. The sun was bright and warm, but it was not too hot. The flowers in the palace garden filled the air with sweet perfume.

Elegguá exclaimed, "What a perfect day."

His courtiers agreed. "It is indeed perfect," they said.

Elegguá said, "On such a day, I should go for a stroll."

The courtiers parroted, "It is indeed a day for a stroll."

Elegguá picked up his walking stick and set off down the road. The jugglers, the musicians, the ladies in waiting, the lords and the cooks followed. The pavilion carts, the palanquins and the cook wagons came after them. When the Prince went for a walk, the whole court went with him to amuse him and take care of his every whim.

They walked for a long distance. The jugglers juggled. The musicians played, drowning out the singing of the birds. The lords and the ladies flirted with each other.

They reached a place where four roads met. Suddenly, Elegguá raised his hand and cried out, "Halt!"

The jugglers dropped their balls. The lords and ladies stumbled into each other. The music came to a discordant stop.

The court ladies pouted and asked, "Why are we stopping? There is no shade and no place to set up the tents."

"We can't stop here," grumbled the lords. "Where can we organize our games and dances?"

Eleggúa was angry with his companions. "Quiet," he said. He pointed at the crossroads. "Can't you see it shine?"

No one saw anything.

"It's coming from where the roads cross," said Eleggúa. He took a few hesitating steps towards the thing only he could see. It was as if he were approaching a holy place.

The courtiers were worried. They didn't want to contradict the Prince, but they said, "There is nothing there, sire."

"Quiet," whispered Eleggúa. He shaded his eyes with his hand. "It's shining so brightly that I can't tell what it is."

A lady laughed nervously. "The only thing shining is the sweat on my nose," she complained.

Eleggúa paid her no attention. He went to the middle of the crossroads. He took a few steps to the left and then a few to the right, searching for the thing that shone so brightly into his eyes. Then he found it, half hidden in a clump of grass.

Eleggúa bent over and picked it up. "Look at how its eyes glow!" he exclaimed.

An astonished lord cried out, "By all the ancestors! He's picked up something with his own hands!" No one had ever seen the Prince do anything for himself before.

Eleggúa turned to his courtiers and showed them the thing he had found. "Look, isn't it beautiful?" he asked.

It was a dry coconut. Just a dry old coconut. But to Eleggúa, it seemed that a brilliant light shone out of the coconut's eyes. To Eleggúa, it was a thing of wonder, a treasure.

He caressed it and murmured with great respect, "This is a message from the ancestors."

All the important personages that accompanied Eleggúa looked at each other in embarrassment.

The glittering courtiers whispered, "How is it possible that the Prince acts with such great awe and reverence towards a small dried coconut?"

Some said, "We know that he is a trickster and capricious. Maybe this is a joke."

Others said, "He is always sticking his nose into everything. This is just another passing fancy."

A cook gave a knowing wink and said, "Our Prince sometimes acts like he is his own best friend. Other times, he acts like he is his own worst enemy."

Elegguá paid no attention to the whispered remarks. He wrapped the coconut in his royal robes.

"Back to the palace," he ordered. "The king must be told about this wonder."

The courtiers assembled and trudged back home. There was no juggling, music or flirting. There was only annoyed silence except for the cook saying, "No good will come of this."

When he arrived at the palace, Elegguá rushed to the throne room.

"Look, father," said Elegguá. "I have brought back a wonder."

The King was annoyed. "Can't you see that I am in council with the elders?" he asked. "Where are your manners?"

"This is more important than the council," said Elegguá. "I bring a message from the ancestors."

One of the elders said, "Let the Prince speak. Then we can get back to the work of this council."

Elegguá knelt before his father. He carefully unwrapped the bundle. No blinding light shone forth. There wasn't even a glow.

"Is this your idea of a joke?" shouted the King. "That is nothing but a dry coconut."

Elegguá stammered, "But it shone with the light of the ancestors!"

Everyone leaned forward and stared at the perfectly ordinary coconut.

The elders shook their heads and mumbled about spoiled princes. The lords and the ladies covered their mouths and snickered.

"Out!" ordered the King. "Get out of the court and take your garbage with you."

Elegguá took the coconut and ran out of the throne room. He made his way through the palace, angry and embarrassed.

A lady laughed at him. "Hail the bearer of the magic coconut," she said.

Another said, "Does it speak to you?"

They knew the King was angry with Elegguá. They knew on which side their bread was buttered. The courtiers had lost their fear of the Prince.

Flustered, Elegguá threw the coconut behind the palace door and ran outside. The coconut remained hidden behind the door, forgotten, gathering dust.

Everyone gave Elegguá a hard time about the coconut. He tried to shrug off their comments by saying, "It was all a joke."

Several days later, Oba Okuboro held a large feast in his palace. The lords and the ladies were resplendent in their finery. The musicians were drumming a frenzied güemilere. The jugglers and the acrobats wandered the great hall amusing the guests with their tricks. The cooks rushed about with immense trays of roast pig and yams.

Elegguá was trying to dance and drink a jug of aguardiente at the same time when a lord bowed before him and said with a smirk, "How fares our Prince of the coconut?"

At that very moment, everyone was blinded by an explosion of light.

The ladies shrieked, "It's the end of the world!"

The palace guards shouted, "We're being attacked!"

The lords yelled, "Hide the women! Bury the gold!"

One of the elders, who had kept his composure, said, "The light is coming from behind the door."

A brave warrior crept forward and moved the door away from the wall with the shaft of his spear. There was the coconut! Intense shafts of light shone out of its eyes.

The ladies huddled together, "It's a sign of evil," they said.

The lords said, "It's witchcraft."

"It's that damned coconut," shouted the King.

Panic spread. Everyone screamed, "Don't look at it! Get down on your knees and pray! It's going to kill us all!"

That last shout made everyone stampede. Some jumped out of the windows. The rest made a mad rush for the back door. The coconut's light shone on a shambles of broken and overturned furniture, trampled food, smashed crockery and torn tapestries.

Three days later, Elegguá died. During his funeral, the coconut shone so brightly that no one could enter the palace.

Eventually, the light faded away. A new door was built for the palace because everyone was afraid of going by the place where the coconut still lay behind the old door.

Years passed. The coconut was forgotten. People forget even the most important things.

Oba Okuboro was now an old man. Since Elegguá's death, his reign had not been an easy one. Great famines had swept his kingdom. A plague of locusts came every year, destroying most of the crops. Droughts had followed floods. Plagues afflicted his people, killing most of the children. Desperate, he summoned all the wise men of his kingdom.

The King sat glumly on his throne. He said, "May your wisdom save our kingdom. Our situation is desperate."

"Tell us what to do, oh King," said the elders.

The King told them, "You must divine the cause of our suffering. Tell me what sacrifices to offer. Tell me what prayers will make our ancestors have mercy and not destroy us all."

The elders went away and began their work. Oracles were consulted. Sheep were slaughtered and their entrails were read. Incense was burnt. There was drumming and chanting. They smeared dung ashes on their bodies. Exhausted, they went back to the King.

They said, "We have done everything we know how to do."

The King asked them, "Do you have an answer for me?"

The elders bowed their heads and said, "No, we do not have an answer."

The King sighed. "Then my kingdom is doomed."

The eldest of the counselors, a man so old that he looked like a shriveled up monkey, tottered to his feet.

"I remember Eleggua's coconut," he quavered. "I made fun of it, that day of the feast."

"What coconut?" asked the King. The cares of decades had taken that memory away from him.

The old man said, "The coconut he found at the crossroads, the one that shone. It was an omen. If we give it homage, we may be saved."

He shuffled to the hangings that hid the old door, the one that had not been used in so many years that all had forgotten it. "It may still be here," he said.

The King himself stepped down from his throne and helped push aside the dusty hangings. The huge door was covered with cobwebs. Its hinges were rusted solid.

The King shouted, "Guards, move this door away from the wall."

The palace guards struggled against the door. It stayed frozen in place. Levers and wedges were brought to bear, but the door would not budge. Finally, a team of oxen was yoked to a thick rope tied to the door. The door creaked, groaned and gave way.

The coconut was covered by rat droppings. Insects had eaten holes in it. There was nothing left but a fragile cracked shell that crumbled as the King touched it.

Seeing the coconut turn to dust, the elders moaned, "We're lost."

"Nonsense," said the oldest of the old. "We'll make a stone coconut."

The King said, "I, myself, will be the first to give it homage."

A stone coconut was made. Homage was paid to it. The kingdom was saved.

As was done that day, so it is done today. Stones are given eyes like those that shone on that ancient coconut. They are placed behind the front door and, all honor Eleggua.

THE BEST AND THE WORST

Mischievous as he is, Elegguá often proves to be far wiser than the other Orishás.

One day, Olodumaré, the Supreme Being, was in a teaching mood. He called all the Orishás. They came and gathered before his throne in the sky.

Olodumaré told them, "I want you to go down to the world and bring me back the thing that is, at the same time, both the best and the worst that can be found there."

Elegguá muttered, "Not another of those stupid tasks." Olodumaré glared at him so, he went to hide behind the door.

The Orishás left the Supreme Being's presence and set out on their mission. Elegguá slammed the door as he left.

Olodumaré flinched at the loud bang. "I wish that I hadn't given him leave to do whatever he wants," he said to himself.

The next day, all of the Orishás returned to Olodumaré's palace. Each one brought the thing he or she considered to be both the best and the worst that could be found in the world.

Oggún said, "I have a knife. It can be used for cooking or killing. That's the best and the worst."

Olodumaré said, "No, that's not it."

Shangó said, "I have a drum. It can be used for dancing or for war. That's the best and the worst."

Olodumaré said, "No, that's not it."

Yemayá said, "I have gold. It can either bring pleasure or destroy through greed."

Olodumaré said, "No, that's not it."

Oshún said, "I brought oñi, the sweetness of love. Everyone knows that it can be heaven and hell."

Olodumaré said, "No, that's not it."

One by one, the other Orishás showed Olodumaré the thing that they had brought. Olodumaré rejected each and every one of them.

Olodumaré shook his head and said, "You are all my children. I made you intelligent and powerful. How is it that none of you has managed to bring me what I want?"

The Orishás grumbled, looked down and shuffled their feet.

Then Eleggua came through the palace doors. "Olodumaré," he called out haughtily. "I have brought you what you asked for."

Eleggua's hands were empty. He had no sack. He brought no package.

"Let's see, Eleggua," said Olodumaré. "Show me what you have brought."

Eleggua walked across the great hall and stood right before the Supreme Being. He stuck out his tongue and gave a loud raspberry right in Olodumaré's face. "Raaaaazz!"

The Orishás were shocked. Eleggua was mischievous and disrespectful, but he had never done anything like this. They all stepped back from the throne, expecting a horrible punishment to come down on his head.

Olodumaré wiped his face and told the assembly, "Eleggua has solved the riddle." He patted Eleggua's head. They were very hard pats. "The tongue," he continued, "depending on the way it is used, can create the most good or the most horrible evil in the world. Congratulations!"

He gave Eleggua another pat on the head that sent him staggering. Eleggua had a headache the rest of the day.

WHITE AND BLACK

This story bears a striking resemblance to a classic Sufi teaching tale. However, instead of teaching, Eshú provokes enmity.

Eshú wanders the world, ever on the lookout for the opportunity to create deviltry. One day, he walked into a small village.

Two men passed him, walking arm in arm. They were laughing and shared a gourd full of beer.

Standing next to Eshú were two women, carrying water jugs home on their heads.

One woman said, "Those two are closer than brothers."

The other said, "Not even brothers love each other so much."

There's nothing that upsets Eshú more than to find harmony and peace. He made the women trip. Their clay jugs went crashing to the ground. Satisfied, Eshú clenched his soggy cigar in his teeth and followed the two laughing men.

They went by a drum maker's shop.

The drum maker waved at them and said to his apprentice, "The friendship of those two is tighter than the lacings on my drums."

Eshú took the time to make a drum head split and hurried after the two friends.

They walked through the market. Everyone they met greeted them. Everyone commented on the men's friendship.

A woman selling yams blew them a kiss. "You two better not stay so close together at night or I won't get to have any fun," she said.

One of the men grinned and said, "You should come to our farms. We'll show you some fun." His friend added, "They're next to each other. You'll have twice as much fun."

Everyone laughed except Eshú. He glared at the market woman's basket. It tipped over. A passing oxcart mashed the yams into the dirt. The market woman screamed hysterically at the driver. The driver cursed and shouted at the woman.

Eshú settled his straw hat on his head and stalked after the two friends.

They walked past an old man sitting on a crate. He was telling stories to a group of children.

The old man pointed at the friends and said, "You should treat each other with the devotion and respect that those two have for each other."

Eshú flicked cigar ashes on the old man's beard. It caught on fire. The old man hopped and yelled until a beer seller poured a jug of beer on his head. The children shrieked with laughter and called him "a crazy old poop."

Eshú grumbled, "Enough is enough. It is time to end this beautiful friendship."

Early the next morning, Eshú painted the left side of his body black and the right side of his body white. He walked slowly along the road that divided the two friend's properties from each other.

Each man was working in his own field. They looked up when Eshú walked by. The man on Eshú's left saw a black man. The one on his right saw a white man. They both gave a friendly wave to the stranger.

The day grew hot. As was their custom, the two friends met in the shade of a huge baobab tree at noon. They shared out their food equally and began to talk.

The friend who had been on Eshú's left said, "Did you see the stranger that walked down the road this morning?"

His friend, who had been on Eshú's right, said, "Of course I did. It's very rare to see a white man walking in these parts."

The man who had been on the left was startled. "Your eyes are playing tricks on you," he said. "The stranger that I saw was black."

The man who had been on the right was annoyed. "It's your mind that's playing tricks" he said. "He was white."

"I know what I saw," said the man who had seen Eshú's left side. "He was black."

"White."

"Black."

121

"White."

"Black."

Just as Eshú had planned, they began to argue. Anger sharpened their tongues. They shouted insults at each other. As they
grabbed their machetes, Eshú walked away happy. The best of
friends had become the worst of enemies.

THE CONTEST

Eleggyá has a very close, though sometimes contentious relationship with Orunmilá, the owner of the oracles. Whoever does not follow what Orunmilá commands risks Eleggyá's wrath.

A very long time ago, Orunmilá taught the babalawós how to use the oracles. He did this so that the oracles could be of benefit to humanity, not so that the babalawós could get rich.

When Orunmilá returned to the world to see how his gifts were being used, what he saw made him sad. He was disappointed in the babalawós. They had become fat, rich and arrogant.

Orunmilá visited one babalawó. The man brushed him off. "I don't have time to talk," he said. "I have a consultation."

Imagine not having time to honor the one who taught you everything you know!

Orunmilá visited another babalawó. This one ran out the door as Orunmilá arrived. "Come back in a few days," he said before rushing off. "I'll have a few minutes to spare."

This man did not even invite his teacher into his house!

The next babalawó Orunmilá visited yelled at him, "I'm with a client," and slammed the door in his face.

Orunmilá became angry. The first babalawós had been upright men but the ones he found in the world now were vain and greedy. They had no respect. He decided that they had to be taught a lesson.

He sent out runners to the four corners of the world to proclaim:

"Orunmilá challenges all the babalawós to prove that they are not big mouthed buffoons. He will challenge their skills with the oracles and they will be shamed!"

This was Orunmilá's plan: He wanted to bring down the current crop of babalawós by humiliating them before the people.

He thought, "Their shame will make them go back to the old ways. They will serve the people instead of themselves. They will seek knowledge, not gold."

Orunmilá went to the nearest town, stood in the marketplace and shouted, "Orunmilá is here to test your babalawó."

The people gathered. A runner was sent to fetch the babalawó.

The town's babalawó was a greedy man who overcharged his clients. A dozen drummers announced his arrival. He was escorted by servants carrying umbrellas of honor. He wore gold rings on every finger. His robe was embroidered with gold thread and covered with cowry shells.

"I am the babalawó," he announced full of self importance. "What is this about a test?"

Orunmilá said, "I am your lord, Orunmilá. I am here to challenge your right to be a babalawó."

The babalawó flicked his horse tail whisk at Orunmilá. "I don't care who you are," he said. "I will not lower myself to participating in some foolish game."

The people began to grumble. "He's afraid."

Some said, "He's not a real babalawó. He's a fake."

Then some said, "If he's a fraud, he's been stealing our money." They began to pick up sticks and rocks.

The babalawó saw that there was no way out of the situation. "Very well," he said grandly. "I agree to the test. It will be amusing."

Orunmilá said, "If you lose, you must give me all your gold so that it can be distributed among the people."

The people cheered. The babalawó saw that things would not go well for him if he did not agree. He consented to Orunmilá's terms.

The first test was with the biague, the coconut oracle.

A woman asked, "Who will I marry?"

The babalawó threw the four pieces of coconut and read their meaning. "You will marry the weaver," he said.

Orunmilá threw the oracle. He peered to see how many pieces had the dark shell up and how many had the white meat showing. "This woman will marry the blacksmith," he said.

A man in the crowd said, "Orunmilá's right. She's already bearing his child."

The crowd cheered. Maybe they would get some of the babalawó's gold.

The second test was with the diloggun, the cowry shells.

Two men brought a very sick man lying on a cot. They said, "Our friend is dying and no one knows what to do."

The babalawó threw the cowry shells. "There is nothing to be done for this man," he said. "Better be resigned to his death."

Orunmilá picked up the cowry shells, blew his ashé on them and threw them before the sick man. "This man has to stop eating pumpkins," he said. "He must also make an ebó to Yemayá with a blue candle and a turtle."

The sick man followed Orunmilá's advice. In a couple of days, he regained his health and was able to get up from his bed.

The townspeople were delighted. They began to plan what to do with their babalawó's gold.

The third test was with the Ifá, the oracle board.

The chief of the region stood before Orunmilá and the babalawó and said, "Our neighbors steal our cattle. Should we go to war against them?"

The babalawó sat down and threw the ekuele, the collars, on the board. He got no results. He tried again. Again, no results. "The problem is too complicated and mysterious," he said. "I cannot read what the Ifá says until I have received three fat cows."

Orunmilá laughed. "You're not getting results because you don't even know how to spread powdered eggshell on the board," he said.

He sat down next to the board. Very carefully, he spread an even coating of powdered eggshell on its surface. Orunmilá threw the ekuele on the board. This time, the collars made marks and tracks that could be read.

"There is no need for war," Orunmilá told the chief, "Offer an exchange of peace for tribute. That will end your troubles."

The chief did as Orunmilá counseled. Within the week, the raids stopped and the danger of war was removed from the people.

The chief threatened to boil the babalawó in a pot of oil.

The people began to prepare a feast to be paid for with the defeated babalawó's gold.

Orunmilá went to the babalawó's house. "Bring me your gold," said Orunmilá. "I will distribute it among the people at the feast."

The babalawó said, "You're not the chief here. I don't have to obey your commands."

Orunmilá said, "You agreed to the terms of the contest."

The babalawó shrugged. "So what? Who's going to make me pay? The chief is gone back to his palace. He never said I had to pay you."

Orunmilá was shocked. "Don't you have any honor at all?"

The babalawó said, "It doesn't matter if I have honor or not. I have plenty of gold."

Elegguá chose that moment to show up. He is everywhere and hears everything. Elegguá loves to jump into an argument. No one knows if he will bring fortune or calamity.

Elegguá said, "May fortune smile upon you, Orunmilá." He looked the babalawó up and down. "What terrible company you keep."

Orunmilá said, "He is not only bad company. He is a liar and a cheat."

Elegguá thought Orunmilá's purple face looked interesting. He tried to see if he could make it change into another color.

He knew what angered Orunmilá, but he still asked, "What has gotten you so upset?"

Orunmilá face turned beet-red. "This fraud refuses to pay up," he spluttered. "He agreed to give me all his gold if he lost. Now, he just laughs at me."

Elegguá thrust his beaked nose into the babalawó's face. "Is what my friend says true?" he asked.

The babalawó saw nothing but a scrawny old man. He did not know he was talking to Elegguá. "What is it to you?" he said.

Elegguá grabbed the babalawó's neck and shook him. Elegguá may choose to appear as an old man or as a child, but he is a powerful warrior. The strength in his hands is immense. He is a dangerous and deadly adversary.

He asked the babalawó, "How long do you want to keep breathing?"

Elegguá's smile reminded the babalawó of a shark he had seen once. "A long time?" he pleaded.

Elegguá shook the babalawó a little bit, just enough to make his teeth rattle. "You wouldn't want to make me angry?" he asked softly.

The babalawó thought of calling his servants for help. He looked into Elegguá's eyes and changed his mind. "Would not dream of it," he said.

Elegguá gave him a hard thump on the head with his garabato, his walking stick. "Then give my friend, Orunmilá, what he wants."

"He can have all my gold," said the babalawó.

Elegguá hit him again and shook him. "I didn't hear you," he said. "Could you repeat that?"

"I will give him all my gold," said the babalawó, talking as fast as he could. "He can also have my house and my fields and my clothes and my cattle and my servants. Just don't hit me any more."

Elegguá slapped the babalawó on the back so hard the man fell on his face. "I'm glad we have settled this little misunderstanding," he said.

Orunmilá said, "This lesson is not over."

The babalawó looked up at him, his face full of dust. "No?" he asked, terrified.

"No, it's not," said Orunmilá. "You have used the oracles to make yourself rich instead of helping others. You may not use them ever again."

Orunmilá and Elegguá gave away all of the babalawó's belongings at the feast. The people were delighted.

When Orunmilá and Elegguá went to the next town, this story had gotten there ahead of them. They had no trouble at all with that babalawó.

AGGAYÚ, SHANGÓ'S FATHER

HOW AGGAYÚ RECOGNIZED SHANGÓ AS HIS SON

In Cuba, some say that Aggayú was Shangó's father and Yemayá was his mother. This is the story they tell.

When Shangó was young, he wandered from town to town. He was always on the lookout for parties to go to and women to bed. He was welcomed everywhere because he was an excellent drummer and renowned as a lover.

When people asked Shangó, "Who is your father?" he answered, "My father is a great king." Or, he said, "My father is a very wealthy man," and let it go at that.

The truth is that Shangó did not know who his father was. His father was Aggayú, the ruler of volcanoes and rivers, the protector of travelers. But Shangó did not know this. Neither did Aggayú know that he had a son.

Aggayú was feared and respected. Everyone was in awe of the mighty Orishá. Proof of this is that he left his door wide open when he went out. His house was full of food and all the good things that men want. But no one dared to set foot inside without Aggayú's permission.

One day, Shangó happened to be passing through Aggayú's village. He had walked all day and was tired and hungry.

Shangó asked everyone he met, "Is there a party tonight?" He expected to eat and drink to his heart's content in exchange for his drumming.

But the people of that place told him, "We have work to do and have no time for such foolishness."

Shangó kept on walking. He saw a beautiful woman and thought, "Maybe she will take me in for the night."

He greeted the woman, "Hello, my lovely. How are you today? I wonder if you cook as good as you look?"

The woman looked down her nose at him and said, "I am happily married today and I have no time for such as you." She turned her back on Shangó and walked away.

Shangó was depressed. "No parties, no women," he said to himself. "What am I to do?" The thought of work never crossed his mind.

He came to Aggayú's house. Through the open door came the delicious smell of food. Shangó's stomach growled.

He peered in and called out, "Hello, is anyone home?"

There was no answer. The baskets of food and the jars of beer called out to him, "Hello, Shangó. We're so glad to see you. Won't you come in?"

Shangó stepped inside and ate and drank as only a very hungry young man is able to do.

When he was finished, he said, "That was great. Now all I need is a nap."

He laid down on Aggayú's sleeping mat. Soon, he was snoring without a care in the world.

When Aggayú came home, he found empty food baskets and beer jars strewn all over the floor and Shangó asleep on his mat.

Aggayú roared, "You dare enter my house? You dare to eat my food?"

Shangó jumped to his feet. But before he could defend himself, Aggayú picked him up in his massive arms and carried him outside. He bound Shangó with strong ropes and built a huge bonfire.

Aggayú picked up Shangó and shouted, "Now you will see what happens to those who defy me!"

He threw Shangó into the roaring flames. The fire burned the ropes away but they did not burn Shangó.

When Aggayú saw Shangó sitting unharmed in the flames, he cried out, "What kind of man are you?"

Shangó stepped out of the bonfire. "How can fire burn fire?" he said.

Aggayú wrestled Shangó to the ground and tied him again.

"Water can destroy fire and water will destroy you," said Aggayú.

He threw Shangó over his shoulder. Taking huge steps, he soon arrived at the sea.

"Now you will see what happens to my enemies," yelled Aggayú.

He waded into the water an threw Shangó in, holding his head under so he would drown. Shangó fought back fiercely, but Aggayú's strength was greater.

Suddenly, a woman's voice cried out, "What are you doing?"

Aggayú turned and saw Yemayá, the Orishá of the sea, standing on the waves.

He took Shangó out of the water and shook him. "This boy has dared to enter my house, eat my food and drink my beer!" he told Yemayá. "He must die."

Yemayá asked him, "Doesn't the son have rights in his father's house?"

Aggayú was bewildered. "Son?" he said.

"Yes, son," said Yemayá.

The waves began to roar about Aggayú. Yemayá's voice took on the fury of a stormy sea. "If you paid some attention to what goes on around you instead of running off and looking at your rivers and volcanoes, you would remember that we have a son you and I!" she said.

"But . . ." said Aggayú. And that was all he could say. The storm beat against him. Even a volcano can't stand up against the rage of the sea.

Aggayú lifted Shangó and sat him on his shoulders. "I was wrong," he said to Yemayá. "I should have recognized my son."

Yemayá calmed the fury of her storm. Aggayú declared, "In this world there is no one with more courage than I. Shangó, you are as fearless as I am. I say for all to hear that you are my son."

HOW AGGAYÚ MASTERED THE RIVER

There are those who say that Yemayá is not Shangó's mother. They say that, back in Africa, Obatalá was recognized as his mother. Obatalá can be both man and woman and, sometimes neither, as befits the power of Olodumaré's child. This is the story of how Obatalá conceived Shangó.

It is also the story of how Aggayú became involved with transportation.

Aggayú was the most powerful man in the village. He was in the prime of life and was able to cut down a tree with a single stroke of his huge double-headed ax.

He was awakened one morning by the shouting of his neighbors, "Aggayú. Aggayú. It overflows."

Aggayú stepped out of his house. "What overflows?" he asked.

His neighbors said, "The river overflows, great Aggayú. You are the mightiest man in the village. You must save us!"

Aggayú shouldered his huge ax. He strode towards the river. His immense steps soon left the villagers far behind.

At the river bank, he sat down to think. How was he going to stop the muddy waters that threatened to flood the countryside?

The villagers surrounded Aggayú and wailed, "The river is going to wash away the village! All our animals will be drowned! We'll all die!"

Aggayú did not say a word. He stood up and walked away from the people.

"Aggayú has abandoned us!" they all cried as the roaring river rose higher.

Aggayú had no thought of abandoning his people. He went into the jungle looking for the biggest tree he could find. He came to the giant grandfather of all the trees. With his ax, he cut it down with one mighty chop. In less time than it takes to tell, he carved a magnificent canoe and two strong oars. Aggayú lifted the canoe on to his shoulders and carried it back to the river.

The people rejoiced when they saw Aggayú. They raised a great shout, "The mighty Aggayú has returned to us!"

They marveled at the size of the canoe. No ordinary man could lift such a weight! Aggayú strode to the rushing waters and shouted at the river, "I will conquer you!" Then he launched his canoe into the furious current and jumped in before it could be washed away.

The water was like a bucking wild horse. Aggayú rode the mighty torrent, shouting at the river, "I will conquer you!"

The river answered back with a roar, "I will kill you!"

Aggayú, crashed through the rapids, cutting the eddies. He flattened out the foaming curls.

As he slashed the river's body with his canoe, he shouted, "I will conquer you!" and the river roared back, "I will kill you!"

For nine days and eight nights, Aggayú and the river battled. The river began to tire. Every new attempt to overturn the canoe and drown Aggayú made the river grow weaker, like a horse when it is ridden to exhaustion.

Mighty Aggayú shouted, "I will conquer you!"

The river did not answer him. Its waters began to quiet down. When the ninth day dawned, the river ran smooth and placid. Aggayú had broken its spirit.

The people praised him, "Long live Aggayú the river tamer! He will be our king forever!"

Aggayú became king. He took good care of his subjects. He put the giant canoe at the service of his people. It became a ferry between the villages on either side of the river. Since Aggayú was the only one with the strength to handle the mighty craft, all who wanted to cross the river had to pay him for his services.

His subjects asked him, "You are the king, why do you do this kind of work?"

Aggayú replied, "People must get to the other side. Besides, I enjoy it. It keeps me in shape."

Very early one morning, Aggayú was repairing his canoe when he heard a soft and melodious voice say, "I wish to cross the river."

He looked up and saw a majestic woman, very beautiful, dressed in an elegant white gown.

"You are welcome to use my canoe," said Aggayú respectfully.

Daintily, she stepped into the canoe, settled herself comfortably and allowed Aggayú to row her to the other shore.

They arrived safe and sound, since the river was now well behaved. Aggayú said, "I must now ask you for payment, madam."

"I have no money," said the woman softly.

"What?" roared Aggayú, always quick to anger. "Everyone must pay!"

The woman began to take off her clothes. "If I must pay, I must pay," she said.

"What are you doing?" spluttered Aggayú.

The woman displayed her body to Aggayú. "I am offering what payment I can," she answered. "I hope it is acceptable."

Aggayú embraced her. They made love right there, lying together inside the canoe.

That day, the villagers thought that the river was flooding again. Giant waves crashed against the river banks. Everyone was relieved when the waters settled down.

Aggayú lay panting on the bottom of the canoe. No one had ever made him feel like that before. The woman calmly dressed and stepped out of the canoe.

She addressed Aggayú. Her voice was full of disdain. "A mountain of strength and there you lay, crumbled," she said. "I have paid you more than you are worth. You have had the honor of possessing Obatalá."

She turned her back on him and, majestically, walked away. The frenzied lovemaking in the canoe produced Shangó.

Aggayú was humiliated and hurt. The episode made him surly and suspicious. From then on, Aggayú required that everyone tell him their names and pay in full before he took them across the river.

ODDUDUÁ AND AGGAYÚ SOLA

This is a re-telling of the classic Catholic story of St. Christopher carrying the child Jesus across the river. Obatalá appears in this story as Odduduá. The oldest of the Obatalás is usually associated with Jesus Christ.

There was once a ferryman called Aggayú Sola. He was as big as a mountain and as strong as an ox. He had to be. The river he ferried people across was wide, with a fast and fierce current.

Aggayú was working on his boat when a child came up to him. "Hello, Aggayú," said the child, giving him a dazzling smile. "Isn't it a beautiful morning?"

"What do you want?" growled Aggayú, for he had a very rude nature.

Instead of running away, the way other children did, he surprised Aggayú by asking, "Will you take me to the other side?"

"Do you have any money?" said Aggayú. "You must pay me in advance."

"I don't have any money," said the child.

"Then you don't get across," said Aggayú.

"But I need to get to the other shore," said the child. "My mother is waiting for me."

Aggayú liked the child's perseverance. "Look," he said. "I have some very firm rules that I never, and I mean never, break. Everyone that I ferry across the river has to pay me in advance. And, everyone has to tell me their name. Everyone."

The child thought for a little while. Then, a smile lit up his face. "Those rules only apply to your boat," the child told Aggayú. "You are big and strong. Pick me up, and set me on your shoulders. Then you can walk me to the other side. That way, you can take me across and not break any of your rules."

Aggayú laughed. He covered his mouth and looked around to make sure that no one had seen. It would not do for people to gossip that he was mellowing. "You're pretty smart," he told the child. "Here, climb up on my shoulders and I'll take you across."

Aggayú stepped into the river. The current roared, but his legs were like tree trunks and held firm.

"Hold on," he yelled to the child. "If you fall, there's no way I can save you."

"Save your breath," the child said. "I'm very heavy and you must make it to the other shore."

"Heavy?" laughed Aggayú. "My lunch is heavier than you."

But it was true. With every step that Aggayú took across the river, the child grew heavier on his back. Halfway across, he felt that he carried a horse on his shoulders.

"You're bewitched," shouted Aggayú. "You weigh more than a horse."

"Go on. Go on," said the child, holding tight to Aggayú's neck. "We're almost there."

Each step was torture for Aggayú. The other bank was no more than three steps away, but he could not take them.

"I have the weight of the world on my shoulders," gasped Aggayú. "I can't go on."

"Hurry up," said the child, spurring Aggayú on with his heels. "Hurry up."

Aggayú made a mighty effort. One step was like lifting mountains. The next step was like lifting the moon. With the last step, Aggayú collapsed on the river bank.

The child leaped lightly off Aggayú's shoulders. "Look at me, Aggayú," said the child.

Aggayú raised his head from the mud. The child was gone. Instead, a glorious personage with a long white beard and dressed in flowing white robes stood before him. "Oddudúa," he cried out, recognizing the creator.

Oddudúa bent down and placed his hand on Aggayú's head. "I name you the river tamer," he said softly.

HOW OSHÚN MARRIED AGGAYÚ

This old African story is part of the cycle that describes the migration of the people of Oyo to their new home in Ilé-Ifé. The story tells of how Oshún bore Aggayú a son.

Back when the great kings walked the earth, there was a terrible drought in the lands around Oyo. It had not rained for months. The springs and rivers had all dried up. People and animals wandered desperately in search of water.

The king of this land, who had a very beautiful daughter called Oshún, needed a solution to his people's desperate situation. He summoned Elegguá into his presence and told him, "Go find water even though you have to go to the other side of the world."

"Your wish is my command, lord," said Elegguá.

Very early the next morning, he set off with an army of servants. Each servant carried a net full of gourds. In this way, if they found water, they could carry it back to the people.

Elegguá opened the way through the forest with his crooked stick. The long line of servants followed him like ants following a child carrying candy.

They walked for three weeks in the forest. They walked for three weeks in the mountains. When Elegguá climbed to the top of the last mountain in the range, he saw, shining down below, an enormous river.

He cried out, "Here is fresh, clear water for our people!"

Elegguá and his servants ran to the river. When they got there, Elegguá was even more excited. The water was sparkling and crystalline, of a purity he had never seen before.

Elegguá knelt at the water's edge. He dipped his hands into the water and brought them to his lips.

Bam! A massive blow lifted Elegguá up into the air. He came crashing down among the river rocks and lost consciousness.

His servants gathered around him. "Owner of the roads, please come to us!" they cried.

Slowly, Elegguá came to his senses. He rose and staggered to the water. When he tried to wash his bruised face, BAM! He was knocked out by another blow.

His servants wailed, "Owner of honors, please come to us!"

Elegguá sat up with as much dignity as he could and called out, "Who dares to strike the Lord of the Roads?"

A very loud and powerful voice answered him out of the air, "I do, Aggayú, the Lord of the Rivers."

Elegguá looked around, but did not see anyone. "Why do you strike me if I have not done you any harm?" he asked the air.

Aggayú's voice said, "This is my river and you are stealing my water."

"My people need this water," said Elegguá. "Without it, they will die and their animals will die."

"If that's the case, I will give you all the water you want, now and forever," said Aggayú.

Elegguá bowed to the river. "Thank you, mighty Aggayú," he said.

Then Aggayú told Elegguá, "In return, your king must give me his daughter, Princess Oshún, as my wife."

Elegguá said to the river, "I will do as you ask." He turned to the servants and ordered, "Fill all the gourds. We are returning with life for our people."

They made the long journey back to their village. The people feasted and rejoiced when they saw uncountable gourds full of water.

Elegguá asked for an audience with the king. It was granted right away.

He presented the king with a gourd full of water and said, "My king, I have found a place that offers life to all our people."

The king drank deeply of the delicious water and said, "I will shower honors upon you, Owner of the Stick."

Elegguá bowed saying, "Thank you my king. But there is something you should know. The owner of these waters, the mighty Aggayú, will not give us more water unless you give him Princess Oshún in marriage."

The king was troubled. He loved his daughter very much. How could he give her away to a stranger? "I will give you my decision tonight," he said.

The king meditated upon what Elegguá had told him. When the sun went down, he sent for his daughter.

"Dear Oshún," he said, "you know that I would not force you to marry someone that you don't love. But the situation is desperate. If you do not marry this Lord Aggayú, our people will die of thirst."

Oshún was a Princess and knew her duty. "Your people will not die because of me," she said. "Take me to Aggayú. I will bow to his wishes and to yours. Do not worry."

Early the next morning, Oshún set off towards Aggayú's domain. She was accompanied by her servants, scores of beautiful young girls. Soldiers guarded them. A few of the men who had made the journey with Elegguá served as guides.

Three weeks they walked in the forest. Three weeks they walked in the mountains. When they arrived at the river, Oshún sent away her companions. She spoke to the air, "Where will I sleep?"

Aggayú's voice thundered around her, "Here."

Oshún did not see any shelter. There were no houses or huts. "Here, where?" she asked the empty air.

The voice repeated, "Here."

Oshún sighed, "Very well."

She gathered the soft moss and ferns that grew on the river bank and made herself a bed in the hollow between two boulders. She laid down and, being very tired, soon fell asleep.

The next morning Oshún opened her eyes to find herself in a huge house, surrounded by all the comforts that a Princess could desire.

She lay on a thickly woven sleeping mat with a beautifully carved head rest. The walls were covered in fabrics of a hundred colors. Baskets of food and jars of beer surrounded an ivory table and stools. All along the walls were large wooden chests holding valuable bolts of cloth and ornaments.

Oshún marveled at all she saw. She went to the door and tried to open it. It was locked from the outside.

She spent the next days trying to escape her luxurious prison. The floor was too hard. She could not dig. The walls were too thick. She could not break through them. The bars on the windows were too strong and closely set. She could not squeeze through them.

By the end of the week, she was resigned to her solitary confinement. Then a strange thing happened.

When she went to bed that night, Oshún felt the presence of another next to her on the sleeping mat.

She asked, "Who is there?" But she could not see anyone nor did she receive an answer.

Every night, she felt someone's presence next to her. Eventually, it comforted her in her loneliness.

One night, she opened her body to her invisible companion. And, every night after that, she received pleasure.

The day came when Oshún felt her belly beginning to grow. She stood naked before a large bronze mirror and confirmed that she was pregnant.

That night, Oshún told her invisible lover, "I am going to have a child." But there was no answer.

Oshún's belly grew bigger. One night, she told the presence next to her, "It is almost time for the child to come. I am very afraid. I cannot give birth by myself."

When Oshún woke the next morning, she found her mother in the house.

"How did you arrive? How did you get in?" Oshún asked her.

"I have no idea," answered her mother, bewildered. "I went to sleep next to your father. Then I dreamt that I was being carried along by a wild river. When I woke up, I found myself here."

Oshún reassured her mother. She showed her all the wonders in the house. When it came time for Oshún to give birth, her mother helped her deliver a beautiful son.

Oshún was happy. Her time was taken up by her baby. She had her mother's company during the days. Her invisible lover pleased her at night. The years passed and they lived in their strange but comfortable isolation.

One morning, after they had eaten, Oshún's mother said, "Daughter, I love you very much, but now your child is grown and you no longer need my help. I miss my house. I miss my husband. I wish to go home."

The next day, Oshún awoke alone with her son. Her mother had gone in the same mysterious manner that she had arrived. She cried for days, but at least she now had her son to keep her company.

He asked her questions all the time. "Mother, what is the world?"

Oshún told him, "The world is what is outside."

Her son was puzzled. "Mother, what is outside?" he asked.

Oshún told him, "It is what the sky covers."

Then her son asked, "What is the sky?"

Oshún cried. How could she raise a child that did not know what the sky was?

"I must go home," Oshún told her invisible lover that night. "My son must know the world. He must know his family. He cannot live here like an animal."

The voice that was thunder spoke for the first time in years, "You may go."

Relieved, Oshún went to sleep. She woke up in her father's palace. Everyone was amazed to see her again. There were days of feasting and celebration. All the people honored her as their savior. Her son was educated by the elders and the wise men. Best of all, Oshún could dance and talk and see people. She was happy to be alive.

However, at night she was lonely. Her bed was cold.

She went to her father. "Father, I wish to return to my husband," she said.

"You wish to leave your family and live all alone in that house?" said the king. "Your mother told me how horrible it was."

Oshún's temper flared up. "It is not horrible and it is my home." she said. "I wish to return."

Preparations were made for Oshún's return. When everything was almost ready. Oshún's sister came to see her.

"Will you take me with you?" asked her sister. "Then you will not be so lonely."

Oshún readily agreed. Her bed would be warm at night, and she would have company in the daytime.

After weeks of traveling, Oshún and her party arrived at the river. When Oshún saw her house, she marveled. It was the first time that she had seen it from the outside. If anything, its exterior was grander than the inside. She unbarred the door and invited her sister to enter. Exhausted, they fell asleep.

When she awoke, the door was still open. Oshún was surprised. That had never happened before. Delighted, she stepped outside, leaving her son with her sister.

When the child woke up, he began to whimper and cry. He had never been away from his mother.

Oshún's sister slapped the little boy. "Shut up, you son of a father no one knows!" she shouted.

From then on, every time that Oshún left the house, the same thing happened. Her child started to cry. His aunt hit him mercilessly shouting, "Shut up, you bastard!" or, "Shut up, you whelp!" or, "Shut up, you no name monster!"

Oshún knew none of this. She was happy that she had the freedom to stroll along the river. She felt comfortable leaving her son in her sister's care.

And then, after a long afternoon of hitting and screaming, Oshún's sister raised her hand to hit the child once again.

She did not bring her hand down. An immense man appeared before her, seeming to fill the house. "Leave my child alone." he thundered.

Oshún's sister ran out of the house. She rushed past Oshún, terrified.

Oshún cried out, "What is happening? What is wrong?"

Her sister screamed over her shoulder, "A monster wants to kill me!"

Oshún ran into her house. The huge man was holding her son in his arms.

Oshún fell to her knees before him. "Please don't hurt my son," she begged.

The voice like thunder rumbled out of the man, "I won't hurt our son. Don't be frightened, Oshún. I am your husband."

He put an arm like a tree trunk around her and took her to a window. "I am Aggayú, the owner of all this," he rumbled.

Oshún was astonished. In a place where there had always been wilderness, stood a prosperous village. A busy market full of people sparkled with wealth. Each house had a courtyard. In each courtyard there was a large number of animals.

Aggayú told her, "You, my darling, are the wife of a great chief."

Oshún looked at him. He was very handsome, dressed in fine woven cloths and gold anklets. He looked every inch a king.

Oshún was never alone again.

The child in the story, although unnamed, might be Shangó.

OGGÚN'S INCEST

OGGÚN AND HIS MOTHER

This story tells of how Oggún seduced his mother and how Elegguá became the guardian of the door.

There was once an Obatalá called Ibaíbó. He was a very old man with a long white beard. He cultivated his fields and lived in harmony with his wife, Yembo. The couple had four sons, Elegguá, Oggún, Oshosi, and Osún.

Every morning, as Obatalá and Oshosi left for the fields, Obatalá told Osún, "Take care of your mother and your brothers. I leave you in charge of the house."

Every evening, when they returned from work, Obatalá asked Osún, "What new thing happened today?"

Osún would replied, "Oggún fixed the roof," or, "We killed a chicken for dinner," or "The neighbor and his wife had a fight."

This way, Obatalá knew everything that happened while he was gone.

Life went along smoothly until, one day, Yembo bent over to pick up a basket. Her dress rode up her legs and Oggún saw her thighs.

"My mother is certainly a very beautiful woman," he thought.

When Yembo went to bathe, Oggún followed her. "What a beautiful body she has," he thought as he spied on her.

From then on he took every opportunity to see Yembo naked.

Early one morning, Oggún was peering through the window as Yembo dressed. "An old man like my father cannot keep such a woman happy," thought Oggún. "I must take her away from him and make her mine."

Elegguá saw his brother crouched next to the house. "What are you doing?" he asked.

"I am fixing this window," was Oggún's hasty reply. "Our father asked me to."

The next time that Oggún followed Yembo to the river, Elegguá came up to him as he hid behind the bushes.

"What are you doing?" asked Elegguá.

"I am looking for a flock of quail," growled Oggún. "Go away before you scare them."

Whenever Oggún followed Yembo, Elegguá followed Oggún. "If I don't stop Elegguá from meddling," thought Oggún, "I'll never have the chance of taking Yembo for myself."

Oggún began to mistreat Elegguá. At the midday meal, Oggún took Elegguá's bowl away and gave him a much smaller one.

"Why is my bowl so small?" complained Elegguá.

"You have been eating too much and not doing enough work," said Oggún. "Besides, Osún is the man of the house during the day. He deserves your portion."

Osún was delighted. "Thank you, Oggún," he said. "My responsibilities make me very hungry."

Elegguá went to bed hungry that night, and the night after that, and the night after that.

Oggún made sure that Elegguá's portion grew smaller every day. "Let's see how much snooping he can do when he's starving," Oggún muttered to himself.

But by this time, Elegguá had figured out what was going on. "I must keep Oggún away from Yembo," he thought. "I must keep our family from dishonor."

Weak as he was, Elegguá followed Oggún. If there was an opportunity for Oggún to be alone with Yembo, Elegguá interrupted and spoiled it.

"Look, mother, I found a pretty stone for you," he cried. Or, he said, "Mother our neighbor wants to borrow a pot," or, "Mother, the peddler is here with some beautiful cloth."

Oggún was furious. He could do nothing to Yembo while Elegguá hovered around the house. He waited until Obatalá and Oshosi went out to the fields. Then he grabbed Elegguá and threw him out the door.

"I'm tired of your spying," shouted Oggún. "I'm tired of your meddling. Stay away or I will kill you."

Elegguá ran around the corner of the house and hid.

"What is going on?" asked Osún. "I heard shouting."

"It was just the goats fighting," said Oggún. "Here, I have something for you." He gave Osún four sacks of corn meal.

Osún cooked all the corn meal, ate it, and was soon fast asleep in the shade.

Oggún went in the house and closed the door. He grabbed Yembo and kissed her. "You are mine at last," he said, fulfilling his evil intentions.

The next day Elegguá peered around the corner of the house. He saw how Oggún gave Osún four more bags of corn meal. Osún ate, fell asleep, and Oggún was able to possess his mother again.

For many days Elegguá watched. Osún ate and slept. Oggún had his way with Yembo.

Obatalá returned from the fields one evening to find Elegguá crying, huddled against a corner of the house.

"What is wrong, my son?" he asked. "Are you ill?"

"I haven't eaten in many days," sniffed Elegguá. "Oggún has thrown me out of the house."

"How is it that Osún hasn't told me anything about this?" asked Obatalá.

"Oggún gives him so much food that he spends the days asleep," said Elegguá.

Obatalá was shocked. "Impossible!" he cried. "Osún never sleeps."

"Yes, he does. And, when he's asleep, Oggún makes love to our mother," Elegguá said in a very low voice.

"Liar!" shouted Obatalá. "How can you say such a thing?"

"It is true, father," said Elegguá. "I can prove it to you. Tomorrow, go to the fields as usual. Wait a short while and come back. You will see everything for yourself."

That night, Obatalá spent a sleepless night next to Yembo.

The next morning, he headed out to the fields with Oshosi.

He told Osún, "Take care of your mother and your brothers, Osún. I leave you in charge of the house."

When they arrived at the fields, Obatalá said to Oshosi, "I have forgotten my sharpening stone. I have to return to the house." With a sad heart, he made his way home and hid in a stand of mangroves to watch.

He saw Oggún give Osún the four sacks of corn meal. He saw Osún eat and fall asleep. He saw how Oggún embraced Yembo and closed the door.

Obatalá cried a river of tears. His pain was so great that he could hardly stand. He cut a mangrove stick for a cane and hobbled slowly to his house. He raised the stick and banged on the door.

"Open the door!" he shouted.

From inside the house he heard Yembo say, "You see? You see what you've gotten me into, Oggún?"

"Open the door!" shouted Obatalá.

"You've had your way with me," he heard Yembo tell Oggún. "You've forced me to lay with you. What could I do? I will go and open the door."

Obatalá banged on the door again. "Open this door!"

On the other side of the door Oggún said, "No, mother. I am a man. I will open the door."

Obatalá raised his stick to the door again. When it opened, Obatalá and Oggún were face to face.

Obatalá pointed his stick at Oggún and cried out, "I curse you!"

"Don't curse me father," said Oggún, lowering his head. "I will curse myself." He took a deep breath and his voice grew stronger. "While the world remains the world, I shall work. I shall work day and night without rest. That will be my curse."

Obatalá pushed past Oggún and into the house, shouting, "Yembo! Yembo, where are you?" He found her curled on the floor, her arms around her head. Obatalá raised his stick.

"My mother is innocent," Oggún told Obatalá. "Lower your stick. She is not to blame."

Obatalá turned to Oggún. "Leave this house. Leave my sight. I never want to see you again."

Oggún never returned to Obatalá's house. Since that day he is known as Oggún Alguede, the blacksmith. He has never found rest.

Osún came into the house, rubbing the sleep out of his eyes. "What is happening?" he asked. "All this shouting woke me up."

Obatalá whacked him on the head with the stick. "This will wake you up!" he shouted. He hit him again and again, chasing him all over the house. "Is this how you obey me? Is this how you keep your trust?"

When Obatalá grew tired of hitting Osún, he said, "From now on, Elegguá will guard the door. If he does not eat, no one in this house will eat. I vow that Elegguá will never go hungry again."

He put his arm around Elegguá and said, "From now on, no one will enter or leave this house without your permission. The fate of this house is in your hands. Good or evil may enter. Be it as you wish."

He glared at Yembo. "I will forgive you, Yembo," said Obatalá. "But if you have another male child, I will kill it with my own hands."

Yembo cried, but she did not dare say anything.

149

OBATALÁ AND ORUNMILÁ

This story tells how Obatalá buried Orunmilá alive and how he was saved by Elegguá. It also relates how Shangó grew to hate Oggún and how Obatalá regained his memory. Lastly, it tells how Orunmilá received the Ifá board.

When Orunmilá was born, Obatalá bundled him up and took him into the forest to kill him. It didn't matter that Yembo, his wife, screamed and begged for the baby's life. Obatalá had vowed that he would kill all the sons born into his house. He kept on walking into the forest. Yembo's voice faded away. Soon, he couldn't hear it any more.

Obatalá arrived at the place where a baobab tree grew. He laid the baby on the ground and began to dig. When the hole was big enough, he put Orunmilá inside. Orunmilá cried and screamed. Obatalá closed his ears to his son's crying.

Obatalá filled the hole, but he left Orunmilá's head above ground. He couldn't bury the baby alive. He couldn't do that. He left the head out for the ants to eat.

Elegguá, who sees everything, had followed Obatalá. He saw his father bury his baby brother alive. He ran back home.

"What did your father do with the baby?" asked Yembo.

"He dug a hole at the base of the big baobab in the forest," said Elegguá. "He put the baby in and covered him up."

"Is he dead?" asked Yembo.

"His head is still above the ground," said Elegguá.

Yembo cried.

When Obatalá returned, he asked, "Why are you crying?"

"You have killed my baby," said Yembo.

"What baby?" asked Obatalá. He had forgotten. He had done a terrible thing. His mind refused to hold on to it.

Yembo prepared the day's meal. When everyone had eaten, she wrapped food in a plantain leaf and headed for the forest.

"Where are you going?" asked Obatalá.

"I go feed the memory of your forgetfulness," said Yembo. Obatalá laughed at his wife's foolishness.

Every day, Yembo took food to Orunmilá. Every day, she fed his head.

Time passed. Yembo found that she was pregnant. The women came and delivered the child.

"Is it a boy or a girl?" asked Obatalá.

"It is a boy," said the women. "His name is Shangó."

"Give him to me," said Obatalá.

The women wailed and screamed.

"Give him to me," demanded Obatalá. "I will not have another son born into this house."

"Don't harm this one," cried Yembo.

"I have harmed no one," said Obatalá. He did not remember Orunmilá. "Give me the child."

The women had to do as he said. They gave him Shangó.

Obatalá looked at the baby. He felt strange. "He is very handsome," he said.

His face hardened. "I have made a vow," he said. "I cannot have him live in this house."

The women wailed.

"Quiet, women," he shouted. "Why are you howling so much?"

"You will kill him," said Yembo.

"I will do no such thing," said Obatalá. "I like children. I was thinking of taking him to Dadá, our eldest daughter. She can raise him."

Obatalá took Shangó to Dadá's house. There, he grew to become a strong, good looking boy.

One day, Dadá said, "Get dressed. Put on your very best robe."

"Why?" asked Shangó. "There is no festival today."

"You're going to visit your father," said Dadá.

When they arrived at Obatalá's house, he said, "What a handsome young warrior you've grown to be!"

Shangó was very pleased at Obatalá's compliment. Yembo just cried and cried.

"Why are you crying, mother?" asked Shangó. "Why are you so sad?"

"It's nothing," said Yembo. She did not want to tell her son about Orunmilá's horrible fate. "Someday I will tell you."

"I want this boy brought to me every day," said Obatalá. "It is not right that a man be taught by women."

After that day, Dadá brought Shangó to see his father every day.

Every day, Obatalá sat Shangó up on his knee and said, "Let me tell you the thing that your brother, Oggún, did to your mother." Or, he'd say, "Today I will tell you about the traitor, Oggún." Or, "This is how Oggún starved your brother and raped your mother."

Naturally, Shangó grew up hating Oggún. Day after day, his hatred grew. When he became a man, he developed a fierce temper. He angered very easily. He wanted to fight everyone, but mostly, he wanted a chance to fight Oggún.

Shangó went to visit his godfather, Osaín. Osaín owns all the magic and medicinal herbs and is very wise.

"I greet you and honor you, godfather," said Shangó.

"What can I do for you, my son?" said Osaín.

"I want a weapon," said Shangó.

"You already have your bow and your spear and your ax," said Osaín. "What else do you need?"

"I need a weapon to make me invincible," said Shangó.

"Very well," said Osaín. "Take this gourd."

"A gourd?" laughed Shangó. "What kind of a weapon is that?"

"A very powerful one," said Osaín. "Fill this gourd with water and hang it in a corner of your house. Before you go out the door, moisten your finger in the water and make a cross on your tongue."

That is what gave Shangó his power. That is why, when he is saluted, fire and smoke come out of his mouth. The fire is the lightning. That is why we pray to Shangó when we hear the thunder, the sound of his voice.

Time passed and things began to go from bad to worse for Obatalá.

Shangó came to visit and said, "Father, why are you so worried?"

"My animals are dying," said Obatalá. "The crops I planted will not thrive. My enemies want my lands. Let them have the land! All the water has dried up on it."

"I must think about this," said Shangó. He stood up and went for a walk. At the crossroads, he met Elegguá.

"Why are you so glum, my brother?" asked Elegguá.

"I have heard disturbing news from our father," said Shangó. He then told Elegguá everything that Obatalá had said to him.

"All these things are due to the division inside his own head," said Elegguá.

"I don't understand what you say," said Shangó.

"Before you were born, there was another son," said Elegguá. "His name was Orunmilá."

"Why have I never heard of him?" asked Shangó.

"Obatalá has forgotten. Our mother will not speak of it. And, I know how to keep secrets," said Elegguá.

"What happened to Orunmilá?" asked Shangó.

"When he was born, Obatalá took him and buried him at the base of a baobab tree. Yembo fed him. I saved him," said Elegguá. "You must talk to Obatalá about these things. When his head has cooled off, his life will improve."

Shangó and Elegguá returned to where their father was sitting.

"Father," said Elegguá. "I have always obeyed you."

"That is true," said Obatalá.

"Father," said Shangó. "I have always given you good advice."

"That is true," said Obatalá. "That is why I have told you of my misfortunes."

"I know the cause of your misfortunes," said Shangó.

"Tell me then, son," said Obatalá.

"Before I was born, there was another baby boy. His name was Orunmilá. You murdered your own son by burying him alive."

Obatalá was stunned. The memory of his horrible act came back to him. He buried his face in his hands and began to cry.

"It is true," he sobbed. "I remember. I killed my own son. I buried a baby alive because of my own pride."

He looked up at Shangó. "What can I do? Now I know that all my bad luck comes from that act. What sacrifice can I make? What will make me clean again?"

Elegguá said, "There is no need to make amends."

"How can you say that?" cried Obatalá. "I killed your own brother."

"You did not," said Elegguá. "It's a marvelous story. One day, I was walking in the forest when I came to a gigantic baobab."

"Yes," sighed Obatalá. "That's where I did it."

"Under the baobab," continued Elegguá. "I found a man buried up to his neck. I dug him out."

"You did what?" said Obatalá.

"I dug him out," said Elegguá. "He turned out to be a great diviner. I did not know his name at the time, but I think that this man could be your son, Orunmilá."

Obatalá leapt to his feet. He wasted no time tracking down the seer that Elegguá had told him about. When he found him, he fell to his knees before him.

"Please forgive me," cried Obatalá.

"Of course I forgive you," said Orunmilá. "But who are you?"

Obatalá told Orunmilá the story of his birth. Haltingly he also told him about how he had tried to kill him when he was just a baby.

"All this you tell me is a long ways into the past," said Orunmilá. "I am just happy that I have gotten to meet my father."

They embraced.

"Will you come to my house and live with me as my son?" asked Obatalá.

"I thank you." said Orunmilá. "But I have made my own way in the world. The baobab tree gave me its wisdom and taught me how to divine. Its roots gave me the cowry shells. Its branches gave me what I needed to make my prophesies. It too is my father."

"I accept your wishes." said Obatalá. But he still wanted to do something for Orunmilá. So, he went to the baobab tree.

"I do this not for me." said Obatalá, "but for our son." And, he took a piece of wood out of the baobab's trunk.

He carved and polished the piece of wood until he had made a beautiful board, an Ifá board.

He took the board to Orunmilá and said, "This is for you, my son, from both your fathers. You are now more than a diviner, you are a babalawó. From now on, all the diviners will have to come and consult you."

And this is just what happened.

HOW OBATALÁ REGAINED HIS MEMORY

This story relates Shangó's birth and childhood. It also tells How Elegguá gave Shangó the secret that restored Obatalá's memory.

You remember how Oggún seduced his mother and was thrown out of the house by Obatalá. Obatalá then swore that if Yembo, his wife, had any more male children, he would kill them with his own hands. Yembo bore Obatalá another son, Orunlá (Orunmilá). Obatalá buried him alive, but Elegguá saved Orunlá's life.

Believing that he had killed his own son, Obatalá went crazy. He lost all memory of what had happened in his house. Only his grief and the conviction that he must kill any male children born to Yembo remained.

Yembo gave birth to another son, Shangó. Crying, she showed the baby to Obatalá and asked him, "Must you kill him, my husband?"

"I swore to kill all the sons you bore me," said Obatalá. "But I cannot do this terrible thing. Send him to our eldest daughter, Dadá. If he is out of my sight, he will be safe."

Yembo took Shangó to the beautiful royal palm that was Dadá's house and told her, "Please raise this child as if it were your own. If he stays with us, Obatalá may have a change of heart and kill him."

"The baby is strong and beautiful," said Dadá. "I will be his mother."

The years went by. Shangó grew and became a handsome young boy.

One day, Dadá called Shangó to her and said, "Shangó, I have decided that it is time that you met your father."

Shangó was surprised. "I did not know I had a father," he said.

The walked to Obatalá's house. "I have come to show you your son," said Dadá. "You can see I have raised him well."

"He looks just like me." said Obatalá.

"He is so beautiful." said Yembo.

They both burst into tears.

"Why are you crying?" asked Shangó. "Aren't you glad to see me? Why did you send me away?"

But Obatalá shook his head and answered, "I don't remember." to all his questions.

"Mother, don't you remember?" asked Shangó.

"I remember," said Yembo, "but I don't have permission to speak of such things."

Obatalá put his hand on Shangó's shoulder and said, "I promise you that the day I remember, I will tell you the story of what happened before you were born."

Shangó had to be satisfied with that.

Dadá and Shangó began to visit Obatalá and Yembo every day. Every visit was the same.

Obatalá said, "He is so tall, so virile, so good looking."

Yembo said, "He is so good, so smart, such a good son."

And then they both started crying. All the crying made Shangó uncomfortable.

"Maybe I shouldn't come." he said. "I don't want to upset you."

His parents always replied, "No, no, we want you to visit."

Shangó thought that it was all very strange.

One time, he asked his mother, "Why is Osún always sprawled on the floor next to the door? Why does he never get up?"

"I do not have permission to speak." said Yembo.

Shangó became angry. He yelled, "What happened to all of you in this house? Why won't anyone talk?"

Yembo bent over and whispered in his ear, "You might want to ask your brother, Elegguá. He knows all the secret things that happened before your birth."

Shangó went to the crossroads, where Elegguá was sitting on a rock and asked him, "Elegguá, will you tell me what terrible thing happened in our house?"

Elegguá thought for a bit before answering. "I have great affection for you," he said. "But if I told you, you would not believe me."

"You won't tell me either?" said Shangó, exasperated.

"I will tell you how to get Obatalá himself to tell you the story," said Elegguá.

"But Obatalá does not remember anything," cried Shangó.

"This is what you must do," said Elegguá. "Take the pulp out of three gourds. Break a coconut and select three pieces. Then, gather three parrot feathers. Get Yembo's bucket and fill it with rain water. Go to the base of the big baobab outside the village. Mix everything into the rain water and stir in some cacao butter."

"Then what?," asked Shangó all excited.

"You must leave the bucket at the base of the tree for seven days," said Elegguá. "When you go back for it, take a handful of powdered eggshell and add it to the mixture."

"Do I put the stuff in Obatalá's food?" asked Shangó.

"No," said Elegguá. "Wait until he sits you on his knee to tell you stories. Then, put a little bit of the mixture on his tongue, on his eyes and on his head."

Shangó ran off to follow Elegguá's instructions. The next time he went to visit his parents, he had a handful of the mixture ready in his pouch.

"Shangó, you are early today," said Obatalá.

"Quick, tell me a story," said Shangó.

He lifted Shangó and sat him on his knees. "Why are you in such a hurry to listen to a story?" he asked.

"Wait," said Shangó, "before you tell the story we must play a game."

"A game?" said Obatalá.

"I'll pretend that you are a house and your walls need fixing," said Shangó. "Close your eyes."

Shangó took a little bit of the mixture from his pouch. "You need a little plaster here," he said, putting some on Obatalá's head.

"You need some more here and here," he said, putting some on Obatalá's eyes.

"And, if you open the door, I'll put some on the floor inside," he said, putting a last dab on Obatalá's tongue. "Now tell me a story."

Obatalá began to remember. He remembered Oggún's evil intentions towards Yembo. He remembered Elegguá's mistreatment. He remembered burying Orunlá. And, as he cried, Obatalá told Shangó everything that had happened before he was born.

YOUNG ORUNMILÁ

This story tells how Obatalá got into trouble because he didn't follow Orunmilá's advice.

Imagine a boy of sixteen being a famous babalawó. That was Orunmilá. He did not even have a beard when his fame was spread all over the world.

People acclaimed him, "Orunmilá is the best babalawó."

"Orunmilá is a genius," they said.

People came from far away to get the young boy's advice. His fame was great. His wisdom was deep. So much so that even the powerful Orishá, Obatalá, visited him one day.

Obatalá had no idea that Orunmilá was the child he had buried alive, the child Elegguá had saved. "I have come for a consultation," he said.

"It is my honor," said Orunmilá. Fame had not gone to his head. He was a humble boy.

Obatalá said, "I am going on a trip. There is good land available. I want to buy it."

"When do you want to leave?" asked Orunmilá.

"I must leave today," said Obatalá.

Orunmilá took out his board, the Ifá board. He took out his cowry shells. He blew on them to give them ashé. He threw the shells and peered at them. Obatalá leaned over to look at the shells too. They were just shells on a piece of wood to him. He could not read the oracle.

"You must not leave today," said Orunmilá.

"Why not?" asked Obatalá.

"Before you go on your trip, you must make ebó," said Orunmilá. "You need the rest of the day to go to the market and buy what you need."

"I don't have time for such foolishness," snorted Obatalá. "I must leave today."

"If you go on your trip without making ebó, you will find yourself in great danger," said Orunmilá.

"There is no danger I can't overcome," said Obatalá. "I am a great Orishá."

Obatalá is a great Orishá, but sometimes, he is impatient. He went home, rolled up his sleeping mat and set off on his trip. He gave no thought to Orunmilá's advice.

Obatalá walked for days. He walked through the forest. He walked over a mountain. He had to swim across a river. He was very tired and hungry.

Then he saw a house. "Hello," he called out, "is anyone here?" There was no answer.

Obatalá said to himself, "I'm very hungry and there's probably food in that house. The owner won't mind if I look inside. After all, the owner should be honored that I visit his house."

Obatalá went inside. There were baskets of yams. There were bunches of bananas leaning against the walls. A delicious smell came from a pot hanging over the fire.

Obatalá spooned out a bowl full of stew, set a couple of yams to roast in the ashes and sat down to eat.

"This is delicious stew," he said. "I must repay this kind stranger when I come back from my trip."

Obatalá finished eating and was about to leave when he saw a drum standing on a little platform. It was across from the door, in a place of honor. Obatalá went to it and gave it a tap with his finger.

"Thrum!" said the drum.

"What a beautiful sound," exclaimed Obatalá.

He hit the drum with his hand. "Pa ta dum!" said the drum.

Obatalá hit it with his other hand. "Pa ta ka ta dum!" said the drum.

Obatalá sat down and began to play the drum.

"Pa ta ka kin la. Kin la pa ta ka!" said the drum.

The song of the drum floated out of the house and over the forest. Shangó was walking in the forest when he heard it.

"Pa ta ka kin la?" said Shangó. "Someone is playing my drum. "Pa ta ka kin la?" he exclaimed. "Someone is in my house!" He hurried home.

Shangó was not the only one to hear the sound of the drum. A troop of monkeys heard the drumming and came to investigate, as monkeys will do.

They peered through the windows and the doors and watched Obatalá drum.

After a while, Obatalá stopped drumming. "What a beautiful drum," he said, and stood up. He tidied up after himself, washed the bowl he had used and left.

The moment he was gone, the troop of monkeys rushed into the house. They spilled and trampled the yams. They bit into all the bananas, spoiling them. They turned over the pot of stew. And, imitating Obatalá, they began to pound on the drum.

"Wakun?" said the drum. "Plaff. Kabum. Konk. Crack!"

With that last crack, the skin broke. The drum was ruined. The monkeys ran away before Shangó arrived. He didn't see them.

When Shangó saw the mess in his house, he yelled, "Who has come into my house? Who has spoiled my dinner? Who has broken my beautiful drum?"

Shangó ran out and went to the palace. It was his palace. He was the king of this country.

"Guards!" he yelled.

The guards ran to him, tumbling over each other in their haste. Everyone knows that it's not a good idea to make Shangó angry.

"Someone has been in my house," said Shangó. "A thief has stolen my food and broken my drum. Go get him!"

The guards went searching in every direction. Soon, one of them caught up with Obatalá. "Stop where you are, you thief!" he shouted.

"Are you talking to me?" said Obatalá. He drew himself up to his full height. "I'll have you know that I'm . . ."

He didn't get a chance to say who he was. The guard's spear was at his throat. "I know who you are," said the guard. "You're the thief who's going to jail."

The next day, the guard went to Shangó and said, "I captured the thief yesterday. What should I do with him, kill him?"

"Let me look at him first," said Shangó. "I may want to kill him myself."

They went to the jail. This was not a modern jail, with television. This was an old time jail. It was a large hole in the ground with a heavy piece of iron to cover it.

The guard opened the iron cover. Inside, in the mud, filth and bugs at the bottom, was Obatalá.

"Father!" exclaimed Shangó. "What are you doing in there?" He turned to the guard. "Where is the thief?"

"That is the thief," said the guard proudly. "I caught him myself."

"That is my father, you idiot," said Shangó. "Get him out of there."

The guard lifted Obatalá out of the hole. The Orishá peered around him, blinded by the sun. "Shangó?" he said. "Is that you? I heard your voice."

"It's me, father," said Shangó. He grabbed the poor guard by the throat. "I don't know what's going on, but I swear I'll make this guard pay for what he has done to you."

"Let him go, son. Let him go," said Obatalá. He knew that everything that had happened was his own fault. He had not made ebó. He had not listened to Orunmilá's advice.

SHANGÓ VS. OGGÚN

SHANGÓ AND OYÁ

This story recapitulates the reasons why Shangó hates Oggún. It tells why Oggún, in turn, hates Shangó.

Shangó is Oggún's younger brother, born of the same mother. They have always been enemies. They have always been at war.

Many years before Shangó was born, Oggún seduced his own mother. His father, Obatalá, discovered Oggún's crime and banished him into the wilderness.

Obatalá swore to kill any more male children born in his house, but when Shangó was born, he took pity on him. He gave little Shangó away. Shangó was raised by his sister. He did not know his mother. He did not know his father.

When Shangó grew up, he learned about his family's shameful secret. He was filled with a great rage against Oggún. He swore to take vengeance. He swore to find Oggún and make him pay for what he had done to his mother and father.

That is the reason Shangó hates Oggún. This story tells of one reason Oggún hates his younger brother:

After learning of his family's disgrace, Shangó set off in search of Oggún. He saw a farmer working his field. The farmer scratched at the hard packed dirt with a pointed stick.

Shangó asked him, "Why don't you use an iron hoe? Your work would be easier."

The farmer said, "Iron, what is that?"

"Just a thing my brother makes," said Shangó and continued on his way. Oggún had not been in that place.

When he had traveled a long distance, Shangó saw a wood cutter. The wood cutter was patiently chipping away at a tree with a sharp stone.

Shangó asked him, "Why don't you use an iron ax? Your work would be easier."

The wood cutter said, "Iron, what is that?"

"It's what my brother makes," said Shangó. Oggún had not been there.

He left the wood cutter and traveled for many days until he arrived at a large town. There, he saw a man clearing a patch of land with a machete.

Shangó asked him, "What is that tool?"

The man said, "This is called a machete. It is made of a thing called iron. It is magic. Its edge can slice through anything."

"Who makes such things?" asked Shangó. He knew he had found Oggún, but he wanted to make sure.

"The secret was brought to us by Oggún," said the man. "Our life is easier because of him."

Shangó asked him, "Where does this Oggún live?"

The man said, "Oggún lives here in town with a woman called Oyá."

"Show me where he lives," said Shangó. "I am Oggún's brother and I have been looking for him for a long time."

The man showed Shangó where Oggún lived. Shangó spent the rest of the day thinking about revenge.

First he thought, "I will kill Oggún." Then he thought, "If I kill Oggún, the secret of iron will die with him. The people in this world would suffer. That is not just."

While he was thinking and debating with himself, Shangó found a house where he could live.

"I can sleep here until I make up my mind," he thought. He went to sleep, still thinking about what to do. When he woke up the next morning, he had the answer.

"I will take Oyá away from Oggún," he said. "Didn't Oggún take my mother away from my father?"

Shangó went to Oggún's house. He climbed a palm tree to watch and wait for an opportunity to get to Oyá.

As Shangó watched, Oggún came out of his house and built a mighty fire. He took rocks and put them in the fire. Then he pounded and hammered the rocks until a pile of machete blades lay at his feet.

Oggún called out, "Oyá! I'm going to the market now." He shouldered the bundle of blades and walked away.

"This is my opportunity," said Shangó. He slid down the palm's trunk and ran to Oggún's door. It was locked.

Oyá heard the door rattle and called out, "Who is that?"

Shangó said in a very sweet voice, "I'm Oggún's brother. I have come to visit."

"I don't open the door to anyone without my husband's permission," said Oyá.

"I don't need anyone's permission," shouted Shangó and sent a bolt of lightning against the door. It burst into a million pieces. Shangó rushed inside to find Oyá, machete in hand, ready to defend herself.

Shangó knocked the machete away. "I like women with spirit," he said and grabbed her.

Oyá screamed and struggled. She scratched and punched but her strength was no match against Shangó's. He threw her over his shoulder and carried her away, breathing fire at the neighbors that came to help Oyá.

When Oggún returned from the market, he saw the smashed door.

"Oyá," he yelled. He ran into his house. It was empty.

He ran back outside. "Oyá," he called.

Oggún's neighbors came when they heard him yelling. They said, "She was taken away by a man who breathes fire."

Oggún raced through the town. He asked everyone for news of a stranger. Finally, he found out where Shangó was staying. Oggún ran to the house.

He got there too late. Shangó already had had his way with Oyá. She lay in his arms sighing with contentment.

"Nobody, but nobody has ever made love to me like that before," she told Shangó, snuggling closer to him.

Oggún began hammering on Shangó's door, shouting, "Oyá!"

Shangó leaned out a window. "Hello brother," he said. "What can I do for you?"

Oggún shouted, "I want my woman back."

Shangó turned his head and called out, "Oyá, there's someone here to see you."

Oyá came to the window. "What do you want, little man?" she asked Oggún.

Oggún's face turned purple with rage. "You come out of there right now!" he shouted.

Oyá smiled. "Go back home," she said. "I'm very happy where I am."

That is how Shangó ran off with Oyá, Oggún's wife. That is one of the reasons Oggún hates Shangó.

WHEN OYÁ BREATHED FIRE

This story combines the tale of Oyá's abduction with her desire to taste Shangó's magic potion, which allows him to breathe fire.

When they were children, Shangó and his brother, Oggún, lived in the same house. There, Oggún seduced their mother while their father was off working in the fields.

Shangó never forgot what Oggún did to their mother, Yembo. He was always looking for ways to avenge his mother's honor.

One day, Shangó heard that Oggún had married Oyá and was living the life of a happy householder.

Shangó was outraged. "This is a man with no honor," he said. "How does he dare pretend that he is a husband?"

Shangó dressed in his warrior's clothing and rushed to Oggún's house.

He banged on the door with his double-headed ax. "Where is the dog that pretends he is respectable?" he shouted.

Oyá opened the door and confronted Shangó. "What do you want making so much noise?" she asked. "We have no need of peddlers."

"Where is Oggún?" said Shangó.

"He is off hunting," replied Oyá. "He works. He has no time to go shouting at people's houses."

Oyá's sharp tongue stung Shangó. He drew himself up and asked her with great dignity, "Don't you know that you have married a man without honor?"

Oyá was not impressed. "And who are you to talk that way about my husband?" she asked.

"I am the great warrior, Shangó," he said. Surely Oyá was going to be impressed now.

Oyá laughed, "Oh, the great party drummer."

Then the insults began to fly back and forth. The insults turned into flirting. They started to laugh. Oyá noticed that Shangó made a fine figure of a man. Shangó saw that Oyá had courage and spirit.

Shangó said. "Leave your husband and come with me."

Oyá pretended to think about it. She knew that she wanted to go off with Shangó. "You please me." she told him. "I will leave my husband and come with you."

To tell the truth. Shangó really wanted to take Oyá away with him to enrage Oggún; make him pay for destroying his mother's honor. He had no idea things would get more complicated.

Shangó took Oyá's hand. "Come with me to Dadá's house," he said. "We can live there."

Oyá drew back. "And who is that?" she asked. "Another of your wives?"

"Dadá is my sister." said Shangó. "She raised me and I love her as a mother."

When Oggún returned from hunting. he found the door open and his house empty.

He went to the neighbors. "Where is my wife?" he asked them.

"Your wife has gone with another man," they said. "A big handsome warrior carried her off."

Oggún knew right away that it was Shangó. He sharpened his machete and went looking for his brother.

They met in the marketplace.

Oggún waved his machete over his head and ran at Shangó. "Thief," shouted Oggún. "Where is my wife?"

Shangó whirled his ax, ready to meet Oggún. "She is mine now, mother raper," he yelled.

The fight was long and horrible. Lighting struck the ground around Oggún. Shangó parried and dodged Oggún's slashes. At last, exhausted, they headed off in opposite directions to take care of their wounds.

Oggún shook his fist at Shangó. "I shall find where you have hidden Oyá," he said. "I will take her away from you."

Shangó returned to Dadá's house. He was bleeding from many cuts. His clothes were in rags.

"What has happened to you?" Oyá asked.

"I met your husband in the market," said Shangó. "He wants to take you away from me."

Oyá shook her head. "If that's the way you look after a fight, he's not going to have too much trouble," she said. "You don't look like a warrior. You look like a rag seller."

Many days went by. Neither Oggún or Shangó had the strength to continue the fight.

Oyá saw that Shangó followed a ritual that never changed. Before leaving the house, he wet his finger in the contents of a gourd that he kept by the door. He then made the sign of the cross on his tongue with his finger.

She asked him, "What is inside that gourd?"

Shangó replied, "That is a gift from my godfather, Osaín. It is full of magical herbs." But he would say no more.

Oyá was curious and wanted to learn more. One morning, she waited until Shangó left the house. She took the gourd down from its nail, wet her finger in the contents and drew a cross on her tongue.

Dadá saw what Oyá was doing and tried to stop her. "Put the gourd down," she said, frightened.

Oyá started to say, "I wanted to see what . . ." before she could finish, a stream of flame and smoke came out of her mouth. She almost burnt Dadá where she stood. The gourd fell from her hands and spilled on the floor.

Oyá was horrified. "I'm sorry, I just . . ." Another flame shot out her mouth, setting the yam basket on fire.

After the two women put out the fire, Dadá gave Oyá a big gourd of beer.

"Drink this down, and then another," said Dadá. "That should put the fire out. That's what comes out of fooling around with magic."

Oyá was ashamed. "I didn't know it would do that," she said.

"Shangó is sure to find out," said Dadá. "His temper is terrible. We must hide where he can't find us. Otherwise, he will punish us."

Deathly afraid of Shangó's punishment, the two women ran out of the house and buried themselves at the base of a royal palm.

Shangó came home. He found his gourd lying on the kitchen floor next to the burnt yams, the precious herbal mixture pooled and spoiled on the floor.

"Someone's been fooling around with my magic gourd," said Shangó. He called out, "Dadá! Oyá!" There was no answer.

He shouted, "Dadá! Oyá!" The house was silent, deserted.

He went outside. "Dadá! Oyá!" he called. There was no answer.

He went to the fields. "Dadá! Oyá! he called. There was no answer, but the royal palm began to tremble.

"That's strange," said Shangó. "The palm is moving, but there is no wind."

"Dadá! Oyá!" he called. The palm tree shook even harder.

Shangó went to the royal palm and called out loudly, "Dadá! Oyá! Come out!" The palm tree shook so hard that a frond fell to the ground.

When Shangó lifted the palm frond, he found the hole where Dadá and Oyá were hiding.

Shangó was very angry. "You disobey me and then hide in a hole?" he asked the two women. "Is that any way to behave?"

Oyá said, "We were afraid."

Dadá said, "We thought you were going to punish us."

The two frightened women looked like rabbits in a hole. "I ought to punish you," said Shangó. "You have ruined my magic and almost burnt the house down. How dare you play with my powerful secret?"

"I was curious," said Oyá.

"I wasn't paying attention," said Dadá.

Shangó said in a stern voice, "If you're so curious, Oyá, you can go see how many weeds are in the yam patch. Dadá, you can go pay attention to the house, wash and repair all my clothes and make me a meal."

Oyá crawled out of the hole and snapped, "You should be declaring war on Oggún instead of on us," she said. "He's the one that ruined your clothes."

That is what Shangó did. Once Dadá had sewn up his warrior's outfit, Shangó and Oyá went to Oggún's house.

Shangó yelled, "Come out, you coward, and fight."

A spear whizzed past Shangó's head. Oggún came charging at him with his sharp iron machete. Oggún was prepared for battle.

Shangó sent a lightning bolt that split open the earth at Oggún's feet. A rain of spears fell around Shangó. The battle went on for hours. The earth shook. The air filled with smoke. Mighty trees fell under Oggún's wild slashing.

Then, Oyá stepped in to fight next to Shangó. Her shooting star flew out and hit Oggún smack on the forehead. He fell to the ground, stunned.

Shangó placed his foot on Oggún's chest. He raised his mighty ax over his head. "I have defeated you in battle," said Shangó.

Oggún spat at him. "You have done no such thing," he said. "It was my wife who tricked me with her shooting star."

Oyá kicked him on the head. "I am no longer your wife," she told Oggún. "I am Shangó's wife." She kicked him again. "And it was no trick. I am as much a warrior and a fighter as Shangó."

Oggún held his head. "You have won, you have won," he said. "Stop kicking me."

Shangó said to Oggún, "Leave these lands and return no more. I am a merciful warrior and I spare your life."

Oyá made a shooting star whizz past Oggún's ear. "I am not such a merciful warrior," she said. "My aim will be better the next time I see you."

Oggún had no other choice than to disappear into the forest. The bloody feud between Oggún and Shangó continues to this day.

THE FRIENDLY DRINK

Another reason that Oggún hates Shangó is that Shangó seems to be able to get the best of him in most situations. Here is an example.

One day, Shangó was walking in the forest when, who should he see walking down the path towards him, but Oggún?

The two enemies didn't think of giving way to each other. They didn't slow their pace. They kept walking until they were face to face, chest to chest.

Oggún thrust his machete between Shangó's feet, deep into the forest floor. He glared at his enemy.

"How dare you come into my forest without permission?" he shouted.

Normally, Shangó would have started blasting with his thunder and lightning right then and there, but he had just fought a long war. He was tired.

He said to Oggún, "Let me pass and I will spare you."

This made Oggún furious. "Spare me?" he growled. "You have forgotten who is the better warrior."

"I haven't forgotten," said Shangó. "It's me."

Oggún was beside himself. "I challenge you," he roared. "I challenge you to fight."

Shangó unslung his huge double edged ax from his shoulder. He tested the edge with his thumb and calmly asked Oggún, "When do you want to have this fight?"

Oggún grabbed his machete. "Right now!" he yelled, swinging at Shangó's head.

Shangó ducked the murderous swing. "Wait," he said. "We have to do this properly."

Oggún lowered his blade. "Properly?" he asked. "All we have to do is fight."

Shangó took a gourd of aguardiente from his belt. He took a long, deep swallow.

"It's too hot and dusty," he said. "Fighting here lacks dignity."

Oggún reached for the gourd. "Let me have some of that while I think," he said.

Shangó gave him the aguardiente. "Have a god drink," he told Oggún. "All this talking makes for a dry throat."

Oggún tilted his head back. The liquor gurgled in the gourd as he took a large gulp. "Ah, that's better," he said, wiping his mouth on the back of his hand. "What is it we were talking about?"

Shangó said, "About how thirsty we were."

"That's right," said Oggún. "I am very thirsty." He took another mighty gulp from Shangó's gourd.

Oggún loves to drink, but he can't hold his liquor. He started to laugh.

"You're funny looking," he told Shangó.

"That's because it's so hot," said Shangó. "Have another drink."

Oggún peered at the gourd he was holding. "Thish ish good," he exclaimed, tilting his head back and pouring the liquor down his throat.

The alcohol rushed to his head, which turned a purplish red. He peered at Shangó with bloodshot eyes.

Oggún mumbled, "Another drinky poo and then we fights."

Shangó smiled and said, "Go right ahead. There's plenty in the gourd."

Oggún took a last drink, staggered a little bit and shouted, "Thish ish it. We fight!"

He took a wild swing at Shangó and promptly fell down. Shangó jumped up and down on Oggún's chest a few times and kicked him in the head for good measure. Then, he grabbed Oggún's ankles and began to whirl him around and around, faster and faster until Oggún's head hit a tree trunk.

"THOCK!" went Oggún's head; like the sound a watermelon makes when it hits the ground.

Shangó bent down and picked up his gourd. He hung it from his belt, brushed the dust off his hands and said, "Well, that's that."

He slung his ax over his shoulder and walked off down the forest path.

Oggún woke up the next morning. He had a horrible hangover. A knot the size of an orange on his forehead did not help his disposition.

He blew the ants out of his nose and scratched at the mosquito bites that covered his body.

"I'll never forgive him for this." he moaned.

Oggún never forgave Shangó. They are enemies to this day. That is why Shangó and Oggún should not be called at the same time. fights will spoil the ceremony.

THE COWRIES AND IKÚ

This is one of the rare stories in which Oggún outwits Shangó.

Even the Orishás get tired. Oggún and Shangó had been fighting for a long time. They had been fighting forever. Oggún wanted a rest from the fighting, at least for a while.

He decided to go and visit Shangó. "Maybe I can talk that jerk into taking a vacation," he said to himself. "I know I can use one."

Oggún went to Shangó's house.

Shangó sat in his yard tuning the bata drums for a güemilere, a party, that night. Before Shangó could raise his ax, Oggún said, "I am tired of so much fighting. I propose that we stop for a while."

Shangó puffed out his chest and strutted up and down his yard shouting, "My strength is greater than yours. I am the greater warrior. I knew that you would surrender to me someday."

This did not go over very well with Oggún. "I have not come to surrender," he said.

"Yes, you have," crowed Shangó. "You have come to my house on your knees."

Oggún was indignant. "I have done no such thing," he said. "I come to offer you a truce."

"A truce?" said Shangó. "Ha! You have come to surrender to me, the superior warrior, the great fighter."

Oggún shouted back at him, "If anything, you're the big buffoon, the puffed up fool."

Shangó's face turned red with anger. "You're the crawling worm, the coward," he said.

Shangó raised his ax. He was panting and covered with sweat.

"Look at you," said Oggún. "All you can do is shout and wave your ax in the air. You don't have the brains to do anything else."

This confused Shangó. He lowered his ax. "What else is there to do?" he asked. "We have been enemies forever. This is what enemies do."

Oggún said, "We've never tried to figure out who is smarter or quicker. I will grant that you are strong warrior; not as good as myself, of course. However, you are as dumb as that stone on the ground."

Shangó's pride was hurt. "I have the lightning," he said. "Nothing is quicker than that. What do you have? That ragged tiger skin and rocks dug from the ground."

Oggún replied with much dignity, "The tools made from those rocks make life in this world easier."

Shangó opened his mouth, but he had nothing to say. What Oggún said was true.

"I can prove that I'm smarter than you," he blustered. "I can beat you at any task you can come up with."

Oggún said, "I propose that we compete at something so simple even you could do it. Lets go to the sea shore tomorrow and see who can find the most cowry shells by the end of the day."

Shangó laughed. "That's ridiculous," he said. "I'll get so many shells that they will bury you and your loud mouth."

"I will meet you tomorrow," said Oggún. "Then we'll see who has the loud mouth."

When Oggún left, Shangó gathered armfuls of palm fronds. Then he began to weave dozens of large baskets.

Oggún did not go back to his own house. Instead, he went to visit Ikú, death. He had a plan.

Ikú was making a seat out of skulls. It was nice, but it seemed very uncomfortable.

Death looked up and saw Oggún. "Greetings, Oggún," said Ikú. "Have you brought more warriors for me to eat?"

"I come to ask your help," said Oggún.

Ikú grinned a bony grin. "What will you give me in return?" death asked.

Oggún said, "If you do what I ask, there will be more weapons in the world and your kingdom will grow."

"I always need more subjects," said death. "What do you desire?"

Oggún told Ikú his plan. "Shangó and I will be at the seashore tomorrow collecting cowries. I want you to meet us there and scare Shangó away."

Oggún knew that Shangó feared nothing except Ikú.

As they had agreed, Oggún and Shangó met at the seashore the next morning.

Shangó had his huge baskets. He was sure that he was going to fill them all. He was going beat Oggún at his own game.

When he saw that Oggún only carried two jute sacks, he said, "I can tell that you've given up already. Even if you fill up those two sacks, one of my baskets full of cowries will beat you."

Oggún shrugged. "You have to fill the basket first," he said.

Shangó began to boast. "A great warrior and king such as myself can find every cowry on this beach before you have taken the first step." He took a deep breath and continued in the same vein. "There will not be one shell left for you to gather. You will have to bow down before me and recognize that I am your superior even at this stupid game you have come up with."

Shangó was just warming up. He had more boasting to do but Ikú appeared before him and kicked Shangó in the shin.

"Boo," said Ikú softly.

Shangó dropped his baskets and ran home as fast as lightning.

That night, Oggún went to Shangó's house. He brought his two sacks. They were stuffed full of cowry shells.

When Shangó came out of his house, Oggún asked, "Where are your baskets? Where are your mountains of shells, Shangó?"

Shangó had spent the day sulking. "It was a stupid game anyway," he said.

"And who won the stupid game?" asked Oggún.

Shangó was ashamed to admit it, but he had to say, "You did."

Oggún got to have his vacation and Ikú's kingdom grew and has kept on growing to this day.

SHANGÓ

SHANGÓ THE KING

This story reveals the historical and political events which transformed Shangó from a feared king into an Orishá.

This is the story of Shangó when he was a man instead of an Orishá. It took place when Shangó was king of Oyo.

Shangó was a formidable warrior. He could run faster, fight harder and throw a spear farther than anyone. He had no fear.

Shangó could go up to a lion or a tiger, grab it by the tail and take it home. That's how powerful a hunter he was.

He was also a sorcerer. Shangó knew spells and had power stones. He could take these stones and work magic with them. He could control thunder and lightning and blast his enemies into a million pieces. If he wanted to, he could breathe fire out of his mouth.

Shangó's subjects were terrified of him. Nobody dared to cross him. Shangó did what he wanted to anybody he wanted.

When Shangó saw a good piece of land, rich with crops and cattle, he went to the owner and said, "That land is mine."

If the owner protested saying something like, "That land belonged to my father's father," Shangó gave the order to his warriors, "Kill him," and, that would be that.

If he saw a beautiful woman, Shangó grabbed her and said, "Come and lay with me."

It did not matter if she resisted and said, "I am a married woman."

Shangó gave the order to his warriors, "Bring her to my palace," and they took her.

Any husband or lover that dared to say, "You cannot do that," would have his head cut off.

The men of Oyo whispered, "Our king is an evil man."

The women whispered, "Our king is an animal."

But when Shangó and his warriors were near, everyone shouted, "Shangó, Alafi Ilé Lodi, he's the castle above the clouds," because they were frightened.

The elders and wise men of Oyo petitioned Shangó. They said, "You have knowledge and power, yet you have become cruel to your people. You have become a tyrant."

Shangó shrugged and told his warriors, "Kill them." There were no more wise men in the kingdom.

The kings from neighboring lands sent representatives to Shangó's court. They said, "We wish to trade our cattle for your crops. We wish to trade our gold for your iron."

Shangó laughed and replied, "My iron is in swords and spears. War will give me your cattle and your gold."

His warriors invaded the neighboring kingdoms, enslaving the people and taking their goods.

Two of Shangó's generals had a reputation for being good men. Their names were Timi and Gbunca.

When Shangó ordered them to confiscate lands, they said to the owners, "Take as many animals as you can and as many yams as you can. Take your tools and what is in your house. We will turn our backs."

When Shangó ordered them to bring him a woman, they told Shangó, "We could not find her." Or they brought Shangó an old toothless hag and said, "We're sorry. We made a mistake. We thought this was the one you wanted."

Shangó knew they were tricking him. He was furious. But he could not have the generals put to death. The generals' troops were loyal to them alone. Shangó could not risk a civil war.

When the people began to shout, "Long live Timi and Gbunca," Shangó's hate grew. Like all bullies, he could not bear to be overshadowed.

Shangó devised an evil scheme to get rid of the two generals. He sent out his agents to spread rumors in the marketplace.

"I heard that Timi said Gbunca is a liar," said the agents.

They said, "I heard that Gbunca said Timi sleeps with young boys."

The rumors flew, "Timi called Gbunca a liar. Gbunca called Timi a thief."

Shangó's plan worked. When the two generals met again, their heads were full of the lying rumors. Their tempers flared.

"I heard that you have been calling me a liar while you fondle your boys," said Gbunca.

"So, it's true that you say I sleep with young boys!" shouted Timi. He spat. "My honor demands satisfaction."

Gbunca thundered, "So does mine."

The marketplace was cleared for the fight. The two generals faced each other armed with swords, shields and spears. Timi drew his sword and attacked. But Gbunca was faster. His spear went through Timi's throat. Timi fell dead in a pool of blood.

Shangó gloated over Timi's death. But this was only half of his plan. He ordered that Gbunca be brought before him.

Shangó said, "You have done a grievous harm to me and my kingdom. But I am generous enough to give you a second chance."

Gbunca kneeled before Shangó and said nothing.

Shangó continued, "You and your men will invade the kingdom to the North. If you are successful, you will live."

"Thank you, my king," said Gbunca, and left to prepare his troops.

Shangó sent agents to the king of the northern kingdom.

The agents told the king, "Shangó is planning to invade your country. He is sending the famous general Gbunca at the head of an army." They told the northern king all the details of the invasion plan.

When Gbunca's army attempted to cross the border, they were massacred. Only one warrior survived. He hid in the jungle.

It so happened that Shangó's agents walked by him when they were returning to Oyo.

The soldier heard them say, "Our king's plan worked perfectly. Not only is Gbunca dead, but all his warriors are dead as well. Now no one will be as great as Shangó."

The surviving warrior rushed back to Oyo. His story spread among the people.

The warriors in the army said, "Shangó is a traitor." They sharpened their spears.

The people vowed to avenge Gbunca. "Shangó is evil," they shouted in the streets.

Everyone came to the same decision, "Shangó must die."

Warriors, peasants, and merchants marched on Shangó's palace.

Shangó only had time to gather a few belongings, shout warnings to the members of his family, and flee into the jungle.

Shangó wandered in the wilderness for weeks.

He begged at farms, "Please, give me food."

The farmers yelled, "There is the monster!" and drove him away with their machetes.

Shangó begged in the villages, "Please, take me in from the storm."

The villagers shouted, "There is the traitor!" A rain of stones sent Shangó back into the jungle.

Hungry and thirsty, Shangó collapsed at the foot of a baobab tree.

He said, "There is no life for me," and hung himself from the tree's branches.

Only one person had stayed at Shangó's side through all his sufferings, his wife, Oyá. She was his inseparable companion. Oyá had fought next to him for years. She had been faithful to Shangó when he was a young warrior. She was faithful to him as a deposed king.

When she saw Shangó hang himself, she lost her mind. She cried and she cried until her tears made the river that has her name, Odo Oyá.

Traders walking through the jungle saw Shangó's corpse hanging from the tree. They rushed to Oyo. "Oba so," they shouted. "The king hung himself."

Shangó's enemies cried out, "Kill the family. Kill the cousins. Kill the aunts. Kill the nephews. Kill them all!"

They wanted to erase the family's power. They wanted to erase Shangó's rule. Anyone who had supported or benefited from Shangó's rule was fair game. Their houses were burnt. Their animals were confiscated. Their women were sold into slavery.

Shangó's relatives said, "If we do not think fast, we are all dead." They came up with a desperate plan to save their lives and their goods.

The plan was this: They hid and waited for the new moon. On that darkest of nights, when everyone stayed at home, they crept into the palace and stole Shangó's stones. These were the magical stones that had given him power over thunder and lightning.

They went to the highest hill overlooking Oyo and called upon the powerful talismans, "Strike!"

The power of the stones worked for them. Lightning struck the kingdom of Oyo. Houses exploded into flames. The people ran in terror, seeking shelter from the lightning. Many were killed.

The next morning, Shangó's family disguised themselves and went to the marketplace.

They whispered to the frightened people, "Shangó is alive. Shangó is in the sky."

The rumors flew, "Shangó's conjured himself up into the sky. Shangó is punishing us. Shangó is an Orishá."

But there were some who did not believe. "It is just a thunderstorm," they said. "Shangó is dead."

The lightning came down on the homes of the doubters. Shangó's family ran through the streets shouting, "Oba ko so, the king did not hang himself. Repent, repent. Shangó has turned into an Orishá. He has risen to heaven."

Since Shangó's family seemed to be the only ones that knew what was going on, the people of Oyo turned to them, "Save us, save us from Shangó!"

This is what Shangó's family had been waiting for. "Bring us your oxen," they said. "Bring us your calves and your palm oil. We will offer them to Shangó so that he will pardon you."

The people believed. They brought their goods. They brought their women. They pledged allegiance to Shangó's family. He became Oba ko so, the king who did not hang himself.

THE KING WHO DID NOT HANG HIMSELF

This is the Caribbean version of how Shangó came to be known as Obakoso. Obakoso, in Yorùbá, means "the king who did not hang himself."

Many years ago, before he was an Orishá, Shangó was a king in Africa. He had many lovers and kept many mistresses, but officially he had two wives.

His wives were always nagging and complaining. Maybe that's the reason Shangó ruled his kingdom with an iron hand. If there is no peace in his home, a man is at war with the world.

There was no peace for Shangó.

When he walked around the palace, Wife Number One complained, "Stop that. It's like living with an elephant."

If he gave orders to the household, Wife Number Two complained, "Stop yelling. Do you think we're deaf?"

His wives nagged him when he left the palace.

"You leave us alone all the time," they said. "Why can't you stay home like other husbands?"

They nagged him when he came home. "Where are our presents?" demanded Wife Number One.

"Why don't you ever take us out to have fun?" said Wife Number Two.

One day, Shangó asked for his dinner. His wives wailed, "All you think about is filling your stomach. You don't love us!"

"That's enough!" shouted Shangó. "I'm going into the jungle where there's some peace and quiet!" He mounted his horse, Enchilé.

His wives called after him, "When will you be back?"

"Never!" said Shangó, and he rode off into the jungle.

"He's so moody," said Wife Number One.

"He'll be back for dinner," said Wife Number Two.

But a week went by and Shangó did not return.

"He's with some woman," said Wife Number One.

"He's probably getting drunk," said Wife Number Two. "Wait until he gets home. He'll be sorry."

But a month went by and Shangó did not return.

His wives became worried. "This is the longest he's ever been away," said Wife Number One.

"Maybe he's abandoned us," said Wife Number Two.

"Maybe he's dead," gasped Wife Number One. The two women burst into tears.

The next day, Shangó's wives sent out a search party. It came back a week later.

"We looked from one end of the jungle to the other," said the captain. "There is no trace of the king."

People spread all sorts of rumors about their king's fate.

"Shangó went and hung himself. He couldn't stand being hated and feared," said some.

"He tied a rope around his neck and jumped off a tree because he couldn't stand his wives," said others.

More search parties were sent out. They had no more luck that the first. Six months had gone by since Shangó rode away from the palace.

The counselors said, "We cannot be without a king. Send out the army to find him."

The army, as well as everyone in the palace, from the youngest child to the oldest woman, marched into the jungle to search for Shangó.

"Shangó!" they called out. "Where are you, Shangó?"

The echo of their voices answered them, "Shangó!"

"Where are you, Shangó?" they shouted. "Have you hung yourself?"

The echo came back, "Shangó!"

Shangó was asleep atop an immense banyam tree deep in the heart of the jungle.

A thousand voices woke him up. "Shangó, Shangó. Where are you, Shangó?"

"Can't a man have some peace?" shouted Shangó.

A mighty roar came from the crowd. "There he is. Shangó is alive. He did not hang himself!"

"What madness has come over you?" said Shangó. "Of course I did not hang myself. I will never hang myself."

A sea of expectant faces surrounded the tree and looked up at Shangó. "Come down, Shangó, come down!" they shouted.

"Quiet," yelled Shangó. The shouting died down. "I'm not coming down. If I come down, I will have to go back to my wives."

"You come right down off that tree," shouted Wife Number One.

"You bum!" shouted Wife Number Two. "You can't run away from us."

"Come down, Shangó. Come down," shouted all his subjects.

Shangó crossed his arms and sat on a branch. "I won't," he told them.

He thought about what to do. One thing was sure, he wasn't going back to his wives.

"Come down this instant!" shouted Wife Number One. "We're hot and sweaty."

"Start having some consideration for others," shouted Wife Number Two.

That did it. Shangó stood up on the branch.

"Come down, Shangó. Come down," shouted his people.

Shangó addressed them, "Listen to me! Ruling you is too much trouble. I'm tired of all my problems."

"Are you calling us a problem?" shrieked Wife Number One.

"We'll show you a problem," screamed Wife Number Two, throwing a rock.

Shangó ducked and went on with his speech. "I will rule you from afar." He flinched as another rock went by his head. "From as far away as I can get. I will rule you from the sky."

Shangó's subjects jumped up and down and shouted. His wives cursed and threw more stones. He ignored them.

He reached up and took hold of a thick iron chain that led from the top of the tree to the sky. Link by link, he climbed up the chain. The people's shouts faded away. Shangó looked down. His wives were two tiny specks.

He climbed until he disappeared into the blue of the sky, where he stayed.

Obakoso now comes down only when he is invited with respect, sacrifice, and ceremonies.

SHANGÓ'S STEPMOTHER

This story is a condensation of the story cycle in which Shangó is conceived by Aggayú and Obatalá, thrown out of Obatalá's house and raised by Yemayá. It also describes how he came to own the Ifá board for a while before giving it up to Orunmilá.

Obatalá came down to the world as a very powerful woman. One day, she walked along a path led to a river. The river flowed fast and deep. There was no way to cross to the other side.

"I must find Aggayú to take me across," thought Obatalá.

She walked along the river bank until she found Aggayú Sola, the ferryman.

"I wish to cross the river," said Obatalá.

Aggayú showed respect to the queenly woman. "You are welcome to use my canoe," he said.

Once Aggayú took Obatalá across the river, he demanded payment. Obatalá, instead of paying him, offered him her body. Months later, Shangó was born in Obatalá's white house.

The first words out of Shangó's mouth were, "Who is my father?"

"You are too young to know," said Obatalá.

A year went by. "Who is my father?" Shangó asked again.

"You are still too young to know those things," Obatalá answered.

Shangó waited another year. "Who is my father?" he asked Obatalá.

"That is a secret," she replied. "You are still too young to learn secrets."

Each passing year, Shangó asked Obatalá his father's name. Each time, Obatalá refused to answer him.

Finally, Shangó told her, "I am tired of being called a bastard. I will no longer accept no for an answer. Is your shame so great that you will not tell me who you laid with?"

Obatalá was angry and lost control of her tongue. "You insolent whelp!" she yelled. "I am not ashamed to have laid with the mighty Aggayú Sola."

Shangó was thrilled. "I now know my father's name," he said. "I will find him and have him acknowledge me as his son."

Shangó left Obatalá's house and went in search of Aggayú. After walking for many days, he arrived at a mighty river. He followed the river bank until he met a huge, strong man ferrying people across the river in his canoe.

Shangó asked him, "Are you Aggayú?"

Aggayú towered over Shangó. "To little shrimps such like you," he said with great dignity, "I am Lord Aggayú Sola."

Shangó spat, barely missing Aggayú's feet. "To Obatalá you're just a boatman she bedded on a whim," he said.

Aggayú struck Shangó with a fist as big as a ham. Shangó went flying into the bushes.

Shangó felt his bruised face. He was delighted. "My father has touched me," he said. "He has recognized me!"

Shangó thought that being punched in the face by his father was a sign of affection. He had no idea how a father should behave towards his son.

Shangó ran back to Aggayú. "Father, does your caress mean you acknowledge me as your son?"

Aggayú was furious. "You dare to come back and mock me?" he roared. "I'll show you how I deal with those who mock me."

He picked up Shangó and threw him into the fire burning under a huge pot of boiling pitch.

Two good women who were walking by, Oyá and Oshún, saw everything. They were horrified and ran to Olodumaré's house.

Oyá told him, "Olofín, we saw Aggayú killing a child!"

Oshún sobbed, "We beg you to use your power to save him."

"I am too old and tired to go there myself," said Olofín. "Oyá, take this shooting star and do with it what you can."

Oyá and Oshún ran back to the river. They found Aggayú prodding Shangó with a log to keep him in the hottest part of the fire.

"Hurry Oyá, hurry." cried Oshún. "The child may still be alive."

Oyá hurled her shooting star at Aggayú. His hair and beard burst into flames. Terrified, Aggayú ran away and climbed to the top of a royal palm.

Oshún ran to Shangó and pulled him out of the fire. "Child, are you all right?" she asked.

She was astonished when Shangó stood up and brushed away the burning remnants of his clothes. "I am very well, thank you," he said. "But I wish you had not interrupted my father and me. We were playing."

Oyá said, "Aggayú was trying to kill you."

"Yes," said Shangó. "It's so much fun."

Oshún said, "We must show this miracle to Olodumaré," said Oshún.

They took Shangó back to Olofín's house. After Oshún and Oyá told him everything that had happened, Olofín turned to young Shangó and said, "I bestow fire upon you, Shangó, since it is obvious that you and fire are one." He said to Oyá, "To you, Oyá, I give the shooting star as a reward for your bravery."

He sat back on his throne all out of breath. "Oshún," he said, "I will reward you another day. Today I've already given out too much ashé."

Shangó rushed back to his mother's house shouting, "Mother, Aggayú has made me the owner of fire." He was excited and confused and misinterpreted what had happened.

Obatalá was annoyed. "What are you saying, child?" she scolded. "Everyone knows that only Olodumaré can bestow that kind of ashé."

Shangó blurted out, "But it's true, mother. I went to see Aggayú and I told him I was his son. He gave me fire after he played with me."

"You liar," retorted Obatalá. "If you had said that, he would have killed you, not given you presents!"

"It's true," insisted Shangó.

"That's enough!" said Obatalá and slapped Shangó.

Shangó was furious. "You are just jealous that Aggayú has acknowledged me as his son." he shouted. "I will no longer be your little boy!" He ran out of Obatalá's house.

That was the beginning of Shangó's wanderings. He went to the bembés and the güemileres, the ceremonial feasts. Despite his tender age, he became famous as a drummer. He also became famous for his hard drinking.

One day he ran out of money. "Obatalá owes me," Shangó said to himself, and made his way to Obatalá's house.

When he got there, he went through Obatalá's chests and found her crown with the nine points.

"Now I have money to go back to the güemilere," said Shangó.

At that very moment Obatalá returned. "You thief!" she screamed. "You abandon me and then you come back to rob me?" She seized Shangó. "You want to ruin me? Before you do, I will kill you."

She carried Shangó outside and threw him from the top of the mountain where she lived.

As Shangó fell, the sky turned black and he became a ball of fire flying though the air.

Down below there was a village. In this village lived Yemayá. She looked up from her housework and saw the ball of fire coming down towards her house. She ran until she was directly under the fireball. She spread her skirt and caught it.

Yemayá marveled to find a young boy on her lap. She asked him, "Boy, who are you?"

"I am Shangó," he answered. "My mother, Obatalá, threw me from the sky."

Yemayá became Shangó's stepmother. She was very happy that she had a child. She loved him very much. She made him huge platters of corn meal and okra. She gave him apples for dessert. She pampered him and coddled him.

She would hold him in her arms and kiss him. She'd say, "How I love my little gift from heaven!"

Shangó took everything Yemayá gave him and still wanted more.

He asked for fancy clothes. "I need a new red suit to go to the güemilere," he said.

"Yes, my dear," said Yemayá. She ran to the market and bought one.

Shangó was always asking her for money. "Give me money for aguardiente," he demanded.

"Is there anything else my little gift wants?" said Yemayá. She gave him the last coins in the house, going hungry herself.

Once Shangó even told Yemayá, "This house is not big enough for the both of us. You can sleep outside."

Yemayá laid her mat on the porch to please her son.

Not once did Shangó say, "Thank you." Instead, one day he told Yemayá, "You do not love me."

This hurt Yemayá very much. With tears in her eyes, she said, "Of course I love you my darling."

Shangó said, "If you loved me, you'd go to Obatalá's house and get me her Ifá board so I can throw the ekueles and read oracles."

Yemayá tried to reason with him. "My dear, you are a drummer," she said. "What do you want with the Ifá board?"

Shangó went into a tantrum. "You don't love me! You are a terrible mother! You never give me anything."

Yemayá's heart was breaking. "Very well," she sobbed. "I'll go."

Yemayá set off for Obatalá's house. She had to take the terrible path of Osanquiriñan to get there.

Sharp stones cut Yemayá's feet. Thorns dug into her skin. She got to the top of the mountain bleeding and totally exhausted. Yemayá sat on a boulder to catch her breath.

A voice said, "That took you long enough!"

Yemayá looked up. Shangó stood there with the Ifá board in hands.

He scolded her, "You took too long. I always said you couldn't do anything." While she had been struggling up the path, Shangó had ridden to the top of the mountain on a thunderbolt. He had searched Obatalá's house and taken her Ifá board.

"I don't need you." said Shangó. He turned his back on Yemayá and flew down the mountain on a ball of fire. Yemayá fainted.

Meanwhile, Obatalá had returned home to find her house turned upside down. She searched the top of the mountain for the culprit and found Yemayá.

Obatalá demanded, "Where is my board?"

"I do not know," sobbed Yemayá. She said nothing about Shangó. She wanted to protect her stepson despite his cruel tricks.

"Tell me where it is or I will punish you for climbing my mountain," threatened Obatalá.

"I know nothing of your board. Punish me if you must," said Yemayá.

Obatalá had Yemayá drag heavy stones to repair the walls of her house. She had her plow the fields and plant yams. She made her dig a new well.

Every day, Obatalá asked, "Where is my board?" and Yemayá answered, "I do not know, mistress."

Obatalá's fury ran its course after forty days. She thought the whole thing over and realized that Shangó must be the thief. Yemayá was so good and her loyalty to Shangó was so great that it moved Obatalá. She was sorry she had punished Yemayá

Obatalá went to where Yemayá was chopping cane. "Put that machete down," she said. She took a necklace from the pocket of her white apron. "This is the ekuele," she told Yemayá. "Without it, the Ifá board will do Shangó no good. Go home. Give it to Shangó in my name. You will be doing him a great favor, even though he doesn't deserve it."

Yemayá took the necklace and rushed home. She gave the ekuele to Shangó and he became the richest and most prestigious diviner in the world.

Being rich and famous did not change Shangó. He became bored with the responsibilities of owning the oracle. One day, while at a güemilere, he met Orunmilá.

"I am tired of being a soothsayer," said Shangó. "I want a life of adventure. I want to get back to drumming and dancing. Take the Ifá board and the ekuele. I don't want them anymore."

That is how Orunmilá became the owner of the oracle.

THE CEMETERY

Even though Oyá is his wife and fights beside him, Shangó is afraid of her charges. These two brief stories tell of Shangó's fear of Ikú, death.

Marriage is an invitation to fight. One time, Shangó and Oyá were having a fight up in heaven.

Oyá was screaming at Shangó, "You're a good for nothing. All you want to do is run after women and get drunk."

"I do not run after women," lied Shangó. "It's all in your head."

"I saw you at the güemilere," said Oyá. "You were rubbing against Oshún."

"That's not true," said Shangó. "We were just dancing."

"Dancing, you call that dancing?" exclaimed Oyá. "You took off most of your clothes."

"It was hot," explained Shangó, as husbands do.

"Oshún was hot," yelled Oyá. "That's it. No more dancing, no more drumming, no more parties."

Shangó was furious. "You can't tell me what to do, woman," he told her. He pushed Oyá so hard that she tumbled out of the sky and fell towards earth.

Shangó looked down and saw Oyá's fiery trail. "I'm in trouble now," he said, and dove after her shouting, "Oyá, I'm sorry. I didn't mean it."

Shangó followed Oyá's shining trail until she landed. But she came down inside a cemetery. When Shangó saw her standing among the bodies of the dead, surrounded by graves and skeletons, he did not dare follow her inside.

Oyá laughed at him. "Where is the great warrior now?" she said with contempt. "He fights women but is afraid of death."

It's true, Shangó is afraid of death, Ikú.

Another time, Oyá and Shangó were walking along. They were having such an interesting conversation that, without realizing it, they wandered into a cemetery. When Shangó saw that there was an open tomb right under his feet with a rotting corpse inside, he ran away.

ORISHÁ OKÓ'S YAMS AND THE DRUMS

These two stories tell of how Yemayá managed to get Shangó his drums. The situation and characters in both stories are the same, but Obatalá's motivation is different in each story.

Obatalá was known as a woman before she was known as a man. Back in those days, she had the best yam plantation in the world. Not only that, she was the only one that knew the secret of how to plant the yam roots. If you plant yams the wrong way, the roots will not grow big and healthy.

One day, a very hot day, Obatalá was working in her fields. She dug with her digging stick, took out a yam root from her bag, bent over and put it in the hole. Obatalá did this over and over and over again until she collapsed in the shade of a banyam tree.

"I can't keep doing this," she said to herself. "This farming is going to kill me."

She thought about her situation. "I've got to get some help," she decided. "I've got to get a farmer to work for me."

Obatalá went to the village square and called out, "I'm looking for a farmer to help me with my yams."

Faster than you can wink, Obatalá was surrounded by men.

"I need work," said one.

"I'm a great farmer," said another.

"I'm big and strong," said a third, flexing his muscles and winking at her.

Dozens of men yelled and jumped to get Obatalá's attention. "Me, me, me," they all said.

Obatalá saw the greed in their eyes. "You don't want to work," she told them. "You just want my secret so you can get rich growing yams." She turned her back on them and walked out of the village.

What was Obatalá to do? Any man that she hired would learn the secret of planting yams. She couldn't entrust a treasure like that to just anyone. She was walking and thinking about this when she passed Orishá Okó's house.

Obatalá's feet took her to his front door. She'd heard of Orishá Okó. He had a reputation for being a man of respect, a serious man, a responsible man. He was also known to be chaste.

Obatalá thought, "A man who doesn't have sex is more likely to keep his mouth shut than one who goes chasing women." That decided it.

Orishá Okó was at home and Obatalá said to him, "Do you want to work for me?"

"Why not?" said Orishá Okó. "I have plenty of free time."

Orishá Okó proved to be a great worker. He arrived at the fields as the sun came up and he left when the sun went down. He only took a few yams for pay. He had no other mouths to feed. Obatalá was delighted at how big the yams grew and how fast they multiplied under his care.

Just as things were going nice and smooth for Obatalá, Shangó showed up at her house and said, "I have waited long enough, Obatalá. I want you to turn over the bata, the drums of the sacred dances, to me."

Obatalá refused. "You are too hot. You're always fighting. You're always chasing after women. How can I give such an important thing to you?"

Shangó returned home. "How did your talk with Obatalá go, my son?" asked Yemayá.

"She still refuses to give me the drums, mother," said Shangó. "She swears I'm not fit to have them."

Like all mothers, Yemayá thought that her son was perfect. "If she won't turn them over to you when you ask nicely, maybe I should take them away from her by trickery," she said.

Yemayá came up with a plan and put it to work the next morning. She went to Obatalá's fields. She took off all her clothes behind a banyam tree. Orishá Okó came along, poking and planting, bending and weeding.

Yemayá jumped out in front of him. "Obini, take me," she murmured. "I have come for you."

Orishá Okó turned red. His eyes rolled in his head. A little bit of steam came out of his ears. He dropped his sack of yams. He dropped his planting stick and grabbed his other stick in his hands.

"Uk, Ik, Uk," went Orishá Okó.

"Come here," said Yemayá. "It's about time a woman taught you something."

She took him standing up. She took him lying down. She took him leaning against the tree and up in the branches. They made love until the late afternoon.

As the sun was going down, Orishá Okó managed to stammer, "You are . . . it was . . . I've never . . . How can I repay you?"

Yemayá ran her hand through his hair. "Making love to such a handsome and virile man is its own reward," she said. "But you could do just a little thing for me."

"What?" asked Orishá Okó. "I would do anything for you."

"Just tell me one thing," said Yemayá.

"Yes," said Orishá Okó. "Anything."

"Tell me the secret of planting yams," said Yemayá.

Orishá Okó told her everything. He told her things he didn't even know that he knew.

The next day, Yemayá visited Obatalá. "I think it's time that you gave my son the drums," she said.

"I've told him and I'll tell you," said Obatalá. "He's not serious enough to own something so important."

Yemayá told Obatalá, "You either tell my son that the bata drums are his to play when he wants or . . ."

"Or what," said Obatalá.

"Or I'll tell everybody how to plant yams," Yemayá yelled in triumph.

"You don't know anything about that," laughed Obatalá. "What can you tell?"

"I can tell them this," said Yemayá, and she began to repeat every secret that Orishá Okó had told her.

Obatalá had to give in and give the drums to Shangó. She then went out to her yam fields. She yelled at Orishá Okó for three hours, maybe four. Ashamed, Orishá Okó went away and hid in the woods.

Another version of the story goes like this:

Yemayá wanted to learn the secret of how to grow yams more than anything else in the world. There was only one person who knew how to grow yams, Orishá Okó, the farmer.

Yemayá brought Orishá Okó tasty things to eat. "You'll tell me the secret of growing yams, won't you?" she asked.

"No," said Orishá Okó and returned to his hoeing.

Yemayá danced through his fields. Her hips moved like ocean waves. "Will you tell me now?" she asked.

"No," said Orishá Okó, turning away to trim a hedge.

Every time Yemayá tried to get Orishá Okó to reveal his secret to her, he said, "No."

One night, Yemayá returned home tired and angry.

"How did it go?" asked Shangó. He was still living with Yemayá, being too young to go and live by himself.

"Terrible," said Yemayá. "He'll never tell me the secret of growing yams."

"There has to be a way," said Shangó. "You've got to find it."

"What do you care?" said Yemayá. "You've never grown anything in your life."

"Obatalá said that he would give me the bata drums in exchange for the secret of growing yams," said Shangó. "They're what I want most in the world."

"What does Obatalá want with yams?" asked Yemayá.

"They're his favorite food," said Shangó. "He wants to make sure that he has a steady supply and . . ." Shangó looked around to make sure that no one could overhear them. "Yams make people talk when they're asleep," he said. "If Obatalá had the secret of the yams, he could listen to what is in people's hearts."

Yemayá was indignant. "You want me to get the secret of growing yams just so that you can give it to Obatalá?"

"That's right," said Shangó. "I know you can do it."

Yemayá huffed and puffed and acted angry. But in the end, she gave in. She always gave in to Shangó's every whim.

The next day, when Orishá Okó was busy cultivating his fields, he heard a sweet song.

"Orishá Okó ogun feye weye tani owi moru mariwo."

(Landlord, medicine of life the one we must love to live. I need to see the one who knows the secret.)

He looked to one side. The field was empty. He looked to the other side. There was no one there. He looked behind a tree. There was Yemayá, gloriously naked, stretching out her arms for him.

". . . the one we must love to live." sang Yemayá.

Orishá Okó was very chaste. He had never been with a woman. He had never even seen a woman naked. He spluttered. He choked. He turned bright red.

". . . I need to see the one who knows the secret," sang Yemayá.

Before Orishá Okó could run away, Yemayá grabbed him and threw him on a soft patch of grass.

She made love on top. She made love standing up. She made love upside down. She made Orishá Okó rise and melt, rise and melt and then rise again.

Early that evening, when Yemayá and Orishá Okó lay side by side, exhausted and sweaty, Orishá Okó said, "I love you."

"How much do you love me?" asked Yemayá, using her hand to make him rise again.

"I love you more than life itself," said Orishá Okó.

"Then I'm sure that you can tell me how to grow yams," said Yemayá.

Orishá Okó told her all the secrets of growing yams. He told her how to prepare the soil, how to plant, how to cultivate and harvest them.

"Will you come back tomorrow?" asked Orishá Okó.

"Of course I will, darling," said Yemayá. Of course, she didn't.

Orishá Okó spent the next day sitting by the tree waiting for Yemayá. He spent the day after and the day after that and the days and weeks after that sitting by the tree. Orishá Okó did not plant that season's yams.

To make doubly sure that Obatalá could not get any yams at all from Orishá Okó, Yemayá sent a drought to shrivel his fields.

Meanwhile she had planted a huge field full of yams. She followed all of Orishá Okó's instructions.

One day Obatalá ran out of yams and went to Orishá Okó's fields to get some more.

"Where are the yams?" he demanded. "My store houses are empty. My stomach is empty. Where are my yams?"

Orishá Okó bowed low and said, "You can see that there are no yams. Not even grass grows in my fields."

"You have no yams?" shouted Obatalá. "What am I to do, then?"

"I have yams," said a sweet voice behind him. Obatalá turned around and there was Yemayá with a huge sack full of yams.

"I have all the yams you could possibly want," she said.

"Thank you, thank you," said Obatalá, reaching for the sack.

"Not so fast," said Yemayá. "You want the yams, but what am I going to get in return."

"Anything," said Obatalá, "anything at all."

Orishá Okó said, "I've heard this before."

"You be quiet," said Yemayá. Then she told Obatalá, "I want your drums."

That's the way it happened. Obatalá gave Yemayá the drums and Yemayá gave Obatalá the sack of yams and the secret of how to grow them. She then gave the drums to Shangó. Since that day, Shangó has owned the bata drums and Yemayá has been the queen of any party where the bata drums are played.

OYÁ

THE GOURD

This story tells of how Oyá accompanied Shangó to war and how she finally got a taste of Shangó's secret potion.

Shangó's gourd hung by the door. Osaín gave it to him. It didn't look like much, but it was powerful, very powerful. The herbs inside had a lot of ashé. Before leaving the house, Shangó always dipped his finger in the omiero (purifying water) inside the gourd, then touched it to his tongue. Just that, and he could breathe fire out of his mouth and smoke out of his nose. What enemy could stand against him?

Shangó guarded his gourd more closely than a jealous husband guards his wife.

"Don't you dare touch my gourd," he always shouted at Oyá, his long-suffering wife. "If you do, I'll lay a stick across your back."

Oyá had gotten Shangó out of enough scrapes to know how full of hot air he could be. She kept saying, "Yes, dear," but secretly she wanted a taste of Shangó's power.

"Imagine, my shooting star and fire, too," she dreamt. "That would be something."

The problem was that if she moved the gourd, even just a little bit, Shangó was sure to notice. Oyá did not want a piece of firewood bounced off her head.

Shangó was always going off on one or another of his interminable wars.

One day, he told Oyá, "Pack my things, we're going to the land of the Bariba." Shangó liked to fight with Oyá at his side. The two of them together were invincible.

"Make sure you bring my gourd," he told her.

Oyá wrapped everything they needed in their sleeping mats, put the bundle on her head and followed Shangó into the Bariba's territory.

Shangó went into battle swinging his great double-headed ax. Each swing killed five men. Each swing killed ten men. But the warriors swarmed over him like ants over honey. He could not get to Oyá. He could not get to his gourd. Without fire, he was in danger of being defeated.

Things were getting desperate when Oyá took Shangó's gourd out of her bundle. She dipped her finger in the omiero and put a drop of the magic liquid on her tongue.

"Make way," she roared, flame shooting out of her mouth. "Oyá fights with Shangó!"

Meteors of flame rained on the Baribas. Trees exploded. The splinters were blown away by a mighty wind.

"Run," shouted the Baribas. "Shangó's wife breathes fire and billows smoke. She is a mightier warrior than her husband."

They left their village empty, their possessions and treasures there for the taking.

"We did pretty good," said Oyá. "We have their food and their animals. We can take their gold and their cloth home in their carts."

"You made use of my gourd," grumbled Shangó. "They said that a woman was a better warrior than me."

"I turned defeat into victory," said Oyá. "You cannot argue with that."

Shangó was disgusted and jealous, but he did not argue. It's best not to argue with a woman that breathes fire.

THE PALM TREE

Oyá tried to keep Shangó from making dates with the many women who admired him. This story tells of one way Shangó tried to fool her.

Oyá, Shangó's long suffering and faithful wife, knew that he fooled around behind her back. She also knew that Shangó needed her more than the other women in his life.

"With me, he's invincible," she told her friends.

"That may be," said her friends, "but how often is he with you?"

This was true. Shangó used every opportunity to run off and spend time with Oshún, or any other woman that struck his fancy for that matter.

What bothered Oyá the most was that she couldn't figure out how Shangó made his dates with the women. She never saw him pass a note. He never sent a messenger. The women did not drop by the house.

"How does he do it?" said Oyá. "I never catch him at it, but those women know just when and where to meet him."

If she could stop him from making his dates, Shangó would spend more time at home, or so she thought. She decided to follow him and discover his secret.

Shangó went to the market, but he just bought apples. He went to get his ax sharpened. He bought skins from the butcher to use as heads for his drums. Nowhere did he even speak to a woman yet, that night, Shangó disappeared. Oyá knew that he had gone to meet a woman.

"How does he do it?" said Oyá. "I was with him all day." Oyá is steadfast. She decided to follow Shangó the next day as well.

In the morning, Shangó said, "I'm going out to the yard. I need to find another turtle shell for a rattle."

"I'll finish cooking breakfast," said Oyá. But she tiptoed after Shangó and spied on him from behind a bush.

She saw Shangó climb the royal palm that grew in the middle of her yard. When he reached the top, he began to wave a red handkerchief back and forth.

Oyá shaded her eyes from the sun and peered into the distance. Way off, on top of a hill, she saw Oshún waving a yellow handkerchief.

"So that's how he does it," said Oyá. "He signals from atop the palm tree. I'll put an end to that."

Early the next morning, before Shangó returned home, Oyá went to the courtyard and climbed the palm tree.

"Is he going to get a surprise when he comes up here," thought Oyá, holding a small shooting star ready in her hand.

But her plan did not work. The rising sun lit up the top of the palm tree just as Shangó returned.

"What's that fluttering on top of my tree?" said Shangó. He looked carefully and saw that it was the nine colored scarves Oyá wore around her waist. "She's not going to catch me that easily," he said and did not climb the palm that day.

The next day, while Oyá was in the market, Shangó filled a large sack with every lizard he could find. He climbed the palm tree and shook out the lizards over all the fronds. "This should scare Oyá away from my palm tree," thought Shangó.

Oyá returned from the market and Shangó said, "As soon as I finish this beer, I'm going out to the courtyard to take a nap."

"Now's my chance to catch him on top of the palm tree," thought Oyá. She rushed out of the house and up the tree.

No sooner had she gotten to the top of the royal palm than lizards began to run all over her. There were green lizards and yellow lizards. There were big lizards and small lizards. There were lizards in her hair and lizards going up her skirt.

Oyá threw the shooting star she held ready for Shangó and blew off the top of the palm tree.

"I better come up with another way to arrange my dates," said Shangó when he saw what Oyá had done.

To this day, Oyá is very fond of blasting off the tops of royal palms.

JEALOUSY

This is another story in which Oyá enlists death's aid in keeping Shangó away from Oshún and of how Oshún tricks death.

Shangó may have been married to Oyá, but he carried on his romance with Oshún out in front of everybody.

One day, Oyá was sitting on her front stoop, cleaning a pan of white rice. Carefully, she took out the little stones and grains of sand. She was cooking rice and black eyed peas that night and didn't want a broken tooth to spoil her dinner.

A neighbor came along and said, "Good morning, Oyá."

"Good morning," muttered Oyá. She didn't like this nosy neighbor very much and could hardly wait for her to go Ilé Yansán, to the cemetery.

"Are you going to the party?" asked the nasty neighbor.

"What party?" said Oyá.

"Why, everyone knows that Oshún is giving a big bembé for your husband, Shangó," said the neighbor. "You mean you didn't know?"

"Of course I knew," said Oyá through clenched teeth.

"I'll see you tonight," said the neighbor and left Oyá fuming.

She threw down the pan of rice. "We'll see about this little party," she said.

Oyá went to Ikú's house.

"Hello, neighbor," said Ikú. "Is there a new war stacking up folk at the cemetery's gate?"

"The war is between Oshún and me," said Oyá. "I want you to help." She told Ikú what she wanted her to do.

The bembé was going good and hot. The drums were singing pickety pack, pickety pock, kin la, kinla. The dancers hips were moving with the rhythm, kin la, kinla. The aguardiente was flowing. A fat juicy goat was buried in the hot coals. Its aroma was making people's mouths water. It was a great party, a wonderful party. There was a knock on the door.

"I'll get it," said Shangó, opening the door.

There was Ikú's bony grin. "Boo," said Ikú.

"AAAAAAAA," shouted Shangó. He ran out of the house, terrified. As everyone knows, Ikú is the only one who can scare Shangó.

Oshún came to the door. She found Oyá standing next to Ikú, laughing.

"What a great party, Oshún," said Oyá. "We're so glad we came."

"Clack, clack, clack," laughed Ikú with her ivory jaws. "Yes, great party, clack, clack, clack."

That was the end of the bembé. All the guests left because, as they said, "How can you have drumming without Shangó?"

Oshún was furious at the way she had been humiliated. "You'll see," she told everyone. "You'll see if I can't be smarter than Oyá and Ikú!"

The following week, Oshún bought aguardiente, a fat goat, candles, and flowers. She hired drummers. She invited everyone in town to another bembé. She made a point of inviting Shangó.

"I don't know," he said. "Maybe it would be better to leave the party for another day. Oyá's found out about it."

Oshún came up very close and smiled at him and rubbed her breasts against his chest.

"Don't worry," she said, giving Shangó the benefit of her most seductive smile. "I have arranged everything. We'll have so much fun!"

Shangó could not resist. "I'll be there with my drums," he said.

Oshún gave Shangó a kiss. "I'll see you tonight," she said, and hurried off to the market.

"Send a dozen large baskets of okra to my house," she told the vegetable seller.

"That's a lot of okra," said the man, "even for a large bembé."

"Never you mind about the bembé," said Oshún. "Just make sure you send the baskets."

Oshún hurried home. When the porter arrived with the baskets, she told him, "Spread that okra all around my house."

"All around the house?" asked the dumbfounded man.

"That's what I said," said Oshún, for she had a plan.

That night, the drums were going pickety pack, pickety pock, kin la, kinla. The dancers hips were moving with the rhythm, kin la, kinla. The party was hot.

Oyá arrived with Ikú in tow. "Just do what you did the last time," said Oyá. "Knock on the door and scare my husband away."

Ikú went to the door, squishing the okra into a slippery mess underneath her bony feet.

Clackety clack, went Ikú's feet as they slipped on the okra. "Help me," shouted Ikú as, clickety click, she flailed her arms.

"Hold on," yelled Oyá. But when she tried to help Ikú, she began to slip and slide on the slippery mess of okra.

Clack ka bam, fell Ikú. Click, click, click, skittered her bones all over the flagstones.

Ker splat, fell Oyá, landing on Ikú's sharp bones.

Ikú pulled herself together and ran home yelling, "Gui! Gui! Gui!"

That's why not even death can ruin a good bembé.

HOW OYÁ SAVED SHANGÓ

Oyá helped Shangó evade his enemies by disguising him as a woman. Then she fought at his side until he was victorious.

Many years ago, Shangó was embroiled in one of his unending wars. He had fought for many days and killed many of his enemies. But more came than he could kill. He found himself surrounded in the middle of the forest.

"Enchilé," he shouted, but his famous magical horse had become lost during the fighting.

Shangó was afraid to yell again. He might be found. He heard his enemies beating the bushes and shaking the trees to find him. If they did, they would kill him.

Without Enchilé, Shangó had to scurry through gullies and cover himself in river mud to hide from his enemies. Days passed. His enemies did not rest. They did not eat. Shangó, tired and hurt, had to keep on running without sleep and without food.

He ran until he reached the place where Oyá lived. It was very deep in the woods. Very few people there knew that Oyá was Shangó's wife.

Shangó pounded on Oyá's door. She opened it and saw Shangó bruised, cut, and panting.

"What has happened to you?" cried Oyá.

"Oyá, they have me surrounded," said Shangó. "They want to hang me from a tree."

"Come in, quick," said Oyá, hustling Shangó into her house.

"My lightning is not effective against my enemies today," He told Oyá.

"That's because you lack the courage to fight," she scolded. Oyá gave him water and a bite to eat.

"It's not courage I lack," said Shangó. "I'm very tired."

"What do you want from me?" asked Oyá.

"If I could escape my enemies, I could rest and sleep," said Shangó. "I could recover my strength and destroy them."

"Why is it that you only come to see me when you need help?" asked Oyá.

In those ancient times Shangó was used to fighting by himself, but he swallowed his pride.

"Help me, Oyá," he pleaded.

Oyá thought for a moment and then said to her husband, "When night falls, put on one of my dresses. The disguise will let you escape."

"They will still recognize my face," said Shangó.

"I will cut off my hair and put it on your head. That will complete the disguise," said Oyá. "I will cut off my hair to save my king's life."

They waited until night. Oyá lit no fire. She was afraid that the smoke from her chimney would be noticed by Shangó's enemies and draw them to the house. When the sun went down, but before the moon rose, Oyá cut off her beautiful hair and pinned it to Shangó's head. Shangó did not know what to do with a woman's hair. It fell across his eyes. It tangled in his ears. Oyá had him sit down and wove the hair into two long braids.

"Here's a dress," she said. "Put it on quickly, before the moon comes up."

Shangó managed to tangle himself up in Oyá's dress. "Stand still," she said. "Just stand still and let me dress you."

Finally, Shangó was dressed as a passable imitation of Oyá. She went to the door and peered out.

"Hurry," she said. "There's no one around."

Shangó stepped outside, imitating Oyá's dignified walk. He reached the forest and came across the line of searching men. He greeted his enemies with an imperious tilt of his head and crossed their line. He did not speak to them because his voice is very deep. It would have given him away.

That is the way Shangó was able to escape his enemies' trap.

Once he was far away from the forest, he made camp. He rested and slept and ate and regained his strength and his will to fight.

Enchilé managed to find his way back to his master. Shangó fed him and groomed him.

A few days later, rested and healed, Shangó mounted Enchilé.

"It is time to kill," said Shangó to his horse, and galloped off to find his enemies.

It was dawn when he reached his enemies' camp. He came rushing at them. His fury was terrible to behold. Lightning flashed from his hands. He shouted wild warrior cries. In his fury, he had not bothered to change clothes. He was still dressed as Oyá.

"Oyá has turned into Shangó," his enemies shouted when they saw the screaming apparition bearing down upon them, long hair flying and a gown flapping in the wind. They panicked.

Behind them, Oyá came striding out of her house, fully armed, and began blasting right and left with her shooting stars. Her short hair bristled and shot out electric sparks.

"If Oyá helps Shangó, there is victory," she shouted, taking off arms and legs.

Shangó and Oyá were victorious. Since that battle, Oyá has been Shangó's inseparable companion in war. With Shangó's thunder and Oyá's shooting star, they are invincible and remain so to this day.

OSHÚN

ORUNMILÁ AND THE HOLE

This is the story of how Oshún saves Orunmilá from Oggún's traps. She then uses her feminine charm and grace to teach Oggún a lesson.

Oggún owned the wilderness. He was greedy and did not allow anyone on his property. No one could hunt. No one could gather wood. No one could harvest the plants and roots needed for medicine.

Oggún thought in this way: "It's all mine. Why should I share my wealth?"

To make sure no one entered his kingdom, Oggún dug giant pits in the paths and hung snares from the trees. When he caught a trespasser, he sat for hours watching his victim suffer.

His victims might cry, "I was cold and needed wood," or, "I was hungry and needed food," or "My child is sick and I needed medicine."

It didn't matter to Oggún. He said, "This will teach you not to steal what is mine."

One day Olofín, the Supreme Being, summoned Orunmilá into his presence. He told Orunmilá, "I need you to go into the wilderness and bring me a coconut from the highest palm tree."

Orunmilá didn't want to go. "That is Oggún's domain," he said. "You know he does not allow anyone to enter. Surely you can use a coconut from your own land, or from mine?"

Olofín shook his head. "No, that won't do," he said. "I am preparing a powerful ebó (sacrificial offering), and only a coconut from a palm in the wilderness will do."

How could Orunmilá argue with Olofín? "Very well," said Orunmilá, "I will go." If Olofín needed that kind of coconut, he needed that kind of coconut.

Orunmilá threw his ekuele, his divination necklace, on the Ifá board before setting out for Oggún's kingdom. He saw how dangerous his trip was going to be. The oracle told him that the wilderness was full of snares and traps.

"I am old, but my body is small and quick," thought Orunmilá. "Maybe I can get away with it." Orunmilá was careful and wise as only an old man can be.

He took his horse hair whisk to brush away any evil influences and set off for the wilderness.

He asked the wild animals to guide him. The animals took him through hidden paths in the undergrowth. They warned him of the traps along the way.

All his wisdom and all his care came to nothing. Orunmilá fell into a deep hole. Oggún was a jealous guardian. His traps were well concealed.

Orunmilá's old body was bruised. The edge of the hole was way beyond his reach. He looked up at the sky, so far away, and said, "There's nothing left to do but wait for Ikú to come visit." He sat down in the mud and rocks and sighed, "She will come by and by."

Orunmilá spent a horrible night in that hole, hungry and tormented by insects.

Early the next morning, three girls came into the wilderness. Their names were Obatalá, Yemayá, and Oshún. They had been sent by their village to gather the herbs needed for an ebó. They were terrified. The skeletons of Oggún's victims rattled in the trees and filled the traps in the ground.

The girls worked fast and soon had gathered everything they needed.

Oshún said, "Quickly, quickly, let's return to our village before Oggún finds us."

Then the girls heard a strange cry. It sounded like "Gui, gui, gui."

Obatalá said, "Oggún has found us!"

"No, it's someone in pain," said Yemayá. "We must go help whoever it is."

They were afraid, but they went deeper into the wilderness. They followed the cries, "Gui, gui, gui."

Soon, they came upon a deep hole. Yemayá peered in. "There is a little old man in there," she said. "How are we going to get him out?"

Oshún said, "Let's knot my sashes together. We can make a rope that reaches down to the bottom."

That is what they did. The three girls, pulling together, were able to pull Orunmilá out of the hole.

Obatalá asked him, "Who are you?"

"I am Orunmilá," he said. "I am on a mission from Olofín. Please help me get back to him."

The three girls carried Orunmilá out of the wilderness as fast as they could and took him to Olofín's house.

When Orunmilá told Olofín everything that had happened, Olofín was furious. "Oggún's greed has spoiled my ebó," he said. "He must be taught a lesson and it is you, Oshún, who will do so."

"Me?" said Oshún. "I am just a girl."

Olofín said, "You are full of love and female grace. It is you who must return to the wilderness and teach Oggún a lesson."

Oshún was afraid, but she did what Olofín ordered. She returned to the wilderness and called out, "Oggún! Oggún!"

Oggún heard her and was furious. "Who dares to disobey my orders?" he shouted. "Who dares to enter my kingdom as if it were a marketplace and shout out my name as if I were a merchant?"

He followed the sound of Oshún's voice until he found her. Oggún lifted his machete and ran towards the girl. Oshún turned and ran away from Oggún as fast as she could.

They raced through the wilderness. Oshún, young and lithe, was always a few step ahead of Oggún's blade.

"You may run," shouted Oggún, "but you can't escape me."

Oshún was in a panic. How could she escape Oggún? Then she did the only thing that came to her mind.

She stopped, turned to face Oggún and let her wrap fall to the ground. "Then take me and know what pleasure is," she said, naked and radiant.

Oggún's machete fell from his hand. His other blade rose. There, in the heart of the wilderness, Oggún and Oshún made love.

Afterwards, Oshún said to Oggún, "You're a great lover as well as a great warrior. Drink a little aguardiente to renew your strength and we will make love again."

Oggún drank and reached out for Oshún.

She thrust the bottle at him. "Drink a little more," she said. "You must be thirsty after such a long chase."

Every time Oggún reached for her, Oshún put the bottle of aguardiente in his hand. Finally, the bottle was empty and Oggún was snoring on the ground. Oshún got up, dressed and tiptoed away.

Many hours later, Oggún woke up with a horrible hangover. He searched for Oshún, but she was nowhere to be found.

"I might as well go home and lay down," said Oggún. "I feel terrible."

When he got home, he found that all his animals were gone. His door was open. He walked into his house. All the chests were open and empty. His mats were gone. His gourds full of beer and his yams had disappeared. When he ran outside again, he saw Oshún's dainty footprints in the yard.

Oggún was astonished. "I have been tricked," he said. "By a girl, at that."

The next morning, he went into his wilderness and took down all the snares and filled in all the traps. He made it known that anyone was welcome to enter his domain and take what they wanted.

When people asked what had made him change, Oggún grumbled, "Why bother with constant watching and building traps? What's the use of all that work when a girl has made it all be in vain?"

THE YELLOW DRESS

his story tells how Oshún fell in love with Shangó and how they went through some hard times together. Things were so bad that she had to sacrificed all her possessions in order to help him.

Oshún was a very beautiful woman. She wore the finest dresses. Golden bracelets jangled at her wrists. A mirror was always in her hand so she could admire herself.

Oshún loved to dance in the güemileres. She covered her body with honey and swayed to the rhythm of the sacred drums.

Her dancing drove the men wild with desire. They offered her gold. They offered her houses. They offered her lands. But Oshún always looked down her nose at them, rolling her hips and laughing.

One day, Oshún arrived at a güemilere. The drummer was a big man. Sweat rolled down his muscled arms as he coaxed screams and moans of passion from the drums.

"Who is that?" asked Oshún.

"That is Shangó," she was told.

Oshún fell in love. That night, her dancing was wilder than ever. She writhed at Shangó's feet. He paid no attention to her. Her eyes flashed messages of passion. He did not notice. Her breasts heaved. He ignored her. No one had ever ignored Oshún.

Oshún chased after Shangó. She gave him gifts. She cooked for him. She sang for him. She made Shangó fall in love with her. They became the perfect lovers.

Shangó forgot about his wives and lived only for Oshún. The Ibedyí, the holy twins were born out of their union.

The sad thing is that nothing lasts. The perfect romance ended in bitter fights. Shangó and Oshún went their separate ways.

Shangó's life changed for the worse. He lost all of his wealth. With his wealth, went all his friends. Friendless and despised, he led a miserable life.

One day, Oshún asked her friends, "How is Shangó? I haven't seen him in a very long time."

Her friends told her, "Shangó is sleeping in the gutter."

A spark of love flared to a flame in her heart. "I must go to him," said Oshún. "I will show him that one person still cares for him."

Oshún sold her dresses and her bracelets. She sold her pumpkin fields. She took the money to Shangó and said, "This is for you."

"Why are you doing this?" asked Shangó.

"What is mine is yours," said Oshún.

When all Shangó's debts were paid and all his enemies pacified, there was no money left.

Oshún and Shangó lived in a small shack. They were so poor that Oshún only had one dress. She wore it every day and washed it every night. The dress lost all its color and became a yellowish rag.

This is why Oshún's "children," her devotees, wear yellow clothing.

221

OSHÚN AND ORUNMILÁ

Orunmilá was married to Oshún but couldn't satisfy her. She found relief in Oggún's arms. The secret of their affair was revealed to Orunmilá by gossipy parrots.

There was once a rich and powerful babalawó named Orunmilá. All paths led to his house, which was as big as a palace. He was visited every day by hundreds of people seeking advice or wishing to get relief from an illness.

They came and said, "Orunmilá, my luck has been very bad. What can I do?"

Orunmilá had the answer, "Crush a handful of laurel leaves into a hot bath and soak in it."

They came and said, "Orunmilá, I need to make money. I'm poor, no matter how hard I work."

Orunmilá had the answer, "Mix cow's milk, goat's milk, and coconut milk with holy water. Wash yourself well with the mixture before sunrise."

Young men said, "Orunmilá, I'm in love with a woman, but she won't even look at me."

He had an answer for that, too, "Crush a little bit of coral and a little bit of anise. Mix the powder with a pinch of cinnamon in a little glass of creme de menthe. When you put this in the woman's food or drink, she will turn into a passionate lover."

Orunmilá had an answer for everyone and for everything except his wife. He was married to Oshún, a young, beautiful woman full of sensual fire. He gave her everything she wanted.

When Oshún said, "Orunlita, I need a new dress to go to the güemilere tonight," Orunmilá bought her a new dress.

When Oshún said, "Dear, I saw the most beautiful gold bracelet," Orunmilá bought her the bracelet.

He didn't care what things cost. He loved Oshún and his clients gave him plenty of money for his advice.

But when Oshún came close and rubbed her breasts against him in the afternoon, whispering, "Dear, let's take a little nap together," Orunmilá could do nothing.

At night, when Oshún kissed him and said, "I want you so much," Orunmilá could do nothing.

He couldn't even do anything in the morning. Orunmilá was old and unable to give Oshún what she wanted.

He tried to solve the problem by taking herbal baths. He tried ebós. He tried potions, but nothing worked.

Orunmilá was desperate. "If I don't do something soon," he said to himself, "Oshún is going to take her need somewhere else."

He was right. One day, Oshún saw Oggún in the marketplace. He was wearing a costly green and black robe. He carried an anvil under his arm as easily, as if it were a pillow. Oshún imagined what it would be like to have his powerful arms around her.

"Who is that man?" she asked a woman selling yams.

"That is Oggún," said the woman, "a very powerful warrior. He owns all the metals."

"Is he rich?" Oshún asked her.

"He owns all the lands and forests from here to the river," said the woman.

Oshún was very interested now. "Where does he live?" she asked.

"He lives by himself in the forest," said the yam seller. "He doesn't like people very much."

The next day, when Orunmilá was busy with his clients, Oshún ran into the forest. She followed the sound of metal being hammered until she reached Oggún's house.

Oggún stood in front of his anvil, making a sword. He was naked except for a small loincloth. The muscles in his arms were like coconuts. His legs were like palm trunks. Sweat rolled down his hard body, making him shine.

"Oh, my," sighed Oshún. She took off her clothes and rubbed her body with oñi, honey. Naked, she walked to Oggún.

When he saw her, Oggún's mouth dropped open. Oshún began to dance for him. The hammer and sword blade clattered to the ground. His hands reached for her and he growled, "Woman, come to me."

Oshún laughed and evaded his arms. She ran into the forest, calling over her shoulder, "Catch me, if you can."

Oggún raced after her, maddened with desire. Every time he was about to catch Oshún, she would laugh at him and slip out of his arms. The game lasted until Oggún gave a mighty leap and captured Oshún in his embrace. They rolled and thrashed on the forest floor until Oggún had Oshún pinned under his massive body.

"I have caught you, woman," said Oggún.

Oshún smiled up at him. "Now that you have me, let's see what you are going to do with me," she said.

They made love like two savage animals, with screams and roars, with scratching and biting. Finally, hours later, they lay in each other's arms.

"No other woman has ever made me feel like this," gasped Oggún. "Promise me that you will come every day."

And Oshún did. Every day she slipped from Orunmilá's house to lay with Oggún.

Orunmilá was old, but he wasn't a fool. He noticed Oshún's satisfied smile. He saw the bits of leaves and twigs in her hair. He could not ignore the bruises and scratches on her body.

When he asked about these things, Oshún said, "I'm clearing a new pumpkin patch," and turned away to make his dinner.

Orunmilá consulted his oracles and confirmed his suspicions. Oshún was having an affair.

"I must find a way to watch her," thought Orunmilá, "but I have to keep the business going. If I ask anyone to keep an eye on Oshún, my reputation will be ruined. What am I to do?"

He thought about the problem until he had an idea. He went to the market and bought five parrots.

When he returned home, he gave the parrots to Oshún. "Look, my love," he said. "These parrots were so beautiful I just had to buy them for you." But he had really bought them so they could spy on Oshún and tell him who she was seeing.

The next day, when Oshún returned from Oggún's house, the parrots flew around the house squawking. "Oshún is an adulteress. Oshún makes love with Oggún Areré."

Oshún lured the parrots back to their perches with handfuls of corn. She fed them cassava. She fed them squash. She gave them aguardiente until they were falling down drunk.

Then she told them, "Onide lepe lepe, gossipy parrots, be silent or there will be nothing tomorrow."

That night, when Orunmilá finished work, he went to the parrots and asked them, "What did Oshún do today?"

"Oshún is the best of wives," said the parrots. "She worked at home all day. Oshún has not gone out."

"Aren't they cute?" said Oshún, cuddling into Orunmilá's arms. "You bring me the most darling presents."

Oshún kept on feeding the parrots and giving them lots of aguardiente to drink.

When Orunmilá asked them at the end of the day, "What did Oshún do today?" the parrots answered, "Oshún has not gone out."

But one day Orunmilá arrived from work early. He found the parrots passed out on the floor from too much food and drink.

He asked them, "What is wrong with you?" The parrots just twitched and did not wake up.

When Oshún got home, Orunmilá asked her, "What's wrong with the parrots? I found them lying on the floor."

Oshún laughed and told him, "I probably gave them too much to eat."

That evening, the parrots recovered enough to slur, "Oshún not go out," before passing out again.

Orunmilá became suspicious. "Dear," he said to Oshún. "I know it's late, but could you go to the market for oguedede? I feel like having plantain foofoo for breakfast tomorrow."

Oshún left with her market basket on her arm. Orunmilá put a little bit of epo, corojo butter, on the parrot's beaks and told them, "This will force you to tell me the truth tomorrow."

LUIS MANUEL NÚÑEZ

Orunmilá left the house the next day and said, "Oshún, don't feed the parrots so much. I don't think it's good for them."

"Of course, dear," she said. As soon as the door closed behind Orunmilá, she went to the parrots and fed them and got them drunk. "Onide lepe lepe, gossipy parrots," she told them. "Be silent or there will be nothing tomorrow." Then she ran into the forest to meet with Oggún Areré.

Orunmilá returned home that night and asked the parrots, "What did Oshún do today?"

The epo did its work. The parrots squawked, "Oshún is an adulteress. Oshún lays with Oggún Areré."

Oshún was so embarrassed, and hurt so much from Orunmilá's beating that she behaved herself for a while.

THE GIANT PUMPKIN

This is the story of how Oshún raised a giant pumpkin that stole Orunmilá's gold. The pumpkin then plotted with Elegguá to destroy Orunmilá.

Oshún's pumpkin patch was very big, bigger than any other in the village. Oshún was a very good farmer. She gave her pumpkins lots of care and love. She took pride in her work. The pumpkins were very happy. They grew big and round.

There was one pumpkin that grew until it was at least twice as big as any other pumpkin in the patch.

Every time she saw it, Oshún said, "How beautiful you are. How round you are. What a wonderful color you have. It's like having the sun in my garden."

She began giving it more care that the other pumpkins. She put extra coffee grounds in its roots. She gave it extra water.

The other pumpkins became very jealous. "Look at fatso over there," they said. "She thinks she's better than us. She's probably full of water and doesn't taste like anything."

The big pumpkin sniffed and ignored them. After all, she was the best pumpkin in the patch.

Oshún gave her pumpkins the best of care. But her love was lavished on the giant pumpkin, which kept getting bigger. One afternoon, she exclaimed, "You are the best pumpkin in the world," and gave it a big kiss.

That night, the pumpkins in the patch jumped on the giant pumpkin and began to beat her up. "You good for nothing monster," they shouted. "You have stolen our master's love. We're going to kill you!"

"Gui, gui," screamed the giant pumpkin.

Oshún heard all the noise in her garden and ran out. "What is going on here?" she said. "Stop all this jumping around."

The giant pumpkin told her, "Oshún, they want to kill me. Hide me in your house."

Oshún carried the giant pumpkin into her house and laid it on the bed. "There, there," she said, patting the pumpkin. "Nothing can hurt you in here."

Orunmilá, who shared Oshún's bed, asked her, "Must the pumpkin sleep in our bed?"

"It's just for tonight," said Oshún. "She's frightened."

Orunmilá tossed and turned, trying to get comfortable with a giant pumpkin in his bed. Finally, he turned over and told the pumpkin, "Get down and sleep on the floor. I can't sleep in the same bed with you."

The pumpkin grumbled, but she spent the night on the floor.

After that night, Oshún kept the pumpkin in the house. Orunmilá kept stumbling over it. "A house is no place to grow pumpkins," he told her. "When are you going to cook that thing?" This made the pumpkin very angry with Orunmilá.

Oshún told her husband, "I love my pumpkin and I'm going to take care of her here, where the other pumpkins can't get to her."

Orunmilá made a lot of money as a respected babalawó. Every night, when he came home, he hid his money in a secret place.

The pumpkin knew this and thought, "If I find out where Orunmilá hides his money, Oshún will love me even more."

She watched Orunmilá closely and discovered where he was hiding his money. The pumpkin waited until Orunmilá left the house to go to work. Then she rolled to the hiding place and put all of Orunmilá's gold inside her body.

She did the same thing every day. As she took Orunmilá's gold, the pumpkin grew fatter and fatter.

One day, Oshún kissed her pumpkin. She heard a strange sound. "What is that noise?" she asked the pumpkin.

"That is gold," said the pumpkin.

"Gold?" exclaimed Oshún. "Where would a pumpkin get gold?"

"I steal Orunmilá's gold every day and hide it inside my body for you," said the pumpkin.

Oshún gave the pumpkin a big hug and said, "You are indeed the best pumpkin in the world."

Orunmilá kept bringing his gold home and the pumpkin kept stealing it and hoarding it for Oshún.

One day, when Orunmilá and Oshún were out of the house, Elegguá, Orunmilá's porter, burst into the house.

"Where's my money?" shouted Elegguá. "Tell Orunmilá I've come to collect what is due me."

"Who are you?" asked the frightened pumpkin.

"I am the one that is going to destroy that old man if I don't get what he owes me," said Elegguá.

"You may destroy Orunmilá for all I care," said the pumpkin. "But don't hurt Oshún. She loves me."

"I won't hurt Oshún if you let me come in the house and make brujería (witchcraft)," said Elegguá.

"You can do what you want," said the pumpkin and gave Elegguá a bottle of aguard iente to close the deal.

Elegguá started to come to Orunmilá's house when no one was around. He poured potions in the corners. He blew powders on the floors. He hid black eggs under the bed.

Soon, Orunmilá began to feel the effects of Elegguá's workings.

He came home with a big bump on his head. "What happened to you?" asked Oshún.

"I tripped and hit my head against a branch," said Orunmilá.

The next day, Orunmilá came home limping. Oshún asked him, "What happened to you?"

"A dog ran out of a house and bit me," said Orunmilá.

The day after that, Orunmilá staggered home bruised and covered with dust. Oshún asked him, "What happened to you?"

"I was walking down the street and a wall fell on me," groaned Orunmilá.

Even more horrible things started to happen to Orunmilá. "Have you asked the oracles what is going on?" asked Oshún one day, wiping the blood from his face.

"I did," sighed Orunmilá. "All they say is to watch out for a round yellow door. I don't understand it."

Elegguá kept working his brujerías in Orunmilá's house when no one was around. He and the pumpkin were now great friends.

"I have him now," said Elegguá to the pumpkin. "Soon, that old man will be dead." He took a long swig from a bottle of aguardiente.

"Remember not to hurt Oshún," the pumpkin told him.

"Oshún is so beautiful," said Elegguá, taking a drink. "I would never," he took another drink, "never," and he took another drink, "never ever," and he took two drinks, "hurt Oshún." He took another drink and fell to the floor, snoring.

Oshún returned home to find Elegguá sprawled out on the floor.

"What are you doing in my house?" she asked, scandalized. "What tricks are you up to?"

Elegguá opened his eyes and gave Oshún a very drunk, very silly smile. "Shhh," he slurred. "It's a secret between me and my friend, the pumpkin here."

Oshún glared at the pumpkin. "What is Elegguá doing here?" she asked her. The pumpkin remained silent. "What are you and Elegguá plotting?"

Oshún grabbed the pumpkin and shook her, making the gold coins inside jingle.

Elegguá sobered up. He ran out the door, knocking over Orunmilá as he was coming in.

Orunmilá picked himself up off the floor. His clothes were in rags and covered with blood.

"What happened to you?" asked Oshún.

"An ox stepped on me as I was making my rounds," said Orunmilá. "I fell into a lion trap that already had a lion in it.

A bull chased me home. Elegguá just ran over me." Orunmilá began to cry. "I think I'm about to die."

Oshún grabbed a kitchen knife and said to the pumpkin, "If you don't tell me what Elegguá was doing here, you're going to be dinner tonight."

The pumpkin began to roll around the house screaming, "You let me get fat on Orunmilá's gold and now you want to kill me!"

Oshún jumped on the pumpkin and split it in two with her knife. All the gold inside the pumpkin spilled out and covered Orunmilá's feet. The sight of so much gold made him better immediately.

"Look at all this gold!" he shouted. "I feel great. I feel like a new man. Look at all this gold!."

He embraced Oshún and gave her a big kiss. "Yalodé," said Orunmilá, "You are certainly the mistress of afefa (gold)."

Orunmilá had to pay Elegguá what he owed him, but that's another story.

THE SECRET OF OSHÚN'S NAME

This story tells how Orunmilá was able to win Oshún's hand with Elegguá's help and how Shangó took her away from Orunmilá.

Oshún is now Shangó's mistress, but her first husband was Orunmilá.

Oshún is irresistibly beautiful. Imagine her as a maiden entering womanhood. She was breathtaking. Hundreds of suitors came seeking her hand. But they were always disappointing.

They came to Oshún's house. "Marry me," they gasped. "Marry me," they shouted. "Marry me," they whispered.

Oshún turned her back on all of them. Their last sight of Oshún was her exquisite hips swinging back and forth, disappearing into her mother's house.

Word of Oshún's beauty spread far and wide. More and more suitors showed up at her house. They brought her mountains of gifts. Their horses trampled her mother's garden.

One day, after a camel ate her rose bushes, Oshún's mother ran out of the house shouting, "That's enough!"

The serenaders stopped playing in mid-chord. The young men fighting over Oshún dropped their spears.

Oshún's mother threatened them with a broom and yelled, "You get out of my garden right now! Don't you dare show your faces around here again!"

A brave young man spoke up, "We're in love with your daughter."

"That's right," said another. "We're here to win her hand."

"You're here to make my life miserable," grumbled Oshún's mother.

However, she realized that the young men had a right to woo her daughter. Oshún was the greatest beauty in the world.

Oshún's mother surprised the suitors by saying, "You may woo my daughter. But," she added, raising her voice to be heard over the shouts of the suitors, "this madness has got to stop."

"We want to marry your daughter," they wailed.

"Quiet!" shouted Oshún's mother. "There is a way for all of you to compete for my daughter's hand without tearing around in my flowers and vegetables."

The young men settled down, eager to hear what she had to say.

Oshún's mother told them, "My daughter's name is a secret. Only I know it. The suitor that tells me her name will have proven that he has the cunning to deserve my daughter's hand. He will have my approval. He will be her husband."

Orunmilá was in the crowd of suitors. He is the Orishá who owns the oracles. He can see the future.

Orunmilá ran home to consult his oracles. "This should be easy," he said to himself, concentrating and asking for Oshún's name.

But no matter what he did or how many times he threw the coconuts and the cowry shells, Orunmilá was unable to find out the secret name of the most beautiful girl in the world.

Orunmilá's other attribute is wisdom. He knew when he needed help. He set out to find Elegguá, the trickster Orishá. Elegguá was Orunmilá's porter. He had taught Orunmilá the sciences and secrets of divination.

Orunmilá found Elegguá sitting at a crossroads. He embraced him and said, "Old friend, you must help me."

Elegguá wriggled out of his grasp. "Do you need money?" he asked suspiciously.

"No," said Orunmilá. "I'm in love and I need your help."

"Even worse," said Elegguá.

Orunmilá pleaded, "Please help me find the name of the most beautiful girl in the world. She has won the hearts of all the men, but I want her only for myself. I want her for my wife."

"And what do you need me for?" asked Elegguá.

Orunmilá said, "Only you, a wily trickster, can find out the secret of her name."

Elegguá smiled modestly at the compliment. "I'll try," he said.

Elegguá went to Oshún's house. He stayed there for days. Some days, he disguised himself as an old man. Other days, he kept his eye on the house disguised as a small child. He acted the fool in the local markets, hoping that a loose word would reveal the secret. Or, he pretended to be asleep in Oshún's doorway, the better to hear what went on inside.

Patience always has its rewards. After many days of waiting and watching, Elegguá was dozing in Oshún's doorway when he heard an argument inside.

Oshún's mother, who was always careful never to say her daughter's name aloud, was very angry. Oshún had knocked over a fresh pot of omiero while trying out a new and exciting dance step.

Her mother shouted, "Oshún, look what you've done!"

Elegguá heard. "Oshún, Oshún," he said. "That Oshún is going to cost you a daughter, dear lady. That Oshún will turn a daughter into a wife."

Elegguá ran back to Orunmilá's house. "Well?" asked Orunmilá anxiously.

"This has not been easy," said Elegguá.

"What have you found out?" asked Orunmilá.

"I had to spend days in the most uncomfortable positions," said Elegguá.

Impatience was killing Orunmilá. "What is her name?" he demanded.

"Days and days I spent wearing itchy beards and a small boy's body," said Elegguá. "I'm all cramped."

"Please?" pleaded Orunmilá.

"Her name is Oshún," said Elegguá. "You owe me."

Orunmilá ran to Oshún's house. He knocked on the door. Oshún opened it and he said to her, "You are going to be my wife because now I know your name."

"What is this? What is this?" asked her mother, appearing behind Oshún.

"Your daughter's name is Oshún," said Orunmilá. "And now she is mine."

Orunmilá and Oshún were married and lived happily for some time, even though Orunmilá was an old man and Oshún was a young girl. But then the problems began.

Men kept making offers and improper advances to Oshún. They said, "That old man can't keep a young girl happy. Come with me and have some fun."

Oshún was a married woman. She paid no attention to any of them. But they were right. Orunmilá could not make her happy.

One day, at a party, she glanced at the drummer. He was able to play heavenly rhythms on his drum. Oshún fell in love. Her heart did not care that she was married. She kept looking at the handsome drummer and saying to herself, "He will be mine."

The miraculous drummer was none other than Shangó.

The men at the party asked him, "Shangó, do you see her? Oshún, the most beautiful of all, is flirting with you."

"So?" asked Shangó, concentrating on a very difficult rhythm.

"Make love to her," said the men. "She is beautiful and wants you."

Shangó smiled at his friends and replied, "I have more women than I know what to do with. They throw themselves at me."

The men thought, "What a braggart," but they didn't want to start a fight.

"Besides," said Shangó, speaking to the beat of the drums. "I'm not ready for any more complications right now."

That was what Shangó said, but who can resist Oshún's enchantments? Who can say no to her grace and her flirtatious ways? Who can let her walk away after seeing her hips swaying? Who can refuse the invitation of her moist lips?

Shangó, the great womanizer, the great conqueror could not resist. He became interested in her. Oshún, for her part, became colder as Shangó grew warmer. She wanted to teach him a lesson for having ignored her on their first meeting.

His desire for Oshún became too much for Shangó. One day, he waited for Orunmilá to leave his house. He went to the door and knocked.

When Oshún opened it, Shangó burst in. "If you don't give me your love," he said, grabbing her, "I'll go off to war and never return."

Oshún's heart melted. "Don't go," she said. "I'll love you forever."

"Forever?" asked Shangó, a little taken aback.

"I'll be with you all your life," said Oshún.

On that day, she left Orunmilá's house and went to live with Shangó. Their love produced the Ibedyí.

THE SEVEN HANDKERCHIEFS

This story tells of how Oshún used Orunmilá's own advice to make him marry her.

Oshún was irresistible. She never had a problem getting men.

They rushed up to her and said, "I want you. I need you. I'm your slave. Marry me."

But after they got what they wanted, the men said, "Goodbye," and forgot all their promises of marriage.

Oshún was not happy with this situation. She went to see Orunmilá.

"Men desire me and love me," she told him, "but they won't marry me. I want to find a man who is serious. I want to get married."

"Let's see what the oracle says," said Orunmilá.

He consulted the Ifá board and told Oshún, "The Ifá says that you must get seven kerchiefs."

"Kerchiefs?" said Oshún. "How is that going to make a man marry me?"

"That, the oracle doesn't say," snapped Orunmilá. He didn't like to be interrupted. "It does say that they have to be of seven colors. They have to be the best you can find. When you tie them around your waist, a man will cross your path. That man will marry you."

"It seems silly to me," said Oshún. "But I will do as you say."

Oshún went to the market and bought seven beautiful kerchiefs in white, red, blue, black, yellow, violet and brown. She tied them around her waist. They looked pretty, but time passed and no man was serious about marrying her.

One morning, as she was walking to the river, she heard cries from far away, "Elp, ulp, aaargh, elp."

"Is that a man's voice, or are those birds?" said Oshún. She listened carefully, but all she heard were the birds. Shrugging her shoulders, she continued on her way.

Then she heard it again, "Help, help. Get me out. Help."

"That is a man in trouble," said Oshún. Without a moment's hesitation, she ran towards the cries until she came to an enormous hole.

"Help. Someone help. Get me out of here," shouted the man.

Oshún peered into the hole. There was Orunmilá, bruised and bleeding.

"What happened to you?" cried Oshún.

"Oshún, help me," said Orunmilá. "I was looking for herbs to make an ebó. I didn't pay any attention to where I was going and I fell into this animal trap. Please get me out."

The hole was deep. The walls were steep. "Stay where you are," said Oshún. "I'll see what I can do."

"Of course I'll stay here," said Orunmilá angrily. "I can't get out."

Oshún found a dead branch lying by the hole. She grabbed one end and lowered the branch into the hole as far as she could reach.

"Grab the end of the branch," said Oshún. "I'll pull you up."

Orunmilá seized the branch. Oshún gritted her teeth and began to pull. There was a sharp snap and a thump. Oshún staggered back and landed on her bottom.

"What happened?" she shouted into the hole.

"The branch broke and landed on my head," sobbed Orunmilá.

"Don't worry," Oshún shouted into the hole. "I'll get you out."

Oshún looked for vines. There were no vines. She found a heavier branch. She couldn't lift it. She had nothing to cut a small tree with. She stamped her foot in frustration and shouted down the hole, "I'm looking. I'm looking, but there's nothing I can use."

Then Orunmilá had an idea. "Do you still have the seven kerchiefs that will catch you a husband?" he called out from the depths of the hole.

"Of course I have them," said Oshún. "They don't work. I still don't have a husband."

"Never mind about that," said Orunmilá. "Tie them together into a rope and lower them into the hole."

Oshún knotted the kerchiefs together and started to lower them into the hole. Then she stopped.

"Come on," shouted Orunmilá. "Don't stop. I can almost reach them."

"I know," said Oshún, coyly. "But I was just thinking, what will you give me if I get you out of that hole?"

"I'll give you anything you want," shouted Orunmilá. He was desperate.

Oshún peered into the hole. "You told me these kerchiefs would catch me a husband, didn't you?"

"Never mind that now," shouted Orunmilá. "Get me out of this hole."

"You said that man would cross my path," said Oshún with a sly smile. "Isn't that so?"

"Yes, yes. That's what the oracle said," howled Orunmilá. "Now, get me out of here."

"Very well," said Oshún very calmly. "I'll get you out of your hole if you agree to marry me."

And that is the way that Orunmilá traded his freedom for marriage. That is the way that Oshún became Orunmilá's wife.

FOOLING THE DEAD

In this story, Oyá uses death's help to keep Shangó away from Oshún. The story also tells of how Oshún fooled death and got to Shangó.

Oyá loved Shangó very much. She suffered terribly every time he ran off with another woman. She really didn't mind his infidelities. What she was afraid of was that one day he would leave and never come back to her.

One time, Oyá had to leave town for a few days. "What am I going to do?" she thought. "The minute I leave, he'll run off with someone."

She put her mind to work until she came up with a plan.

She went to the cemetery and said, "Spirits of the dead, I summon you."

The white faces of the dead appeared and moaned, "We stand before you, mistress."

Oyá told them, "I command you to circle my house while I am gone. Do not let Shangó out of the house."

"We hear and we obey," said the spirits of the dead.

They went to Oyá's house and began to shuffle slowly around and around.

"Now Shangó will be mine alone," said Oyá. "He will be too afraid of Ikú (death) to leave the house."

That is exactly what happened. When Shangó tried to go out, the moaning spirits of the dead barred his way.

They pointed back to the house with bony, rotting fingers and moaned, "Return, Shangó. Return."

"Certainly, of course," stammered Shangó. "I have everything I need right here. I don't want to go out." He ran back to the house and slammed the door on the army of white faces with sightless eyes.

Every time Shangó tried to sneak out of the house, he was confronted by the dead and ran back inside. He was a prisoner in Oyá's house.

One day, there was a knock at the door. Shangó opened it a crack, afraid that it might be one of the dead. It was Oshún.

"Inside, quick," said Shangó, "before the dead get you."

Oshún allowed Shangó to pull her into the house. "The only men I care about are live ones," she said, giving Shangó a big kiss. "Why haven't you come to visit me?"

Shangó hung his head. "Oyá set the spirits of the dead to guard me. They make me a little nervous."

Oshún laughed her tinkling laugh. "I'll soon put a stop to that," she said. "There's a big party that I want us to go to."

She sat Shangó on a stool and painted his face white with powdered eggshell. Then she stirred a lot of honey into a bottle of aguardiente and opened the door.

She called out to the shuffling line of corpses, "Your bony feet must be tired after marching around this house for days. Stop for a minute and have a drink. Even the dead need a drink now and then."

Soon Oshún had all those pasty-faced spirits laughing and dancing. After a couple more bottles of aguardiente, Oyá's army of the dead was stiffer than they had been in their graves.

"Come with me, Shangó," she called out. "It's safe to come out now."

Shangó ran out of the house. The dead ignored him. They were so drunk, that his white face paint fooled them into thinking that he was one of them.

Oyá was furious when she came home and found Shangó gone. But she forgave him when he returned from Oshún's house.

OBBÀ

These two stories demonstrate Obbá's extreme devotion to Shangó.

OBBÁ'S EARS

Obbá was unhappy. Shangó was no longer interested in her. There was nothing she could do to make him share her sleeping mat.

When she bathed in cinnamon and mint, Shangó sniffed and said, "You smell like the Ibedyí's candy. Why can't you be more like Oshún?"

When she wore her best clothes, Shangó looked at her and said, "You look like a market stall. Why can't you be more like Oshún?"

When she rubbed her body with palm oil and sang to him naked, Shangó said, "That reminds me, I have to go buy a pig for Oshún's feast." Obbá sat alone and cried.

She decided to go see Oshún.

"Obbá, what can I do for you?" said Oshún. Casually, she added, "Shangó just left, if you are looking for him."

"No, it is you I am looking for," said Obbá.

"Whatever for?" asked Oshún. She raised her hand mirror, just in case.

"You know that Shangó desires you more than me," said Obbá.

"That's true," said Oshún, looking in her mirror and fixing her hair.

"I love Shangó," said Obbá humbly. "Please tell me what secret you have that attracts him so."

Oshún gave a tinkling laugh. "The secret to a man's heart is
through his stomach," she said.

"But I cook him all his favorite food," said Obbá.

Oshún shook her head and her big earrings jangled. "That
is not enough," she said. "A really good wife must know how to
prepare rare and exotic dishes."

"That, I don't know how to do," admitted Obbá.

"You see?" said Oshún. "Come to my house tomorrow and
I will teach you how to prepare a delicious soup that Shangó
just loves."

"You will?" said Obbá, surprised.

"Yes, I will," said Oshún.

Obbá was so happy that she did not notice the sly look in
Oshún's eyes.

The next morning, Obbá returned to Oshún's house.

"Come in," said Oshún. "I've been getting everything ready
for you."

Oshún was wearing a large kerchief around her head. It was
so large, that it hid her ears.

"Why are you wearing a kerchief in the house?" asked Obbá.

"Oh, it is nothing," laughed Oshún, patting her head. "It's just
that I cut off my ears so that I could make a truly delicious soup
for Shangó."

Obbá was shocked. "You put your ears in the soup?"

"Yes," said Oshún. "Shangó loves it." She took the lid off the
cooking pot. "See? There they are."

Obbá saw two ears floating in the pot. What she did not
know was that Oshún had trimmed two sheep's ears so that they
looked like human ears and put them in the soup.

"That's horrible!" exclaimed Obbá.

"Shangó likes it," said Oshún calmly.

Shangó arrived at that moment. "Come here, you sweet thing,"
he said, grabbing Oshún and giving her a big kiss. "What's that
delicious smell?" He ignored Obbá.

"I've made you your favorite soup, darling," said Oshún, and she winked at Obbá.

Shangó sat down and ate five bowls of the soup.

"It's delicious," he exclaimed. He turned to Obbá and scowled. "Why can't you cook like this?"

Poor Obbá didn't say anything and went home.

The next day, she prepared a huge pot of soup. Just before Shangó arrived for his midday meal, she cut off an ear and threw it in the pot.

Shangó stomped in and demanded, "Isn't there anything to eat? I'm hungry."

With trembling hands, Obbá gave him a bowl of soup.

"Soup?" shouted Shangó. "Is that what you give me after a hard morning's work?" He peered into the bowl. "What's this?"

He picked out Obbá's ear. "This looks like an ear." Then he looked closely at Obbá. "What's wrong with your head?"

"I've cut off my ear so you can have soup the way you like it," stammered Obbá.

Shangó stood up and threw the bowl to the floor. "Are you crazy?" he roared. "Are you trying to poison me?"

"I was just trying to please you," said Obbá, reaching for him.

"Keep away from me," said Shangó, backing away from her. "You have turned into a monster. You want me to eat your ear. You have gone mad." With that, he turned and ran out the door.

Obbá didn't know what to do. Desperate, she ran to Oshún's house.

"Oshún, Oshún," she shouted. "Help me, Oshún."

Oshún opened the door and said, "Don't tell me you've had another fight with Shangó."

"I made him the soup just like you said . . ." Obbá's words died away. She saw that Oshún's was bare. Both of her ears were perfectly all right. "Your ears," she cried. "You have both your ears."

"Of course I do, silly," said Oshún.

"Silly? I'll show you silly," shouted Obbá, picking up a large stick and swinging it at Oshún.

"You liar!" Whap, went the stick.

"You trickster!" Pow, went the stick.

"You whore!" Bam, went the stick.

"Whore?" shrieked Oshún.

The two women became a whirlwind of sticks, fists, legs, teeth, pulled hair and spit. The whole neighborhood turned out to watch Shangó's women go at each other.

The elders sent for Shangó.

"They're your women," they said. "You pull them apart. No one else dares."

Shangó had to breathe fire on them. He had to blow smoke out his nose and shoot lightning out his eyes before they stopped fighting. He was so angry with the two women that he turned them into rivers.

Another version of the story goes like this:

Obbá stayed faithfully by Shangó's side during every campaign of his eternal wars.

When Shangó came home wounded, she said, "My poor husband, do not worry. I will heal you."

When his ax became dulled in battle, she said, "You are too tired. Rest, I will sharpen your ax."

When his clothing became soiled or torn, she said, "Here's a new red shirt for you."

She did all this even though he always said, "Hurry up, I want to go visit Oshún."

Still, Obbá remained faithful to Shangó. She would say things like, "That's the way men are," or "He always comes back."

When he did come back, from Oshún or from fighting, Obbá sang to him in her sad voice, "Shangó Oba o mangue alado yina," which means, Obbá is Prince Shangó's esteemed wife. She soothed the Thunder Orishá's heart.

In the evenings, Obbá prepared Shangó's favorite dish, amalá (corn meal and okra with chunks of lamb).

Shangó never thanked her. Instead, he said, "Hurry and bring the food. I'm going out."

Every day, Obbá went to the market to buy the ingredients for Shangó's amalá. But one day, there was no lamb to be found.

"I'm sorry, Obbá," said the butcher. "I'm out of lamb today."

"I'm sorry, Obbá," said the sheepherder. "I sold my last lamb yesterday."

"What am I to do?" said Obbá, desperate. "It is time for Shangó to return and dinner is not ready."

She hurried home and searched her yard for the rooster. But the rooster was not to be found.

"What am I to do?" said Obbá. "Shangó does not like chickens."

She rushed into the kitchen. With the big kitchen knife she cut off her ear and threw it into the pot.

"Now, at least he'll have meat," said Obbá as she covered her mutilated head with a turban.

Shangó arrived, tracking mud into her house.

"I ran into Oggún in the forest today," he said. "I was so weak from hunger that, if I had not tricked him and gotten him drunk, he would have defeated me."

"You are always the better warrior," said Obbá, handing him a bowl of amalá.

"Why are you wearing a turban in the house?" asked Shangó.

"I . . . I wanted to see how it looked," said Obbá.

"Don't you know that it's bad luck to have your head covered inside?" shouted Shangó. "Do you want me to lose tomorrow's battle?" He snatched the turban off Obbá's head.

"Woman, what have you done to yourself?" he cried when he saw Obbá's wound.

Obbá began to cry. "I needed meat for the amalá and there . . ."

"I can't love a woman who is mutilated," said Shangó, pushing her away. "I can't love a woman who is not beautiful."

Obbá screamed like a wounded bird. She ran out of the house and deep into the forest.

"I am a woman without ears," she screamed. "I am a woman without beauty."

Shangó ran after the screaming Obbá. He was not able to catch her before she killed herself. On stormy nights, people hear a high, sad keening. It is Obbá's lament. It is Obbá's desperate appeal to Shangó, "Return my love!"

THE IBEDYÍ

OBATALÁ'S MONEY

The Ibedyí are often Shangó's partners in his schemes. This story tells of how the Ibedyí helped Shangó get Obatalá's money.

Obatalá was famed for his generosity.

If a poor man said, "Please give me money for food," Obatalá not only fed him, he gave him seed and enough land to grow his own food.

Obatalá was able to be generous because he saved his money. He only spent what he needed to live on. He put the rest aside to help the poor. He did not throw big parties like Shangó. He didn't spend money on clothes and ornaments like Oshún.

The problem with saving money is that people want to take it. Thieves watched Obatalá's house night and day. When he went out, they went in and cleaned him out.

Obatalá was always trying to find a safe place for his money.

He hid the money under the bed. That didn't work. Thieves broke in and stole the money and the bed.

Obatalá hid his money up on his roof under the tiles. That didn't work. The thieves took the money and the roof.

When he buried his money in the yard, Obatalá came home to find the yard dug up. His goats, his chickens, and his fruit trees were gone, so was the money.

Obatalá couldn't stay home all the time and guard his money. He had to take messages back and forth from the Orishás to

Olodumaré. Every time he went out to do this important work, the thieves took advantage of his absence and turned his house upside down.

Obatalá's generosity extended even to the thieves. "If they weren't in need, they wouldn't rob me," he said. But he did want his roof to stay over his head and his chickens to stay in his yard.

When the thieves stole his outhouse and everything it contained, Obatalá's prudence won over his patience. He went to see Oshosi.

"Make me the tallest ladder in the world," said Obatalá. "I also want a sack big enough to hold an ox."

Oshosi said, "Very well. You'll have them tomorrow."

The next day, Oshosi carried the ladder and the sack to Obatalá's house. "The ladder is tall enough to reach the moon," he told Obatalá. "The sack will hold the world."

Obatalá put all his money in the sack. He threw the sack over one shoulder and the ladder over the other and set off for the middle of the jungle. He walked until he reached Iroko, whose branches touch the sky and whose roots hold the world together.

Obatalá set his ladder against Iroko's trunk. He shouldered his sack full of money and climbed until he reached Iroko's highest branch.

He tied the sack securely to the branch. "Now my money is safe," he said. "I won't have to worry about it any more." He was wrong.

The Ibedyí, the twins, had seen Obatalá leave his house with the ladder and the sack.
"What is the old man up to?" wondered Taebó.

They followed him through the jungle. They hid in the bushes and saw Obatalá carry his heavy sack up into Iroko's branches.

"That must be his money," whispered Kaindé.

The Ibedyí watched and waited until Obatalá came down the ladder, put it on his shoulders and headed back to town. Then they ran to find their father, Shangó.

Shangó was playing drums in a bembé. He was surrounded by beautiful women and was very drunk.

The Ibedyí ran up to him shouting. "Shangó! Come with us! Come with us!"

Shangó frowned and waved the twins away. "Go visit your mother," he said. "I want to stay and drum."

The Ibedyí didn't pay him any mind. They hopped and skipped around Shangó. "We know where Obatalá hid his money," they sang. "We know where Obatalá hid his money."

Shangó stopped drumming. He was instantly sober. "Where?" he demanded.

"In a tree in the jungle," said both twins at once.

Shangó had ransacked Obatalá's house more than once. The money had gone to bembés, women, and aguardiente.

He hugged the twins. "You are the best children a father could have," he told them. He squeezed harder. "Now tell me where Obatalá hid the money."

The twins struggled to get free. "Give us some candy and we'll tell you," said Kaindé.

Shangó didn't let them go. "I'll give you all the candy you can eat," he said. "Where is the money?"

"Give us the candy first," said Taebó. "Then we'll tell you." The twins knew Shangó's memory was very bad when it suited him.

Shangó took the Ibedyí to the market and stuffed them with candy. When they couldn't eat any more, he said, "You are as round as gourds. Take me to the hiding place while you can still walk."

The twins led Shangó through the jungle until they came to Iroko. "It's up on top of that tree," they said.

But when Shangó and the Ibedyí approached the tree, ferocious wild animals bounded out of the jungle and attacked them. They had to run for their lives. Obatalá had set the animals around Iroko with orders to attack anyone who got too close.

As soon as they ran out of the clearing where Iroko grew, the animals stopped chasing Shangó and the twins.

"There has to be a way to get at that money," said Shangó.

"We don't want to get eaten," cried the twins.

Shangó thought of one scheme after another. Even if he got to the tree, he couldn't outrun the animals with a big sack on his shoulder. There were too many animals for him to fight.

Then he had an idea. "Do you have any candy left?" he asked the twins.

"We have these bags," said Kaindé.

"Remember, it's our candy," said Taebó.

Shangó grabbed the bags. "Never mind whose candy it is," he told them. "When I have the money, you can eat candy every day."

They walked back to Iroko's clearing. The animals roared and attacked them again. Shangó and the Ibedyí were ready. They threw the candy at them. The wild animals stopped the attack. They sniffed the candy and began to gulp it down.

Shangó ran to Iroko's trunk and climbed it quick as lightning. He grabbed Obatalá's sack, tied it to his shoulders and slid down the tree as fast as he could. The animals paid him no attention at all. They were too full of candy to move.

When Shangó and the Ibedyis returned to town, he bought them every piece of candy in the market. The twins ate candy morning, noon and night until they were thoroughly sick of it. Shangó went on a month-long drunk.

HOW THE IBEDYÍ MADE SHANGÓ COME DOWN

During a ceremony, Shangó may refuse to "come down" and make himself manifest. The Ibedyí are invoked as intermediaries to persuade Shangó to possess a participant. This is the story of how this first came about.

Oshún and Shangó had a passionate affair. The Ibedyí, the twins Taebó and Kaindé, came along nine months later.

The Ibedyí are not ordinary children. After all, their parents are Orishás. They inherited some of their parents qualities. One is arrogant, courageous, and loves adventures, like Shangó. The other is sweet, extravagant, and whimsical, like Oshún.

Neither of their parents had the temperament to raise children. The Ibedyí were left to fend for themselves. Taebó and Kaindé hopped and skipped their way from village to village as their whim took them. People everywhere showered the twins with love and affection because the Ibedyí brought peace and happiness wherever they went.

The Ibedyí grew tired of wandering and went to live with their grandmother, Yemayá.

One day Shangó visited Yemayá. "What are my kids doing here?" he asked, surprised.

"Somebody's got to raise them," snapped Yemayá.

Shangó sat down and lifted Taebó and Kaindé on to his lap. He sang to them stories about his numerous wars and victories.

To his surprise, Shangó discovered that he liked being a father. He began to visit his children regularly. Every time he came to Yemayá's house, he sang to them about his adventures.

One day, Shangó came to Yemayá's house and called out, "Taebó, Kaindé, your father is here."

There was no answer.

Louder, Shangó called out, "Taebó, Kaindé, your father is here."

Yemayá came out of her house and told him, "The twins are not here yet. They're playing in the jungle."

Shangó was annoyed. "They know it's my visiting day," he said.

Yemayá shrugged. "Maybe they forgot that you were coming," she said.

"Forgot? They forgot their own father?" shouted Shangó full of indignation. Of course, he didn't think about all the years that he had ignored his own children.

"They'll be here in a little while," said Yemayá, trying to soothe him.

Shangó shouted at her, "I don't care. I'm not going to wait." He stalked to a royal palm near Yemayá's house and climbed to the top. The palm fronds began to beat the morning air as if a hurricane were blowing through them.

When the Ibedyí returned to Yemayá's house, they found Yemayá, Nana Burukú, Oshún, Oyá and Obbá running around like chickens with a hawk after them.

"What's wrong?" asked the twins.

"It's Shangó," said Yemayá. "He was angry that you weren't here to greet him. He's climbed that palm tree and won't come down."

The Ibedyí saw that it was up to them to calm everyone and restore harmony.

"Let's all go into the house," said Taebó.

"It's too hot out here," said Kaindé. "We'll have something to drink and something to eat. I'm sure we'll come up with a way to bring Shangó down from that palm tree."

Everyone regained their composure. that is the twins' power. They all went into Yemayá's house. Hope and good humor filled it as soon as the Ibedyí entered.

After eating and drinking a little palm wine, Yemayá said, "We have tried everything we can think off to get Shangó to come down. But he's so angry that he won't listen to any of us."

Oyá said, "I reminded him of our nights of love under the royal palm. But he won't come down."

Oshún said, "I went to talk to him naked. I showed him my firm breasts and my exciting body." Oyá sniffed loudly and turned away. Oshún ignored her. "But he won't come down," she said.

Obbá dabbed at the tears in her eyes and said, "I sang him all the songs that used to get him into a loving mood at night. My throat is dry from singing." She took a little sip of palm wine. "He won't come down."

Nana Burukú said, "I put plates of his favorite foods under the palm tree. He ignored the food. He won't come down."

Elegguá walked in saying, "I offered Shangó some of my aguardiente. He didn't want to drink."

Stunned silence greeted this announcement. Shangó loves to drink.

The Ibedyí calmed everyone down. They said to the gathering, "Don't worry. If we all work together, Shangó will come down."

"But we've all tried," said Oshún.

"Yes, but we did not do it together," said the twins. "This is what we're going to do. Elegguá, you play the drums and imitate Shangó's style. Oshún and Oyá, you dance. You too, Yemayá. Obbá, you sing your sweet songs. Nana, you bring him his food."

They followed the twins to the palm tree, which still shook furiously, even though there was no wind. They circled the trunk as Elegguá began to play.

The women danced. Their hips moved in seductive rolls. Their arms made beckoning motions. Their lips parted in sensual smiles. Their heads rocked to the beat of the drums.

"Kabie sile, Shangó," they sang, repeating over and over the respectful greeting to the Orishá of thunder. The song flowed from them and entered the wood of the palm tree. It traveled up the trunk and reached Shangó.

Slowly, the lashing of the fronds calmed down until it was nothing more than the rustling of a gentle breeze. Shangó came down, his anger forgotten.

He embraced the Ibedyí and said, "How can I remain angry with my children?"

There was drumming and feasting all night long. Shangó had come down.

YEMAYÁ'S MONEY

The twins are also intermediaries in the frequent arguments between Shangó and Yemayá.

Shangó was tired of adventures. He was tired of getting hurt in battles. He was tired of drumming all night. He decided he needed a rest.

He went to Yemayá's house. On the way there he met the Ibedyí, the twins.

"Where are you going, Shangó?" they asked.

"I'm tired and I need a vacation," he said. "I'm on my way to visit Yemayá."

"We'll all go together," said the twins. "We'll have a great time."

When the Ibedyí arrived, Yemayá's house was filled with life and happiness.

Every morning, Shangó rode his beautiful horse, Enchilé. He made his own paths, cutting branches out of the way with his double-edged ax.

At noon he ate a huge plate of corn meal and okra. Then he played with the Ibedyí before taking a nap.

Every sunset he drummed. The Ibedyí always joined him and sang the songs to the ancestors.

Life for Shangó went on at this easy pace for a long time. Yemayá was delighted that he was living with her. During the day she was busy with the housework, but the twins helped her turn it into play. In the evening she joined in, dancing around Shangó and the Ibedyí like the sea dances with the shore.

Every day at midnight, Yemayá made sure that everyone was asleep. Then she went to her secret hiding place. This was the place where she kept her solid gold coins. She loved to count and play with them. It soothed her.

One day Shangó said to Yemayá, "I am growing fat and lazy here. If I keep eating your good food, Enchilé won't be able to carry me. It is time for me to go."

"I'm sorry to see you go," said Yemayá. "I've enjoyed your company and your music. But I understand. It's not good for a warrior to get too comfortable."

"Will we have a feast?" shouted the Ibedyí.

"We will have a huge feast," Yemayá told them, smiling.

Yemayá went to the market with the Ibedyí. They bought five sheep, fifty ducks, roosters and quail. When she returned, she gathered coconuts, bananas, okra, and corn from her garden.

She called Elegguá. He cut off the ducks' heads and poured the blood into a gourd containing red beads. The Ibedyí helped him by stepping on the other birds' heads and tearing them off. They poured the blood into a gourd containing white beads.

Yemayá tied the sheeps' legs together and muzzled them. She marked their foreheads with yellow ochre. She sheared the sheep very carefully, so none of the wool blew away. Then she cut a sheep's throat while singing:

> Lubeo lubeo yembo eh (to the prince, flame)
> Lubeo amalá eh (to the prince, corn meal)
> Lubeo aguede eh (to the prince, plantains)
> Lubeo akuko eh (to the prince, roosters)
> Lubeo akara (to the prince, burning embers)
> Lubeo obi eh (to the prince, coconuts)

Yemayá drank a little of the blood dripping from the sheep's head. Then she offered blood to all the people that had come for the feast and they cried, "Kabie sile, Shangó! Olofín, Olodumaré, forgive me!"

The heat produced by the sheep's blood was too much for Yemayá. She fell to the ground. Two women rushed to her and covered her face with a white cloth.

"Come back to life, Yemayá," they said and blew gently into her ears.

Four more times Yemayá cut a sheep's throat. Four more times she fell into a trance and all present cried, "Olofín, Olodumaré, forgive me!"

Shangó arrived at Yemayá's house in the middle of the preparations for the feast. He was very hungry, so he began to eat.

"Wait, Shangó," said Yemayá. "Elegguá hasn't eaten yet."

He pushed her aside. "I don't have to wait for anyone."

Yemayá was furious at his lack of manners. Everyone knows that Elegguá always eats first.

Yemayá's voice cut like a knife. "Oh, you are so brave you push a woman around," she said full of sarcasm. "If you are so brave, why do you have such fear of Ikú (death)?"

The sheeps' blood was too hot, too hot. Enraged, Shangó slapped Yemayá.

"You bastard!" shrieked Yemayá. "I raised you!"

Five men jumped on Shangó to keep him away from Yemayá. The women screamed. The men shouted. The food was spilled on the ground and trampled. The feast ended in total disaster. The blood of five sheep was too much for Shangó.

That night, while Yemayá sobbed in her room, Shangó crept to her secret hiding place and stole all her money. This is the way he repaid her kindness.

Shangó began a life of debauchery with Yemayá's money. He went to güemileres every night. He dressed in the most expensive clothes and wore the finest jewels. Both men and women admired him and welcomed him saying, "Shangó oyo!"

Shangó made love to all the women. He was such a good lover, that they stood impatiently in line to get into his bed. He mocked the men. He spent Yemayá's money by the fistful.

One morning, he woke up hung over. He staggered to a food stall.

"Give me a plate of foofoo (yam porridge) and a gourd of beer," said Shangó.

The food arrived. When he reached into his pouch to pay, he found it empty.

"No money, no food," said the cook, taking the plate away.

He went to a woman's house. They had spent many nights in each other's arms.

She said, "Shangó, I'm so happy to see you! There's the most beautiful kente cloth in the market."

"I don't have any more money," said Shangó.

"No money, no love," she said, slamming the door in his face.

That night, at the güemilere, the crowd gathered around Shangó. He always bought drinks for everyone.

"I don't have any money," said Shangó. "Would someone buy me a drink?"

"You bum!" shouted his ex-friends. They threw him out.

Shangó found himself broke, alone and unloved. His only companion was his faithful horse, Enchilé. The only thing he could think of was to return to Yemayá's house.

He mounted Enchilé and rode out of town with a bowed head. The dust of the road settled on him, making him look like a ghost.

When Shangó arrived at Yemayá's house, Elegguá stood at the door, barring his way.

"Get out of here, you thief!" shouted Elegguá.

Shangó reached into his ragged red shirt and brought out his last bottle of aguardiente. "Just have a little drink with me for old time's sake," he said.

"Well, maybe just one," said Elegguá.

When Elegguá was drunk, Shangó crept into Yemayá's house.

Yemayá was sound asleep. The Ibedyí napped next to her.

Shangó woke the twins and told them, "I am destroyed. I need to regain Yemayá's affections so I can return to this house."

"What can we do?" the twins whispered.

"When she wakes, sing her this song.

> Yemayá koro ni (Yemayá don't be bitter)
> Yemayá koro ni
> Ka ma wa ero (Calm yourself, mother)
> Shangó lorisa (Shangó brings happiness)."

The Ibedyí waited for Yemayá to wake up. Then they began to sing the song.

"You are wasting your time," said Yemayá. "Shangó will never be welcome here again."

She spanked them both and forbade them to mention Shangó's name in her presence.

That night, Shangó returned to Yemayá's house.

"Taebó, Kaindé," he called. "Come out. It's your father."

When the twins came out of the house, they were upset.

"Chakuto mio," said the twins. "We did as you said."

"What happened?" asked Shangó.

"Yemayá whipped us," they complained.

"I have another idea," said Shangó.

"We don't want to be whipped," said the twins.

"Quiet down," whispered Shangó. "You won't be whipped. All I want is for Kaindé to come with me into the jungle."

Kaindé agreed to follow his father. Shangó hid the twin in the jungle. Then he waited behind a thicket, watching Yemayá's house.

The next morning, Yemayá asked Taebó, "Where is Kaindé? Breakfast is ready."

"I haven't seen Kaindé," lied Taebó.

Yemayá went through the house calling, "Kaindé!" There was no answer.

She went out in the yard and called, "Kaindé!" There was no answer.

She ran up and down the street shouting, "Kaindé!" But there was no answer.

"What is wrong Yemayá?" asked her neighbors. "Why are you shouting?"

"Kaindé has disappeared," sobbed Yemayá. "He's nowhere to be found."

"We must organize a search," said the neighbors. They went back into their houses to get their machetes, for the jungle was a dangerous place.

The whole village spent the morning searching for Kaindé. Yemayá sat in front of her house crying.

Shangó walked up and said, "I have walked far, Yemayá. I have climbed high mountains. I have searched in dark caves. I have looked out over the world from the top of the royal palm. I have seen no sign of Kaindé." Yemayá cried harder.

Shangó went on, "I am afraid that Ikú (death) has taken the child. Without him, there are no Ibedyí, there are no twins. Since death has taken one, I will take the other."

"You can't leave me alone," wailed Yemayá. "You can't take Taebó."

Shangó walked past her, went into the house and came out carrying Taebó.

"Don't take him!" cried Yemayá, but Shangó carried Taebó off into the jungle.

The search party saw Shangó walking through the forest with Taebó.

"Shangó has found the twin," they shouted. "Yemayá will be so happy when she finds out." They rushed back to the village

"Shangó has found the child," they told Yemayá.

"No, he hasn't," sobbed Yemayá. "He's gone into the jungle with Taebó."

"But Taebó is here with you," said the villagers. "We saw Shangó with Kaindé."

While all this confusion was going on in the village, Shangó had doubled back and gone to Kaindé's hiding place.

"Come," said Shangó. "It's time to go back home."

"I won't be whipped for hiding in the jungle?" asked Kaindé nervously.

"Everyone will be so happy to see you back, they'll give you presents," said Shangó.

That is exactly what happened. When Shangó came out of the jungle with Taebó and Kaindé, he was greeted as a hero.

"You see?" they said to Yemayá. "He has brought back the twins. And we thought just one was missing."

Yemayá was ecstatic. She said. "Oh. Shangó. you've found Kaindé and brought Taebó back. This makes up for all the awful things you've done."

"Do you forgive me?" asked Shangó.

"I forgive you everything," said Yemayá. "I want you to come back to my house. You need someone to take care of you."

And this is the way Shangó managed to get back into Yemayá's house. He lived with her a long time. The Ibedyí grew up and left to spread good luck and prosperity all over the world.

THE RAIN AND THE DEVIL

This story tells of how the twin's mischievous ways were too much for the devil himself.

A long time ago, the African land of Oyo suffered through a long, severe drought. A year had gone by without a single drop of rain. This was all the devil's work.

The devil went to the clouds and told them, "Withhold your rain from the people of Oyo. I don't want them to have water for their crops. I don't want them to have water for their animals."

The clouds refused. "We will not do this thing," they said. "We need to rain as much as cows need to be milked."

The devil bound the clouds with a word of power. They had to do what he said.

"There will be no rain until all the Orishás bow down to me," he commanded.

The clouds suffered. The people suffered.

The people of Oyo offered prayers and sacrifices. "Help us, Shangó. Protect us, Oshún and Yemayá," they cried.

The devil appeared before them and said, "There will be no rain until you bow to me and forget the other Orishás."

The people of Oyo shuddered with fear, but they said, "We honor the Orishás as our ancestors did. We will not do as you say."

The devil was furious. He made the sun burn even hotter on the people of Oyo. "Help us Shangó. Protect us Oshún and Yemayá," they cried. And, taking the last sheep left alive in Oyo, they sacrificed it to the Orishás.

The devil laughed and bound the clouds even tighter. He had blocked all the paths to the Orishás. They could not hear the pleading of the people of Oyo.

The people's skins cracked and wrinkled. They became dried skeletons grubbing in the ground for the few insects they could find. There was no food. There was no water. Their children's bellies swelled and their hair turned red. They died and their mothers did not have the strength to bury them.

The people lay on the ground, too weak to move. They implored the Orishás. "Help us Shangó. Protect us Yemayá."

The devil walked among the starving people. "Make your sacrifices to me and forget the other Orishás. You will have rain. Your children will not die."

"Never," said the people of Oyo. The devil laughed and watched them die.

While the devil gloated, the Ibedyí were playing in the jungle. They headed towards Oyo and saw the dried-up river and the withered trees.

The Ibedyí looked at each other and said, "We must seek the source of this evil."

They followed a dusty river bed until they came to the abandoned farms surrounded by the shriveled corpses of people and animals.

"The devil himself is at work here," they said. "We must help the people that are left alive."

Taebó went one way and Kaindé set off in the opposite direction. They meant to find the devil and make him stop his evil work.

Kaindé went to the square and saw the devil striding among the dead and dying. The twin walked up to him and stood in his way.

The devil was very surprised when he saw someone standing and in good health. "Who are you?" he asked.

Kaindé said, "I am Kaindé and I have come to put an end to your work."

The devil cackled. Flames danced in his eyes. "There is nothing you can do here. Better run before I decide to play with you too."

Kaindé did not flinch. He stood firm in front of the devil and asked him, "What will it take for you to release the rain?"

The devil said, "The clouds are bound with a word of power that only I know. I will not release them until the Orishás bow down to me and these people worship me."

Kaindé knew that the devil loved to bargain, so he said, "I wager my life and the lives of these people if you will release the rain."

"I will get my way in the end," said the devil. "But the idea of a wager amuses me. What do you want to bet on?"

"I bet that I can dance longer than you," said Kaindé.

The devil laughed and laughed. "Dance! Everyone knows that no one can outdance the devil."

"I can," said Kaindé, calmly. "I can dance until you drop."

"I accept," said the devil. "I'll have fun making your soul scream and dance for a long, long time."

"I will meet you here this afternoon," said Kaindé and left the devil standing in the square, chuckling and shaking his head.

Kaindé went in search of Taebó. When he found him, he told him of his bet with the devil.

"He does not know that we are twins," said Kaindé. "This is what we will do. You will hide while I dance. When I get tired, we'll switch places and I'll rest while you dance."

"We'll be able to keep him dancing forever," said Taebó.

That afternoon, Kaindé and the devil met in the central square.

The devil told three bata drums lying on the ground, "Let the drumming begin." The drums began to play a rhythm all by themselves, without a hand touching them.

Kaindé and the devil began to dance. When Kaindé grew tired, he waited until the devil turned his back on him and traded places with Taebó.

All through the afternoon and all through the night, Kaindé and Taebó traded places and danced with the devil.

When the sun came up, the devil said, "Well, are you ready to give up?"

"I haven't even warmed up yet," said Taebó.

"Neither have I," growled the devil.

On the second day, the devil said, "I don't think you can last much longer."

"I'm not even sweating yet," said Kaindé.

On the third day, the devil was breathing hard. "You must admit you're tired," he said.

"I haven't even showed you my best moves," said Taebó.

On the fourth day, the devil gasped, "I can see you are tripping over your own feet."

"That was a skip," said Kaindé, and he twirled around the devil.

At the end of the fifth day the devil was staggering. He could not even keep the beat "I can see . . ." he began to croak and collapsed at Taebó's feet.

The spell was broken. The clouds were freed from their cruel bindings. Joyfully, they spilled their life giving rain on Oyo.

ORUNMILÁ

DEATH AND OKRA

This story tells of how Orunmilá was able to keep Ikú (death) away from a child.

Death is no mystery to Orunmilá.

A long time ago, back in the days when the Orishás still walked the earth, a woman threw herself at Orunmilá's feet, sobbing and crying.

"Ikú is circling my house," she sobbed. "Ikú is trying to get in."

Ikú is death, so the poor woman had good reason to be upset. Death is very patient. When she wants to carry someone away, she will wait outside the person's house. The moment a door or a window is opened, even if it's just the smallest crack, Ikú will slip in and make off with the person she seeks.

"She is at my house," wailed the woman. "I saw her. Ikú wants to make off with my little boy." She plucked at Orunmilá's robe. "Hurry, hurry. She has sent a fever to take my boy. I locked the doors and the windows before I left, but she can find a crack and get inside." She pulled at Orunmilá's hand. "You must help me before she takes my boy."

Orunmilá laid his hand on the woman's head. "Be calm," he said.

"Tell me what to do," she said.

Orunmilá helped the woman to her feet. "This is what you must do," he said. "Go to the market and buy four baskets. Fill the four baskets with okra. Then meet me at your house."

"But Ikú is sure to take my child while I'm gone," wailed the woman.

"I will guard your child," said Orunmilá. "I will make sure that Ikú does not take him. Now go and do as I say."

The woman ran to the market and bought four baskets. She ran to the okra seller and filled them with okra. She balanced the four baskets on her head and raced home as fast as she could.

"Here is the okra you wanted," she said, gasping for breath. "How is this going to save my child?"

"Quiet, woman," said Orunmilá. "I too have seen Ikú sneaking around your house. There is no time to explain."

Orunmilá took the baskets inside the woman's house. He emptied one basket around the child's bed. He emptied another basket around the hearth. He emptied the third basket in the front room. He spread the contents of the fourth basket around the door and windows. He covered the floor with okra. He made sure that not even an inch of the floor could be seen. Then Orunmilá stepped outside and stacked the baskets under the porch.

Orunmilá wiped his hands and said, "Your child is now protected. Ikú can't carry him away."

"I thank you and you may be right," said the woman, "but I'm going to sit here by the door and make sure." The moment she sat down, she fell asleep. She was that tired. She hadn't slept for days worrying about her child.

Inside the house, the child's fever rose. "It's time to take the child," said Ikú. She made the fever soar.

Ikú stepped up on to the porch. She did not make any noise. Silently, she stepped over the sleeping mother. Ikú went to the door. It was unlocked. An evil breeze blew it open a crack.

That was all death needed. Ikú slipped in. She wanted to take the child before the mother woke.

Ikú took a step. Her foot came down on the okra. It burst open, releasing its slippery goo. Her foot slipped out from under her. Ikú flapped her arms and tried to regain her balance. Everywhere she stepped, the okra popped. Slippery sliding slime covered the floor.

"Morondongo," shouted Ikú. Her feet flew up into the air. She came down with a loud crash. Every joint in her bony body creaked and cracked. A couple of little bones went skittering across the floor.

"Mondongo," groaned Ikú. She put herself together and shuffled outside. Orunmilá was waiting for her.

He bowed politely. "Are you having a pleasant day so far, Ikú?"

"Burundanga on you, Orunmilá," she cursed, spitting out some of the slimy okra that had gotten into her mouth. "This is all your doing. I curse you and that snoring woman who went whining off to you."

"When are you coming back?" asked Orunmilá. "We want to make sure we have a proper welcome for you."

Ikú hobbled off down the path. "It's not going to be for a long, long time," she groaned. "And I'm going to make sure that there is no okra for sale in the market when I do."

THE TEN STONES

This story tells of how Orunmilá liberated a people from their evil king.

A long time ago, in Africa, there was a very small kingdom close to Ilé-Ifé. It was ruled by an evil and bloodthirsty one-eyed king. His disfigurement made him bitter. He hated everyone. If you had asked him what he wanted most in all the world, he would have spat out, "I want to kill everyone."

Luckily, this evil king did not have the power to do as he wished. However, he was able to come up with many clever ways to kill as many people as he could. One of the most wicked things he did was to place ten stones on a tray.

He then proclaimed a law, "Everyone that enters my kingdom is to be brought here. They will then count the stones on this tray. Whoever is able to count the stones correctly, will be proclaimed your new king."

One of his counselors asked, "You mean you will step down?"

"Of course not," screamed the king. "Anyone who is proclaimed king is a traitor. I will then kill that person to protect my kingdom from traitors."

The counselor, very wisely, said nothing else.

A lot of unfortunate people had to cross the evil king's territory. They could not help it. Ilé-Ifé was a large place and lots of travelers had to go there and come back from there. Many tried to go around the murderous little kingdom, but not all could do this.

The moment a traveler set foot inside the kingdom, he was arrested and dragged to the palace.

The tray with the ten stones was brought out and the one-eyed king screamed, "Count!"

When the poor victim began to count, "One . . . ," the king always shrieked, "One! He's mocking me. He's laughing at me because I only have one eye! Kill him!"

If the traveler begged for mercy, "Please forgive me your majesty, I was not mocking you . . . ," the king shouted, "He's contradicting me! Torture and then kill him."

In this way, the nasty little king got to kill everyone who had the bad luck of setting foot in his kingdom. It gave him a lot of pleasure.

Ilé-Ifé was in an uproar about the tiny neighboring kingdom. Everyone had had a friend, a relative, or an acquaintance killed.

Why didn't they do anything about it? The answer was this: A powerful kingdom can't just go and squash a neighbor. If they did that, all the other kingdoms would start to worry that they would be the next ones to be squashed. All of Ilé-Ifé's neighbors would band together and declare war on Ilé-Ifé. The evil one-eyed king knew this and laughed with joy that his powerful neighbor could do nothing about his cruelty.

One day, there arrived in Ilé-Ifé one of the greatest sages of all time, Orunmilá. Great honor and respect was bestowed upon him.

When the people of Ilé-Ifé asked him why he was honoring them with his presence, he said, "I have heard that your neighbor is a cruel murderer. I understand that your kingdom cannot move against this tyrant. I have decided to visit his kingdom and put and end to all of his abuse and murder."

"No, no. You cannot go!" the people pleaded. "If you go, you will be murdered, just like everyone else. We cannot let you do it."

They begged and they prayed. They groaned and cried and smeared their heads with ashes. Nothing could stop Orunmilá from doing his duty as he saw it. He left for the neighboring kingdom early the next morning.

No sooner had he crossed the frontier, that a dozen warriors jumped on him, wrapped him up in chains and took him to see the king.

They threw Orunmilá in the dust before the king. "Not even sages can defy my power!" laughed the king. "Bring the stones!"

An counselor brought the tray. All the members of the court and all the people in the city came to see what horrible fate awaited Orunmilá.

"Put them in front of his nose," said the king. "Let's see if he is wise enough to count a few stones."

Even though he was lying at the tyrant's feet, Orunmilá did not lose his dignity.

He looked the king straight in the eye and said, "That one on the end, the first stone on the tray, it does not have a name. If it did, and it were said out loud, it would mean death for the one who said it. I can't count that stone. However, the one next to it, that I name two, then three, four, five . . ." In this way, he kept counting until he reached the tenth stone.

The evil king was flabbergasted. No one had ever gotten past one before. "I declare you king of my kingdom," said the king. "But it doesn't matter, because that makes you a traitor. Kill the traitor!"

"Excuse me," said a counselor, a scholarly sort of man.

"What is it? What is it?" shouted the king. "You're holding things up."

The counselor said, "With your own mouth you declared him king. That makes him king. We cannot disobey your word."

The king was impatient with all this talk. "Yes, I declared him king. Now kill him."

The counselor shook his head and said, "We cannot do that. It would be treason. Also, you have threatened the life of the king. By your own law, you're a traitor."

Orunmilá raised his head from the dust and said, "Let justice be done."

All the people that were standing in front of the palace rushed to take justice into their own hands and tore the evil king apart with their bare hands.

BABALÚ-AYÉ

THE DANCE

Chaponó was the plague, the epidemic that could wipe out whole regions. This African story tells how Babalú-Ayé became a feared outcast among the Orishás.

All the Orishás were gathered in Obatalá's palace for a great feast. The serious part of the ceremonies were over. The güemilere was in full swing. Shangó was making the drums sing while Oshún and Yemayá danced together. In the middle of all this laughing and singing, Chaponó walked in.

Chaponó was old and crippled. His wooden leg scraped on the floor. The stomping of his cane threatened to ruin Shangó's rhythms. He was dressed in sackcloth rags which looked even worse when compared to the finery of the other Orishás.

Oyá was his best friend and even she said, "He stinks."

Chaponó stomped his way to the middle of the dance floor. He gave a flirtatious wink to the women, for he had once been quite a ladies' man. When he tried to dance with Oshún and Yemayá, his wooden leg got tangled up with his cane. He went crashing to the floor.

All the Orishás laughed.

Shangó was not very diplomatic. He roared, "Will somebody get that silly cripple out of here?"

"Maybe he needs his wooden leg trimmed," laughed Oggún, waving his machete.

Yemayá helped Chaponó up off the floor. She said kindly, "Dear, maybe you should sit and watch." But even she could not hold back a giggle.

Chaponó struggled to stay upright. "You dare to laugh at me?" he yelled. "I call down the pox on you. May you all rot in life!"

All the laughter stopped. The clown had become a wrathful killer.

Obatalá said, "That is enough. I apologize for the laughter, but I must ask you to leave."

Chaponó tried to kick him with his wooden leg. "You cannot get rid of me," he said. "I am Babalú-Ayé, the Father of the World."

"You may be the father of the world," declared Obatalá, "but you are not welcome in Heaven." He banished Chaponó from his palace.

Since that day Chaponó does not associate with the other Orishás. He became a pariah that wanders the desolate regions of the world.

THE HALF-BROTHER

Moving to Cuba rehabilitated Babalú-Ayé. In this story he is still shunned by people, but is pitied rather than feared. The story holds out the hope of redemption, for he is no longer avoided by the other Orishás.

This story reveals Shangó's relationship to Babalú-Ayé. It also tells why he is always accompanied by two little dogs.

There is this story told about the time Shangó still owned the Ifá board.

He wandered from town to town, giving the people advice. Huge crowds gathered to hear his oracles, since they always revealed the truth.

If Shangó said, "Do not marry that woman," no marriage would take place.

If he advised, "Watch your husband closely," sure enough, the husband's adultery would be brought to light.

One day, he was surrounded by a large crowd that watched as he threw his necklace on the Ifá board. A leper dressed in sackcloth rags hobbled up to him.

The leper asked, "Why don't you say anything to me? Can't you predict my future?"

The crowd drew back from the leper. Many picked up stones, ready to drive him out of town.

Shangó raised his arms. "Stop!" he told the people. "This man has the right to my oracle."

He spread a fresh layer of powdered eggshell on the board and threw the necklace. Shangó then read the oracle.

He looked up at the leper, his face full of surprise. "My father has told me that, on this earth, I have a brother and a half-brother," Shangó told the leper. "They are both older than me."

"What is that to me?" asked the leper.

The crowd gasped when Shangó said, "You are that half-brother."

The leper was suspicious. "Are you making fun of me?" he said, raising his crutch, ready to hit Shangó.

"Listen to me carefully, and put down your crutch." said Shangó. "I could not remain in the place where I was born. Now, I am called Oni Shangó everywhere I go, even though I am a stranger and a wanderer. It is the same with you."

"I wander and I am strange," said the leper, "but nowhere am I called a king."

Shangó said, "That is because your future and good luck are far away from here. Turn your back and go."

"Are you driving me away, too?" said the leper.

"No, I am not against you." said Shangó. "What you must do is cross the jungle. On the other side, you will find the lands where you are to be king."

The leper laughed. "How am I going to travel in this miserable state? My body falls apart even as I talk to you."

Shangó rose up from his divining board and went to Oggún, who happened to be standing near. Oggún owned two enormous dogs and he was very proud of them. He took them everywhere he went.

"Give your dogs to this man." said Shangó.

"What, are you, crazy or something? shouted Oggún. "I have had enough of your orders! Just because I need fire for my iron you always want to order me about. And, another thing . . ."

Oggún flew off into one of his rages. He was so busy waving his arms about and shouting and spluttering, that he let the dogs' leashes fall from his hand.

Shangó snatched up the leashes and handed them to Babalú-Ayé, for that was the leper's name. Guided by the dogs, Babalú-Ayé reached the lands where he became king.

When Oggún calmed down, he saw that his dogs were gone. "My dogs! I want my dogs back!" he shouted, but Shangó paid no attention and sat back down to his Ifá board. Oggún never got his dogs back, which is another reason why there is such hatred between him and Shangó.

BABALÚ-AYÉ'S KINGDOM

This Cuban story tells of how Babalú-Ayé finally got his promised kingdom. He is treated much more sympathetically than in the previous stories.

The transition from an African figure of fear and horror to a Caribbean incarnation full of compassion is evident.

Olodumaré's punishment left Babalú-Ayé covered with enormous suppurating sores. No one wanted to get close to him.

He went to buy food. The vendors drove him away from their stalls. "Get away from here!" they shouted as they pelted him with rocks. "Who would buy my fruit after you've touched it?"

He tried to find a place to sleep. The innkeeper said, "A bed? If you sleep on my bed no one else would dare to stay here." He pushed Babalú-Ayé out the door.

He went to buy decent clothing. The tailor said, "I will not sell you clothing. No one would buy my cloth after they'd seen you wearing it. It would be bad luck." Babalú-Ayé had to dress in sackcloth he scavenged from the trash heap.

No doctor would try to heal him. "Olodumaré will strike me down," they said. "Worse, he'll make me look like you."

Babalú-Ayé had to wander the world, despised by all. His only companions were the flies that fed on his sores.

Every now and then, he sighed, "I wish I had cared less about making love." There was nothing he could do about it. Olodumaré had cursed him. Wearily, he snugged his crutches in his armpits and wandered off to the next town. Of course, he knew that he would not be welcome there.

Doors were slammed in his face. "Get away. You bring the plague," the people said.

People spat on him. "You're disgusting," they said.

Children threw rocks at him. "No one wants you here," they yelled.

Women screamed. The men chased him off with sticks. That was Babalú-Ayé's life.

Even his brothers and sisters, the Orishás, turned their backs on him.

Oshún said, "Olodumaré gave you your life back because of me. That is all I can do. Now, please leave. I can't bear to look at you."

Oyá said, "Olodumaré has his reasons. It is not up to us to question his decisions. Please go, you look worse than the bodies in my cemeteries."

"Olodumaré is an old fart," said Elegguá. "I would help you if I could. But what can I do?"

"I can't bear this life," said Babalú-Ayé. "I would rather live like an animal. They don't care what I look like."

"At least have Orunlá throw your oracle before you leave," suggested Elegguá. "Then you would know what road to take."

"The last oracle spoke of misfortune," shrugged Babalú-Ayé, "and, it was right."

"Did you do ebó?" asked Elegguá. "Did you follow the prescribed sacrifice?"

"What's the use? Look at me. What sacrifice would make me clean?" Babalú-Ayé gathered his crutches and hobbled away to find an inhospitable waste where there would be no one to hate him.

Elegguá sat down in the dust of the crossroads and thought. "There is no worse errand than that not done," he said to himself.

Elegguá got up and ran after Babalú-Ayé until he caught up with him. "Come with me to Orunlá's house in Ile-Ifé," he said.

"What's the use?" moaned Babalú-Ayé. "Leave me alone."

"There is no worse errand than that not done," said Elegguá. "What have you got to lose?"

"That's true," said Babalú-Ayé. "I can't get any sicker or any uglier."

Elegguá led Babalú-Ayé to Orunlá's house. The courtyard was full of people waiting patiently for Orunlá to tell them how to cure their sickness, what the future had in store, how to tie their lovers down, or how to improve their lives. They had the same questions and problems that people have today.

Babalú-Ayé said, "Look at all these people. We're going to have to wait for days."

A man heard him. "It's not so bad . . ." the spit dried in his mouth when he saw Babalú-Ayé. "Aaaaa," he screamed.

"Aaaaaaa," screamed all the people in the courtyard. In a second, all that was left in the courtyard was a hat, a sandal and a cloud of dust kicked up by running feet.

Orunlá ran out of his house. "Quiet!" he shouted into the empty courtyard. "Hello? Where did everybody go?"

"We're next," said Elegguá.

"It was you," said Orunlá pointing his finger at Babalú-Ayé. "You've ruined me. How can I make a living with you driving my customers away?" He picked up the sandal and threw it at Babalú-Ayé's head. "Get out of here!"

"You see?" said Babalú-Ayé to Elegguá. "It's no use."

"We've come for an oracle and an oracle we're going to get," said Elegguá.

"Not from me, you're not," said Orunlá.

"Then Babalú-Ayé is going to camp in your courtyard until you decide to give him one," said Elegguá, sitting down and dragging poor Babalú-Ayé down next to him.

Orunlá picked up a rock. "He is not."

"If you drive him out, all the people in the town will run away," said Elegguá.

Orunlá lowered the rock.

"You will have no more customers," continued Elegguá. "You will starve."

Orunlá threw the rock away.

Elegguá was merciless. "And I will tell Shangó that you are keeping all the money from using the Ifá board. You're not sharing it with me."

"He is?" asked Babalú-Ayé. "That's terrible."

"Yes, it is." Eleggua was becoming indignant. "And Shangó is going to be very angry that you have not been giving me my share, isn't he?"

"Well, I've just been keeping it for you," said Orunlá.

Eleggua went on. "And Shangó is going to hit you with a thunderbolt, isn't he?"

"Maybe we can work something out," sighed Orunlá. "Come on in."

Eleggua and Babalú-Ayé went inside and washed their hands and feet before sitting down on the mat. Orunlá set the Ifá board before them and spread a fresh layer of powdered eggshell on it. He threw the necklaces.

"I see here that in a land far from here," he peered at Babalú-Ayé and Eleggua, "very far from here, you will become a king."

"Where is this land?" asked Babalú-Ayé.

"Let me finish," said Orunlá. "First you must make a sacrifice and you must become the owner of a dog."

"A dog?" said Babalú-Ayé. "What does a dog have to do with me being king?"

"Remember what happened the last time you did not follow advice," said Eleggua.

Babalú-Ayé still did not believe what Orunlá told him, but Eleggua nagged him until he made the prescribed ebó and began to look for a dog.

"People still run away from me," said Babalú-Ayé to Eleggua, "but maybe I'll find a nice dog to keep me company in my travels. Good-bye and thank you for your help." Babalú-Ayé made his way down the road.

One day, he arrived at a town. A large group of people was gathered around a very handsome man.

"I am Shangó," said the man. "I have been told that I have a brother in these parts."

Babalú-Ayé went closer. As usual, the people ran away from him. He was left alone in the village square.

Shangó pointed at him. "I know that I have a brother in these lands and I can divine that you are him."

Babalú-Ayé did not know what to say. He did not know that he had a brother.

"It is good that we met," said Shangó. "I have a message for you."

"I did not know that I had a brother," said Babalú-Ayé, "but I will listen to your message."

"You will be a king," said Shangó, "and all will respect and adore you. Take this road and you will find the place where you will rule. This dog will keep you company."

Babalú-Ayé was astonished. This was the second time that he had been told that he was to be king. What's more, he now had his dog.

"Thank you for your advice and thank you for the dog," said Babalú-Ayé. He set off on the road that Shangó had indicated.

He walked for days, but now he was no longer lonely. He had his dog. Finally, he arrived at a town. He wondered if this was the place that Orunlá and Shangó had promised him.

Babalú-Ayé stopped before he entered the town. He did not want any more yelling and screaming and rock throwing. He was still standing on the road, undecided, when a man came up to him.

"You better get out of here, stranger," said the man.

"I thought that I would be welcomed in this place," said Babalú-Ayé sadly.

"I welcome you," said the man, "for all the good that it will do you. Our king is a monster without compassion. He kills all who will not give him their wealth. Then he sells the families as slaves and takes their property."

Babalú-Ayé was indignant. "Why do the people stand for this?" he asked.

"There is nothing we can do," the man replied, "His warriors are strong and that makes him powerful."

"But what of the governors and the elders?" asked Babalú-Ayé.

"We went to them and petitioned them for justice," said the man. "There was nothing that they could do. They are afraid, too."

Babalú-Ayé forgot his pain and his sores. "Justice must be done," he said. "I am not much, but I am an Orishá."

The man sighed and said, "There is a prophecy that some day a stranger covered with hideous sores and accompanied by a dog will arrive and govern our country. I see you and your sores and your dog, but I don't believe a word of it."

"Oracles are to be heeded," said Babalú-Ayé firmly and headed into town.

When they saw him, some people said, "It's the man with the sores."

Others said, "He's our future king. He's the prophecy come true."

More and more people followed Babalú-Ayé. When he arrived in the marketplace, he was surrounded by a huge crowd.

"The king of the world! The king of the world!" they shouted.

Then, from the edge of the crowd, came the sounds of blows and cries of pain. A voice shouted, "Make way, you scum! Make way for your king!"

The crowd parted to reveal the king. He was a big fat man with a cruel smile. On either side of him were six foot-tall warriors with sharp spears and knives.

The king looked Babalú-Ayé up and down. He sneered, "So you are the great king that has come to save the people? You look like a bundle of rags to me." He turned to his soldiers and said, "Kill him."

As the soldiers closed in, Babalú-Ayé opened his sackcloth robe. When the soldiers saw the hideous sores on his body, the maggots crawling in and out of the purple flesh, they turned green. Some threw up. Some fainted. Some screamed and ran away. The king found himself alone before Babalú-Ayé. He was so sickened and terrified by Babalú-Ayé's hideous body that he covered his eyes and fell to his knees.

"Konfieddeno kofidenu," cried the king. "Compassion and clemency!"

"Long live the Father of the World!" shouted the people. "Death to the evil king!"

Babalú-Ayé said, "Leave him alone. I have suffered too much to be cruel." He said to the king, "Free the slaves, give the people back their wealth and give up all your lands to the families of those you killed and I will forgive you."

The king promised to do as Babalú-Ayé said and he was pardoned. The little dog did pee on his leg.

"Oba lou aye, the King of the World!" shouted the people, and Babalú-Ayé became their king.

A few days later, Elegguá went to visit Orunlá.

"It is just as you predicted, Orunlá," said Elegguá. "Babalú-Ayé has indeed become king."

"He has?" asked Orunlá, surprised. His oracle had mostly been a way of getting rid of Elegguá and Babalú-Ayé.

"Don't be bashful," said Elegguá and slapped him on the back. "I used to think that you made up a lot of stuff, but you are a true diviner."

After Elegguá left, Orunlá felt both proud and ashamed. He decided to go see Olodumaré.

Orunlá said, "I have come to you, Olofi, with a very important petition."

"You have more than enough power and influence," Olodumaré replied. "You don't need to ask me favors."

"It is not for me, Supreme Being, it's for Babalú-Ayé," said Orunlá humbly.

This so surprised Olodumaré that he listened carefully to Orunlá's request.

So, it came to pass that Olodumaré sent a very heavy rain to the town where Babalú-Ayé was king. When Babalú-Ayé stepped outside his palace to see the unusual rainstorm, the rain washed away all his sores. He was made whole again.

This happened in the land of the Dahomeys, among the Arara.

OSAÍN

OSAÍN AND ORUNMILÁ

In this story, Shangó and Oyá save Orunmilá from Osaín's evil spells.

Osaín spent all his time learning about plants. He got to know the ashé (power) of all the plants that grew in the world. He studied the properties of the rare and exotic plants that grew in the wilderness. He also knew the power of all the little weeds that grow on the side of the road and in people's yards.

Osaín knew which plants healed and which killed. He knew which plants were needed for ebós (sacrifial offerings) and omieros (purifying waters). There was no ceremony where his knowledge was not needed.

As Osaín's knowledge of herbs and magic grew, so did his pride. He began to resent the sacrifices made to the other Orishás. He especially resented the praise and respect given to Orunmilá, the owner of the oracles. Envy made his thoughts black.

Osaín thought himself to be Orunmilá's superior. His thinking went like this: "If I get rid of Orunmilá, I will have his powers and gifts as well as my own. I will then be the most powerful Orishá."

Osaín began to brew powerful potions and cast evil spells aimed at harming Orunmilá.

All of a sudden, Orunmilá was plagued by evil influences. They wove a black web around him. He began to have accidents and his health began to suffer. He attempted to use his oracular powers to find out who wished him harm, but Osaín had been very careful to hide himself from Orunmilá's vision.

Finally, Orunmilá went to Shangó's house. "You must help me, Shangó," said Orunmilá. "Someone is trying to harm me. My powers are not strong enough to see who it is."

Shangó said, "If you join your vision to mine, we're sure to discover who your enemy is."

Shangó is a great diviner in his own right. When he added his sight to Orunmilá's, a wall opened and they both saw Osaín's face. Not only that, they saw Osaín busily brewing his spells against Orunmilá.

Shangó was furious. "There is your enemy," he told Orunmilá. He gathered his warrior aspects around himself. "Don't worry any more. I will rid you of the evil that is out to harm you."

He stalked off to find Osaín. First, he stopped off at Oyá's house since he brought her along whenever he prepared for war.

He explained the situation to her. "I not only want to punish him" he told Oyá. "I want to take all his powers and knowledge away from him."

Oyá nodded her head. "I agree. We have to make him harmless."

Shangó then whispered in Oyá's ear, "Better yet, we will then have all his knowledge to ourselves."

Oyá walks faster than Shangó, so she arrived at Osaín's house first. She knocked at his door.

"What do you want?" asked Osaín. A great cloud of herbal vapors swirled around him.

"I was just passing by and I saw all the smoke," said Oyá. "I want to offer you a little aguardiente, since you seem to be working so hard."

Osaín took the gourd from her hands and took a good long drink. "Thank you, Oyá," he said. "But now I have to keep working."

Oyá offered him the gourd again. "Have another little drink," she said. "It's not good to work all day."

"That's true. It affects the health," said Osaín, taking another drink.

The aguardiente was already rising to Osaín's head, so he didn't protest when Oyá walked into his house. "I think I'll have another little drink." said Osaín, following her inside.

"Drink up. I have plenty." said Oyá.

Osaín drank and drank until he had to lay down. He fell asleep. Oyá put her hands on his head and began to take his secrets. But she had underestimated Osaín's capacity for drink.

He woke up and grabbed her wrists. "So, that's why you came," he shouted. "You wanted to steal my secrets."

Oyá broke away and ran out into the garden with Osaín close behind her. "You can't get away. I'm going to kill you," he shouted.

He leaped and landed on Oyá's back. Oyá bit and clawed him. They rolled over and over among the plants. "Shangó! Shangó, help me!" screamed Oyá.

Shangó heard her screams. He ran around the house and jumped over the garden wall. "You are brave enough to fight a woman," yelled Shangó. "Let's see if you are brave enough to fight a warrior."

He threw a thunderbolt that tore off Osaín's left arm. Holding the spurting stump, Osaín ran back to his cauldrons and grabbed a gourd that held his most potent and dangerous magical herbs. Before he could throw it, Shangó let loose with another thunderbolt meant to strike Osaín blind. Osaín ducked his head just in time. It tore off his ear, leaving a little nub. The pain made him drop the gourd. It shattered on the ground.

"I'm going to take chunks off you until there is nothing left." growled Shangó.

He could have whittled Osaín down to nothing but his aim was off that day. He only hit him a couple of times. As Shangó was winding up more thunderbolts, Oggún, that terrible warrior and Shangó's sworn enemy, came by. Oggún changed himself into a lightning rod and prevented any more thunderbolts from reaching Osaín.

Since that fight, Osaín has been a small shriveled Orishá. He only has one arm and one leg and a very small nub of an ear. He gets around by giving little hops, like a bird.

SHANGÓ'S GOURD

Osaín has a much more benevolent aspect in this story. He is an abused forest spirit who is saved by Shangó. As a reward for his kindness, Osaín gives Shangó the potion that allows him to breathe fire.

Shangó was out one day, hunting in the forest. Suddenly, he heard a man's cries. "Help. Please help me."

Shangó ran behind a tree and peered back the way he had come. He had many enemies and the man's shouts might be a trap.

"Help, help," cried the man.

Shangó carefully made his way from tree to tree until he came to a clearing.

"Help me. Please help me," shouted the man. He lay in the middle of the clearing. One of his arms had been torn off. One of his legs had been torn off. A great wound cut across one eye. When he saw Shangó, the man gasped, "Help," one last time and passed out.

"This is no enemy," said Shangó. "I must help this man."

He went in search of medicinal plants. He crushed leaves and roots and flowers into the water gourd he carried at his waist. When his gourd was full, he rushed back to the clearing and knelt next to the wounded man.

"Drink this," he told the man and poured a bit of the potion down his throat.

The man coughed and opened his remaining eye. "Who are you?" asked the man.

"I am Shangó," he told him. "Drink more of this and I will take care of your wounds."

Shangó washed the man's stumps with the potion and bound them with his own shirt, red as the man's blood. He nursed the wounded man for many days, going into the forest for fresh meat and more of the healing plants.

When the man recovered his strength, he told Shangó his story. "My name is Osaín," said the man. "I have always lived in this wild forest. I am the owner of the forest and all green things not planted by men. I stay away from the places people live. I do not like people. They come into my forest and cut down my trees. People come and burn and take, but they never give anything back. They never help me take care of the forest."

"How did you come to be wounded?" asked Shangó.

"I sleep in the branches of my trees," said Osaín. "I was asleep when a party of hunters began to chop down the tree. I shouted at them to stop, but when they saw me in the branches, they threw rocks until I fell." He showed Shangó his stumps. "Then they did this to me."

"What will you do now?" asked Shangó.

"I will stay in the forest," said Osaín.

"But you are mutilated," said Shangó. "How will you survive?"

"Do not worry about me," Osaín told him. "Olodumaré gave me the forest and the plants. I will stay with them." He put his remaining arm around Shangó's shoulders. "You have saved me and protected me. Now, I will do the same for you. From now on, make all your weapons and your magical instruments out of wood. Wood belongs to me and I will protect you."

"I cannot do that," said Shangó. "Wood cannot stand against Oggún's metals."

"I will give you a weapon against your enemies," said Osaín. "Keep the gourd that you used to mix my medicine. Every morning, dip your finger in the gourd and make the sign of the cross on your tongue with the mixture you will find inside."

"What will that do?" asked Shangó.

"You will be able to breathe death upon your enemies," said Osaín.

Shangó did as Osaín said. This is why Shangó is able to breathe fire.

YEMAYÁ

SHANGÓ'S SEDUCTION

This story tells of how Yemayá seduced her stepson, Shangó.

Everyone knows that Shangó is the fruit of the union of Obatalá and Aggayú Sola. As many women have done before and since, Obatalá kept this encounter a secret and never told her son the truth about his father.

Children always want to know what they're not supposed to know. The first words out of Shangó's mouth when he learned to talk were, "Who is my father?"

No matter how many times he asked her, Obatalá refused to tell him. Shangó did not give up. His need to know drove the boy out into the world to search for his father.

There are many stories that tell of how Shangó found his father, Aggayú, and of what happened between them. This is a story of what happened after that meeting.

Shangó ran back home to tell Obatalá that Aggayú recognized him as his son and had shown him favor. Obatalá refused to believe this and accused Shangó of lying.

After many troubles and disagreements, Shangó ran away from home but returned to steal one of Obatalá's prized possessions. Obatalá caught him and threw him out of her house.

Shangó fell to earth as a ball of fire. Yemayá found him and raised him.

Yemayá showered Shangó with love and affection. He was a headstrong and ungrateful boy, but Yemayá always excused this.

"After all," she used to say, "his own people threw him out to fend for himself."

Shangó grew up and became a powerful warrior, feared by all his enemies and respected by his friends. He became popular because he was the best drummer in the region and much sought after to play in bembés. He became prosperous because of his skill in divination, providing Yemayá with everything she needed. She was full of pride over her stepson.

Shangó returned home every afternoon to share the midday meal with Yemayá and to nap during the hot hours of the day.

One day Yemayá looked at the sleeping Shangó. "How beautiful he is," she said. "What mother can boast of a son such as this?" Then she laid down on the mat next to Shangó and fell asleep cuddling him with motherly warmth.

When Yemayá awoke, her body was filled with sexual desire, a desire that flared into passion when she brushed against Shangó's well muscled body.

Yemayá drew closer to her stepson. She began to caress him. Her caresses grew more and more intimate.

"Mmm," murmured Shangó, still half asleep. He awoke to find Yemayá's lips on his. "Mother what are you doing?" he said, pushing her away.

"I am so lonely," said Yemayá, holding him tight. "I have need of you, my son."

Shangó sprang to his feet saying, "Mother, I am ashamed of you," and ran out of the house.

Yemayá was on fire. Her body needed pleasure and pleasure she was going to get.

She chased Shangó across the yard. She chased him through the bushes. She made him seek refuge atop a tall palm tree.

"Come down, Shangó," she cried. "Come down."

From atop the palm tree, Shangó shouted, "Leave me alone. You are the shame of all women."

Yemayá began to rub herself against the palm's trunk. "I need you," she moaned. "I can give you the greatest pleasure in your life."

Yemayá was beautiful. Her words were sweet. Her motion against the palm tree was enticing.

Shangó came down.

He tried to be furious, saying, "Is this the way you act before your son?" But Yemayá stroked his cheek and moved her hips in such a way that Shangó became interested. He embraced her.

Their bodies moved together with the gentle roll of waves on the ocean shore. Then they shuddered as the rocks do when pounded by a fierce sea. Finally they settled as calm and still as the ocean on a summer morning.

Yemayá belonged to Shangó against all the laws of nature.

HOW YEMAYÁ TAUGHT SHANGÓ A LESSON

Obatalá was Shangó's mother. He stole a treasure from her and she threw him out of the house. Yemayá took the child in and raised him as her own.

Shangó grew into a handsome young man. He left home and discovered the pleasures that women give. He made love to hundreds of women, thousands of women. He loved them and left them and forgot them the minute he left them. He forgot so many that he also forgot about his step-mother, Yemayá.

Women weren't Shangó's only love. He also loved to party. He loved to drum. It was while he was drumming in a güemilere that he looked up and saw an exquisite woman. She was Yemayá, but Shangó did not recognize her. He had forgotten his mother's face.

Shangó's heart raced faster than the drums. "I don't know what it is about her," he said. "But that is the woman for me."

He didn't know that he felt the love of a son for his mother

Shangó put down his drum and went to Yemayá. "I thought I knew all the beautiful women in town," he whispered in her ear. "But now I've met the most beautiful of them all."

Yemayá recognized Shangó right away. How can a woman forget her son?

"He doesn't recognize his own mother," she thought. "I should teach him a lesson."

Shangó caressed Yemayá's shoulder. "This party is very crowded," he said. "Why don't we go and have a party of our own?"

Yemayá smiled at him and said, "You work fast, sir. Where should we go?"

Shangó stole a kiss and whispered, "Let's go to your house. We can be alone there."

He couldn't take Yemayá to his house. His wives wouldn't be too happy about it.

Yemayá took his hand. "Mmm, that would be delicious," she said. "Follow me, I'll show you the way to my house."

Shangó followed her like a little puppy follows a bone. "I'm such a stud." he thought.

Yemayá led Shangó through the town and out onto the beach. A little boat bobbed up and down on the water. She stepped into the boat.

Shangó said, "Don't you think the sand would be more comfortable?"

"Don't be silly." said Yemayá. "I thought you wanted to go to my house."

"Where is your house?" asked Shangó.

Yemayá pointed out over the waves. "Over there," she said. "It's not far."

Shangó could not swim. He did not like the water. He did not like boats. But he wasn't about to tell a woman that. He got into the boat.

Yemayá began to row. The boat shot over the water with Shangó holding on for dear life. In no time at all they were out of sight of land.

"This is far enough," said the nervous Shangó.

Yemayá just said, "Aren't the stars beautiful?" and kept on rowing.

Shangó took the oars out of her hands. "I said this is far enough," he said roughly. "Who are you? No one has the strength to row as you do."

Yemayá said, "You wanted to come to my house. This is where I live."

"No one lives in the middle of the ocean," said Shangó.

Yemayá daintily stepped over the side of the boat and stood on the water. "I do," she said, smiling.

Fear gripped Shangó. "You're not going to leave me here, are you?" he pleaded.

Still smiling, Yemayá slowly sank beneath the waves.

The little boat was tossed by the sea. Shangó put the oars in the water but he didn't know how to row. All he managed to do was to thrash around until he lost one oar and the other hit him on the head.

Yemayá watched and laughed. She stirred the sea with her hand and made a huge wave. She gave it a little push and sent it racing towards Shangó.

When Shangó saw the mountain of water coming, he tried to hide beneath the coils of rope in the bottom of the boat.

"I give up!" he shouted. "I can fight men and women, but I can't fight this!"

The wave crashed over Shangó and swept him off the boat. He sank like a stone. Water filled his mouth. He knew he was going to die and was afraid.

Yemayá came to his aid. She grabbed Shangó's hair and pulled him up to the surface.

Shangó coughed and gasped. The little boat floated next to him. He scrambled aboard.

Yemayá rose out of the water and said to him, "I hope you have learned your lesson."

Shangó wheezed and coughed some more. "I know you now, Yemayá. I'll learn whatever lesson you want," he said. "Just get me back to the shore."

"I will do so on one condition," said Yemayá.

"Anything," said Shangó.

"You must learn to respect your mother," said Yemayá.

Shangó was indignant. "My mother?" he shouted. "My mother threw me away when I was a baby!"

Obatalá came down and appeared in the boat next to Shangó. "My son," she said. "You have to respect Yemayá. She is your mother, too."

Rage filled Shangó. "You abandoned me," he yelled. "You threw me out of your house!"

"I brought you into the world," said Obatalá. "It was up to another to bring you up."

Yemayá said, "Shangó, you either forget women or hate them. You hate your mother and you have forgotten me, your second mother."

"You have two mothers, Shangó," said Obatalá. "You have two mothers in a world where many people have none."

A wind blew over the ocean. It smelled fresh and clean. It blew away the hate Shangó had kept in his heart since he was a little boy.

Shangó sighed and said, "I'm sorry I hated you, Obatalá. I'm sorry I forgot you, Yemayá. It is indeed wonderful to have two mothers."

Shangó changed. He respected women after that. But he still chased them.

YEGGUÁ

YEGGUÁ'S SEDUCTION

S hangó seduced Yegguá. This story tells how Oddua, her father, discovered her shame and disowned her.

High upon the highest mountain in the world, Oddua built a castle for his daughter, Yegguá. There she lived in splendid isolation, her beauty a feverish rumor in the town below.

"Her cheeks have the softness of clouds," said the young men. "Her eyes sparkle like the stars," they said.

"And her body? What about her body?" asked those who had not heard the tales.

"Her body moves with the grace of a summer breeze," they were told.

The young men sighed and yearned after a perfection that could never be theirs.

Shangó wandered the face of the earth. He fought those who angered him. He thrilled those who danced to his drums. He seduced women and dismayed their husbands. He was young and virile. He came to the town at the foot of Oddua's mountain.

"Who is this woman you sigh over?" Shangó asked the young men. "Who is this treasure no one has touched?"

"She is Oddua's daughter, Yegguá," they told him. "He lets no man get near her."

"You mean no man here has dared to climb the mountain and claim her?" said Shangó.

"No man can climb that mountain," said the young men.

Shangó laughed and said, "You mean no one here is man enough to climb the mountain."

"Even a warrior such as you cannot do this thing," they said.

"I have had my way with princesses," boasted Shangó. "I have bedded queens. What is a mountain to me? I bet you I can reach Oddua's palace and seduce Yegguá."

"Perhaps you are so big because you are puffed up with hot air," scoffed the townsmen.

Shangó knocked a few of them down, just on principle. "Have your money ready," he told the ones still standing. "When I return, Yegguá will no longer be a virgin."

It took three days for Shangó to climb the mountain. Three days he fought the wind, desperately grasping the rocks with fingers and toes so as not to be blown off. At night, his teeth chattered from the cold. Nothing grew on the mountainside. He could not make a fire. There was no shelter. If Shangó had not been full of fire, he would have frozen and died. But he made it to the top.

Oddua's castle had strong gates that were forever shut. The walls were smooth like glass and impossible to climb. Shangó went around the castle trying to find a crack, a chink, a chance to get in.

"If I can get up, I can get in," said Shangó, looking at a balcony high above his head. And then his eyes grew wide and his jaw dropped, for the loveliest woman he had ever seen in his life stepped out on the balcony and gazed down at him with eyes of incomparable beauty. She was Yegguá.

"Who are you?" she asked. Her voice was soft and sweet and musical. "No one has ever come here before."

"I am Shangó, the great warrior and lover," he said. "I have come for you."

No one had ever spoken to Yegguá in this way before. She had never seen desire burn in the eyes of a man before. Her heart beat faster in her chest. Her eyes sparkled. Her breasts swelled.

"What do you want with me?" she asked.

"Let me in this castle and I will show you," said Shangó.

"My father will kill you if he finds you here," said Yegguá.

"I am afraid of no man," replied Shangó.

Yegguá was won over. She had never met anyone who could say that. She ran down the stairs and opened the gates to Shangó.

He took her in his arms and Yegguá was lost. She burned with love. She gave herself to Shangó, to the only man who had ever dared to seduce her. Shangó had his way with her and left her, as he had left many others.

Several days later, Oddua noticed a change in his daughter.

"What is wrong, my child?" he said. "Why do you sigh and mourn?"

"It is nothing, father," said Yegguá. The truth was that she pined for her lover.

Time passed and Oddua said, "I'm glad to see you are feeling better, daughter. You seem to be putting on weight."

Yegguá was nervous and did not answer her father.

When it became obvious that she was pregnant, Oddua roared, "You have dishonored me and this house. Who is responsible for this?"

"A great warrior came to me," said Yegguá.

"A great warrior? He didn't even have a name? I'll send you to a place where you will see no more men, warrior or not!"

So Oddua sent Yegguá to live in the cemetery, where there were no men, only bloated corpses and carrion birds. It is her sad duty to turn over the corpses to Oyá. Oyá then takes them to Babalú-Ayé so he can cart them off to Orishá Okó who eats them.

HOW YEGGUÁ BORE SHANGÓ

In another version of the story, Yegguá abandoned her illegitimate child. Yemayá raises the child and his true identity is discovered.

Oddua kept his daughter, Yegguá, locked up in his palace like a precious jewel. No man had ever looked upon her face. No man had ever touched her breasts.

Way atop a high mountain was Oddua's palace. "No temptation can reach my daughter up here," he said. "Yegguá will remain pure and untouched."

But no barrier can keep away temptation. A high mountain will not deter a determined man.

Such a man heard of Yegguá and said, "She will be mine."

So it happened. He struggled to reach his desire. He braved storms. He went hungry. He reached the top of the mountain, where Yegguá fell into his arms.

A child was conceived out of this union. When Oddua found out, he cast out Yegguá saying, "You are no child of mine. You acted like an animal. Go into the wilderness and live with the animals."

Yegguá wandered in the wilderness. She dug for roots. She harvested berries and ate small animals. All the while, her belly grew bigger. One day, her time came. She gave birth to a beautiful baby boy.

"You come alone into the world," Yegguá told her child. "May you grow up as strong as the trees that surround us."

The baby began to cry. Its cries attracted a fierce lion who sprang between Yegguá and her baby. She screamed and threw stones to drive off the beast. The lion bounded towards her. Terrified, Yegguá fled into the jungle, leaving her child behind.

She lost her mind there in the jungle. She was sure the lion had eaten her child. Yegguá wandered for days, babbling and crying.

She picked up stones and branches. "My baby, my poor baby," she sobbed. "You are all right now, see? Eat, eat so you will grow up to be big and strong."

What about the child? The lion sniffed at him. The baby hit him on the nose and squalled. Startled, the lion went away to look for quieter prey.

Yemayá was in the jungle when she heard the baby's cries. She followed the sound until she found the newborn child.

"Who has left you here by yourself?" she said, brushing the ants off the child. "What kind of mother abandons her baby in the jungle?" She picked him up and carried him home. "You will have a home with me little one. You will lack for nothing."

Years passed. The baby grew into a strong handsome youth under Yemayá's care.

One day, Oddua's messenger came to Yemayá and said, "Honorable Yemayá, Oddua is having a bembé and requests your presence at the palace."

"Tell Oddua I will be honored to attend," said Yemayá. "I will bring my son, since he has become an excellent drummer."

Yemayá's son was the center of attention at the bembé. His drumming made even the oldest get up and dance.

Oddua was entranced. He could not take his eyes away from the handsome youth.

"What is your son's name?" he asked Yemayá. "His bearing is that of a king's son."

"His name is Shangó," said Yemayá, "but he is not my son. I found him abandoned in the forest many years ago."

"My daughter's son was born in the wilderness," said Oddua. "I now wish I had never sent her away."

"How did this thing happen?" asked Yemayá.

And Oddua told her the story of Yeggua's seduction and of her madness.

"She now rules the cemetery," said Oddua, "where she remains apart from all men."

"When did Yegguá give birth?" asked Yemayá. "Where did she leave the child?"

Oddua said. "It was at such and such a time in such and such a place."

Yemayá exclaimed. "It was in such a place and at such a time that I found Shangó!"

So it was revealed that Yegguá was Shangó's true mother.

THE LETTERS
(ODDUNS)

THE COWRY SHELL ORACLE

he cowry shell oracle is extremely popular. It consists of tossing sixteen medallions made of cowry shells that have been filed flat. When thrown, the shells will land either natural open up or filed side up. Twelve of the possible combinations can be read by a santero (someone initiated in Santería). The last four combinations can traditionally only be read by a babalawó (Santería high priest).

Each of the combinations is associated with advice and its apatakis (stories).

The throws are listed by the number of shells that land with the natural opening up.

1. OKANA SODDE
The world began with One. If there is no good, there is no evil.

There once lived a man who did not believe in Osha, the religion. When he needed anything, he went to a magician or a witch. Even worse, he went to sorcerers.

His friends told him, "If you need something, you should make ebó to the Orishás. They will get you what you want."

The man laughed at their advice and said, "The Orishás? I have no need of that foolishness. I can pay a powerful magician to get me what I want."

His friends said, "It's not wise to laugh at the Orishás. They will be angry with you and place obstacles in your way."

The man made fun of his friends and said, "Why should I be afraid of things that don't exist? You take food, aguardiente, and money to people that fool you."

"The babalawós are wise," his friends told him. "They heal people and get them out of difficulties."

"It's all smoke and lies," said the man. "You want me to give money to a pretender? I only give money to proven witches when I have a problem. Then I get results."

This misguided man took every opportunity to mock the followers of Osha.

If he saw an iyawó (novice) walking down the street, he shouted, "Look at the fool walking around dressed in white. He looks like a burnt match with that black head sticking out of his white shirt."

If he saw a man who had been initiated, who was asentado, he laughed at his necklaces, saying, "Look at him, he looks like a woman wearing those colored beads." He had no respect.

One day, this man was invited to a güemilere. "You know I don't believe in that trash," he said, "But I like the drumming and the dancing. I'll be there."

That night, after the ceremony had been going on for a couple of hours, Shangó came down and took possession of a woman. Her eyes opened wide and bugged out of her head. She stuck her tongue out as far as it would go. She lowered her head and butted people like she was a goat. Then she fell to the ground and rolled to where the bata drummers were playing.

The unbelieving man laughed and said, "This is what you worship? Look at that crazy woman make a fool of herself."

The woman walked up to him and said in a man's voice, "I am Shangó. It is you who are a fool for laughing at the Orishás."

The man laughed even harder. "Oh, so you are an Orishá, are you?" he said. "I suppose you know everything?"

"I know that you are doing yourself harm by laughing at the religion," said Shangó.

The man pointed at the house across the street. "Well, if you're so smart, how many people live in that house over there?"

"Sixteen people live in that house," replied Shangó.

"You see?" crowed the man. "That proves that all this is a pile of lies. Eighteen people live in that house. I know because I go there every day. Do you see how this woman is lying and taking advantage of you?"

"It is you who take advantage of these people's good nature," said Shangó. "They invite you to parties and you bring nothing. You laugh at them and they don't break your neck."

The man took a resguardo (talisman) out of his pocket and shook it in Shangó's face. "That's because I have this," he said. "I paid a witch good money for it and it protects me." He took out a large knife from another pocket. "And this protects me from the people who might want to break my neck."

"If you're so sure of yourself," said Shangó. "Take sixteen beads from your resguardo and throw them in front of that house you know so much about."

The man was going to argue some more. But when he looked around, everybody at the güemilere was watching the argument. Knives and machetes were out.

"I will do as you say," said the man. "Only to prove to these people that you are a fake."

He took sixteen beads from his charm and threw them in front of the house. The door opened and sixteen people came out to pick up the beads.

"Where's the other two people that live in this house?" asked the man. "I know there's eighteen people living here."

"They moved to Guanabacoa yesterday," said a woman. "We're all the people that live in this house now."

"Osha is truth," exclaimed the man, sinking to his knees. He worshipped Shangó and the Orishás from that day on.

2. EYIOCO

Arrows among brothers. Today your brother is your enemy.

Once, there was a man whose life was nothing but trouble. He had lost all his money. He had lost his house. His woman left him for another man. On top of that, he had lost his health. Nothing he ate agreed with him. He was wasting away.

One morning, the poor man got up off the piece of cardboard that was his bed. He looked at the rags that were his clothes.

"I can't live like this anymore," he said. Right then and there, he decided to go and seek his fortune.

"I'll go out into the country," he said to himself. "A farm always needs workers. At least I will have fresh air and always find something to eat."

The man put his machete inside an old patched sack and set off.

He went to a farm and said to the owner, "I will work hard for a place to sleep and food to eat."

The farmer said, "You are too weak and skinny. I couldn't get enough work out of you to pay for the food you'd eat."

The man was disappointed, but he walked to another farm and said, "I will work hard for a place to sleep and food to eat."

The owner said, "I already have a scarecrow," and laughed at him.

The poor man walked for miles that day. He went from farm to farm. The answer he got was always the same: No. No one would give him work.

When night fell, the man was very tired and discouraged. He ate wild onions and yucca he found growing by the side of the road. After he ate, he crawled under a bush and slept.

The next morning he continued his search until he came to the largest farmhouse he'd ever seen. It even had glass in the windows.

"Surely a place this big always needs another worker," thought the man. He found the owner and told him, "I will work hard for a place to sleep and food to eat."

"I was just thinking that I needed another worker," said the owner. "You can sleep in that lean-to over there. I'll give you a ration of rice and yam every day and chicken once a week."

"Thank you," said the man, happy to find work. "When do I start?"

"Here is a hoe," said the owner. "Go weed the yams. They are out over there."

The man shouldered the hoe and set off whistling. He stopped whistling when he saw the field. It was longer on a side than a man could walk in an hour and it was choked with weeds.

"Well, I can't complain," said the man. "I asked for work and here is plenty of it."

He worked all day. He worked until the sun went down and he was dizzy with hunger. He went back to the farmhouse.

"Here are your rations," said the owner. He gave the man a handful of rice with sand in it and a yam that had rotten spots.

When the man went into the lean to he had been given, he found plenty of spiders and scorpions but not even a mat to lie on.

The farm owner came and woke the man at dawn. "Sharpen your machete and go cut sugar cane," he told him.

The man did as he was told and spent the whole day laboring by himself until he had cut two ox cart loads of sugar cane. That evening he was given another handful of rice and a rotten yam.

Day after day, the farm owner worked the man from sunup to sundown and gave him a handful of rice and a spotty yam. On Sunday, the owner said, "We don't take a day off around here. I can't stand lazy people. But tonight, you get a chicken dinner."

The man worked all day long for a handful of rice, a rotten yam, and the leftover chicken bones from the farmer's dinner.

The man realized his misfortune. "The farmer is greedy and an exploiter," he said to himself, while sucking on the chicken bones. "If I don't do something to improve my situation, he'll work me to death."

That night, the man made ebó with two coconuts, two eggs, and two candles. He took the bundle and buried it in the field.

The owner happened to look out his window and saw the man digging. He was suspicious and thought, "What is he doing out there at night? I better watch that man closely tomorrow."

At dawn, the owner went to wake his new worker. He found him singing and dancing and ready to get to work. "What's wrong with you this morning?" he asked. "You've never acted like this before."

"I've never felt healthier or happier in my life," said the man. "All my cares seem to have been lifted off me."

The owner didn't like this at all. "Then you better lift these sacks of corn and go feed the hogs," he said.

The man spent the day singing songs in praise of the Orishás while he worked.

A passerby heard him and asked him, "What makes you so happy? The Orishás must have surely been good to you. Did they make you rich?"

"Better than rich," answered the man. "They have given me back my health and happiness."

"Then you should give a bembé, a party, in honor of the Orishás," said the passerby.

"I would like that," said the man, "but I have no money."

"My cousins are drummers," said the passerby. "I'll see what I can do. It would be a blessing."

That night, the farm owner was astonished to see drummers and dancers singing Eyioco in front of the man's lean-to.

"He has robbed someone," he thought. "That's where he got the money for a party. Perhaps he has robbed me!"

He went running to the police. "The new man I hired has robbed me of a fortune," he told the cops. "I saw him bury it out in the yam field."

"This is a serious charge," said the police. "We will come with you to see what this man has done." Of course, what they wanted was a reward if there was any money involved.

The farm owner and the police got back to the farm. The bembé was still going on.

"There he is," he told the police. That's the man that robbed me."

The police grabbed the poor man, who said, "I have robbed no one. I am poor, but I am honest."

"Then come with us," said the police, grabbing hold of him. "We'll see what's going on." No man is innocent in the eyes of the police.

"Follow me," cried the owner. "The loot is out here."

The police, the bembé drummers and the dancers all trooped out to the yam field.

"Right here," said the owner. "Right here is where I saw him digging last night."

The police took shovels and dug up the field.

They found the bundle. "Aha!" they said. "And what's this?"

The owner started hopping around. That's how excited he was. "That's it," he said. "That's my fortune.

The police unwrapped the bundle. "This isn't money," they said, stepping back in fright. "This is somebody's ebó."

"That's my sacrifice," said the poor man. "Now you have disturbed my gift to the Orishás."

The police wiped their hands on the grass and on their uniforms.

They grabbed the owner. "You've made us come out here in the middle of the night to get cursed," they shouted while they shook the owner back and forth.

One of the drummers said, "He should pay for a despojo (cleansing)."

"That's right," said the police to the owner. "You're going to pay for a despojo, for our time, and for this man's sacrifice." The owner had to pay for everything.

The poor man was very happy with the result of his ebó. He had his health, his happiness, and money in his pocket. The mean farm owner even had to pay for the bembé.

Another story related to this oddun is:

Odé and his wife lived in a conuco, a small patch of cleared land, far from other people. He made his living by hunting doves.

Odé woke before dawn every day, kissed his wife and went into the forest with his bow and arrows. He was a skillful hunter. By the time afternoon came, he usually had his bag full of doves. Then he headed home.

On the way home, Odé had to pass by a small cotton patch. He always gathered the white cotton fluffs into a pile. Then he laid the doves on top of the cotton. Odé did this with great respect. He sang a song of praise to Obatalá who always came down and enjoyed the blood. This is the way Odé offered thanks to Obatalá. Then he put the birds in his bag and took them to his house.

When he arrived, he shouted, "Greetings, wife, we eat again today," and gave her the birds he had killed.

One day Odé's wife was cleaning the doves, getting them ready for supper, when she thought, "This is very strange. These birds don't have any blood in them."

This made her curious. The next day, she looked over Odé's catch very closely. "I have never seen anything like this before," she thought. "Where is the blood?"

Every day she checked the birds before cooking them. Her curiosity grew. "Maybe Odé is practicing some sort of magic and not telling me," she thought. This thought grew in her head. After a few more days, she thought, "Maybe he is making magic against me."

The next time Odé gave her a bag full of doves, she asked him, "Why is it that none of these birds have any blood in them?"

"It is a secret," Odé told her, since he thought it improper to speak to his wife about his private sacrifice to Obatalá.

"Are you making magic out in the forest?" she asked. But Odé remained silent.

When Odé left the house the next morning, his wife followed him into the forest. "I'll find out if he's making magic against me," she thought. "If he is, I can run away. If he's not, there is no harm in me watching him."

All through the morning Odé's wife watched him hunt. "There's nothing strange here," she said.

She followed Odé until he filled his bag and headed for home.

"He acts as he always does," thought his wife. "There's nothing strange here." But she was still suspicious.

Odé stopped in the cotton patch and laid out the doves on the white fluffs. His wife crept closer and hid in a thick bush. "He has never told me about this," she thought. "There is something strange here."

Odé began to sing and Obatalá arrived.

"Who is here with you?" asked Obatalá.

"There is no one with me," said Odé. "I come alone."

"You do not come alone," said Obatalá.

"Of course I do," said Odé. "Who else is here?"

"Look behind you, in that bush," said Obatalá.

Odé went to the bush, parted the branches, and there was his wife.

His wife accused him. "I knew you were making magic against me," she said.

Odé dragged her out of the bush and told her, "This is not magic. I am giving thanks to Obatalá for our food."

Obatalá walked to Odé's wife and told her, "The blood that is missing from the doves that your husband brings to you every day you will now see flow from your belly every month."

Since then, women have menstruated.

3. OGGÚNDA
Family fight. Tragedy over something.

Laquin and Adafin were the best of friends.

If Laquin had too much work to do in his fields, Adafin said, "All my work can be done tomorrow. I will come and help you."

If Adafin had to take heavy baskets full of yams to market, Laquin said, "Let me help you. I need the exercise today."

If either one was sick or injured, the other said, "I will stay by your side, for you are like a brother to me."

They shared everything, the good and the bad, as brothers should, but seldom do.

It so happened that Laquin had to go on a trip. He had to sell his crop at a big market in the next village.

"What am I going to do with my money?" he asked himself. "If I leave it in the house, someone is sure to come in and take it. If I carry it with me, someone is sure to rob me on the way."

He thought a while longer and decided what to do. "The only person I trust is Adafin," he said. "I should take my money to him and let him keep an eye on it while I'm gone."

He put all his money in a sack and went to Adafin's house.

Adafin said, "Laquin, how good to see you. What do you have in the sack?"

"I'm going on a trip," said Laquin. "I want you to take care of my money while I'm gone. You're the only one I trust."

"Your money will be safe here," said Adafin. "Now come in and eat before you go."

Adafin and Laquin ate together. Then Adafin said, "I will bury the money under my bed. It will be safe there until you return."

"You have lifted a great worry from my mind," said Laquin. "I will return soon."

After a couple of days, Adafin became bored. He sat by his front door with a sad face.

"What is the matter, Adafin?" asked a neighbor.

"My friend, Laquin, has gone away," said Adafin. "I miss him."

"The best remedy for sadness is a party," said the neighbor.

"That's a great idea," said Adafin. "I'll throw a bembé tonight. Be sure to come."

Adafin invited a few more people and hired drummers. The party was a big success. Everyone danced and sang and drank a lot of aguardiente. Everyone went home drunk that night. Adafin staggered to bed and slept off his drunk.

In the morning, Adafin looked under the bed to make sure his friend's money was safe. All he saw was a hole.

"The money is gone!" he cried.

He looked everywhere, under cushions, in his pots and baskets, but there was no trace of Laquin's sack or his money, nothing.

"Someone must have taken the money during the party," thought Adafin. He rushed out to question the people who had been at the party the night before.

"I saw no sack, Adafin," said one.

"I never went into your house," said another.

"I was too drunk to remember anything," said a third.

Adafin asked everyone. No one knew anything or had seen anything. He returned to his house with a heavy heart to await Laquin's return.

The next day, Laquin knocked on Adafin's door. "Adafin, my friend," he shouted. "I am back safe. I have sold everything. Let us celebrate."

"Laquin, my friend, I have sad news," said Adafin.

"What is the matter?" asked Laquin. "Have you fallen ill?"

"No, it is not that," said Adafin.

"Then get my money," said Laquin. "We'll buy beer and drive the problem away."

"That is the problem," said Adafin. "Your money is gone."

"Gone?" cried Laquin. "How can that be? You buried it under your bed."

Adafin hung his head, ashamed. "It was under the bed," he said. "But I threw a party while you were gone. Someone stole the money when I was drunk. It's gone."

"I don't believe what you are saying," said Laquin. "How could someone go in your house and make a big hole without you seeing anything?"

"It's the truth," said Adafin. "I can't explain it either."

"I can explain it," shouted Laquin. "I think you took the money."

"I am your best friend," said Adafin. "How could I steal from you?"

"You are no friend," said Laquin. "You have stolen my money and are now making up a ridiculous story!"

"But that is what happened," said Adafin. "You are a brother to me. How could I lie?"

Laquin yelled, "You are no brother. You are no friend. You are a thief and a scoundrel!"

That was the end of their friendship. Laquin never again spoke to Adafin. He even crossed the street and spat when he saw him coming.

When people asked him, "How is your friend Adafin?"

Laquin said, "I have no friend. He has mocked me and conspired with other thieves to steal everything I owned."

"Is that really true?" they asked. "He stole from you, his best friend?"

"That is the truth," said Laquin.

People take truth to be what they think is true. Adafin was never able to clear his name.

4. IROSO

No one knows what is at the bottom of the sea.

It happened that the king of Ilé-Ifé had to appoint a new governor to rule a distant province. The old governor had died.

The king asked his advisors, "Who shall I send?"

One advisor said, "Send your treasurer."

"He steals from me now," said the king. "If I send him where I can't watch him, he would steal more."

Another advisor said, "Send your chief of ceremonies."

"He doesn't have the courage to steal from me," said the king. "But if I send him where I can't watch him, he will raise taxes and steal from my people."

A third advisor said, "Send one of your generals."

"My generals have been hardened by battle," said the king. "That is good in a soldier, but they lack compassion. They will ignore the needs of my people. The generals may even abuse them."

Then the advisors asked, "How about one of us?"

"I need you here at my court," answered the king. "Besides, you are too old to make such a long journey."

The first advisor said, "Appoint one of your messengers. They come from respected families and they are already in your service."

The king asked him, "How will I know which of those young men is trustworthy enough for such an important position?"

"We will test them," said the advisor.

The king sent for his three messengers. The three young men were tall, strong, and good looking. They were brave and intelligent. Their names were respected. They were Iko, Obe, and Jamu.

He gave each of the messengers a bag containing sixteen cowry shells (this happened at a time when cowry shells were still used for money) and said, "Take this to the market and buy new robes. Your work has pleased me. Then, return to me."

Iko went to the market. "Why should I pay for clothes?" he thought. "I work for the king. The tailor should give me the robe as tribute." Besides, he could keep the money for himself.

He went to the tailor's shop and told the man, "I am a king's messenger."

"You honor my shop," said the tailor.

Iko said to him, "The king has sent me to demand tribute."

"What does the king desire?" asked the tailor.

"A robe of honor for myself," said Iko.

"I hear and obey," said the tailor. He made Iko a beautiful robe and gave it to him for free as a tribute to the king.

Then Obe went to the market.

"Why should I be satisfied with just one robe?" he asked himself. "I have worked hard and deserve at least two."

He went to the tailor's shop and said, "Hey, you!"

"Yes, sir?" answered the tailor.

"I am a king's messenger, in high favor with the king," said Obe.

"You honor my shop," said the tailor.

"Make me two robes of honor," said Obe, "and be quick about it."

The tailor made him two beautiful robes.

"Here's your money," said Obe, throwing the sack of cowries on the counter.

"But there's only enough here to pay for one robe," protested the tailor.

Obe grabbed the tailor and shook him. "You should be thankful that I give you my trade," he shouted.

"I am, sir, I am," said the tailor, his teeth chattering.

Obe threw the merchant to the ground, took the robes, and left.

Then Jamu went to the market. "What an honor the king has given me," he thought.

He went to the tailor's shop. "Good morning," said Jamu.

"You honor my shop," said the tailor.

"Thank you," said Jamu. "The king has sent me for a new robe."

"Do you want a robe of honor?" asked the tailor.

"Oh no," said Jamu. "I am just a messenger. I need a robe that will stand up to rough travel through the forest."

The tailor made him a warm robe of goat's hair tightly woven to keep off the rain and tough enough to withstand thorns and brambles.

"That's just what I wanted," said Jamu. "Here is your money."

"That is more than what this robe is worth," said the tailor.

"The king gave me this as a gift," said Jamu. "I'm sure that he would want me to share it with an honest tailor like yourself."

Jamu, Obe, and Iko returned to the palace. Obe and Iko were resplendent in their robes of honor. Jamu wore his new traveling robe. The king's advisors were there. So was the tailor.

The tailor pointed at Iko. "That one kept the money and did not pay. He also abused the king's name," he said.

He pointed at Obe. "That one threatened me and stole a robe."

Then the tailor pointed at Jamu. "He is not only honest but humble, practical, and generous as well," he said.

Buying the robes was the test the king's advisors had devised.

The king told Jamu, "You are now my new governor. Prepare to leave for the province."

Jamu was overjoyed. He went home and said to his mother, "Mother, today our house has great honor. The king has named me governor of a province."

"And where is this province, my son?" asked the mother.

"It is by the sea, mother," said Jamu.

"That is a very long ways away, my son," said Jamu's mother "It is a dangerous trip."

"I am going with Obe and Iko." said Jamu. "They are my best friends. Besides, the king is not too happy with them right now, so it's best that they keep out of sight for a while."

Preparations were made for the trip. Gifts for the head men in the province's villages were packed in boxes and made ready for the porters. There were baskets of food for the journey and mats and cushions to sleep on.

While everything was being readied for the journey, Obe and Iko plotted against Jamu.

"Jamu has some nerve, taking us along as his servants," said Iko.

"Either one of us would make a better governor," said Obe.

"And that's what we're going to be," said Iko.

"How do you propose to do that?" asked Obe.

"When we come to the sea, we must pass through three caves," said Iko. "We'll wait until we go into a cave and then kill him."

Obe laughed. "Or let the tide do it for us," he said.

Everything was ready. Jamu, Obe, and Iko set off.

It took them weeks of traveling to get to the sea. Their path took them to the caves where Oba and Iko planned to kill Jamu.

The mouth of the first cave was dark as night. The ocean roared in and out and the path was slippery and treacherous.

Jamu said, "Let me walk ahead and see if the way is safe." He went down into the first cave.

Oba and Iko looked at each other and smiled.

"This is going to be easy," said Oba.

But Jamu came back out of the cave and shouted, "We will have to go slowly, but it is quite safe."

The line of porters made their way through the first cave and arrived at the mouth of the second cave. The tide was coming in and the waves roared against the rocks.

Jamu said, "I will go in first and make sure the path is safe for our porters." He went into the second cave.

"Maybe the ocean will do our job for us," said Iko.

But Jamu came back out of the cave and shouted, "The sea is rising, but we can still get through."

When they arrived at the mouth of the third cave, the waves crashed against the path itself.

Jamu said, "I will go see if we can pass."

"We will come with you," said Iko. "It is not safe for you to go in there alone."

Jamu, Iko, and Oba entered the cave together. The sea roared through the cave and flooded the path they would have to take.

Jamu said, "We will have to wait for the tide to go down before we cross. It is not safe to go through this cave."

"It's not safe for you!" shouted Oba as he pushed Jamu off the path.

Jamu's robe caught on the rocks and saved him. The tough material held and did not tear.

Jamu hung suspended above the crashing waves. "Help me!" he shouted to Iko and Oba, but they stood on the path looking at Jamu, laughing.

Suddenly a huge wave roared over Iko and Oba. The were swept off the path and out to sea, where they drowned. Jamu's robe held him fast to the rocks. He was saved.

Jamu's cries for help brought the porters, who were able to pull him back to safety. Jamu was able to fulfill his destiny and served his king as a great governor.

Another story related to this oddun is:

A long time ago, when cowry shells were still used as money, there lived a poor man named Obi.

"I must do something to improve my condition," he decided.

He went into the business of collecting rags, but children set his cart on fire.

He went into the business of selling vegetables in the market, but all the women said, "I'll pay you tomorrow." They never did.

He even tried cleaning out latrines, but he fell into one and almost drowned.

"This is shit," said Obi. "I need some advice."

He went to see Orunlá. Perhaps Orunlá's oracles could tell him what to do.

Orunlá threw the cowry shell oracle for Obi. He also consulted his ate, his oracular board.

"Am I Shangó's son?" asked Obi. "Is he my Orishá?"

"Never mind whose son you are," said Orunlá. "You have a sickness in your belly."

"That's because it's empty all the time," said Obi.

"Ikú (death) is hunting one of your friends," said Orunlá.

"That's because they are starving too," said Obi. "What shall I do?"

Orunlá said, "Don't dress like your friend or in your friend's clothes. Ikú may mistake you for him and take you instead."

"But how can I change my luck?" asked Obi.

"You have to make ebó," said Orunlá.

"What kind of sacrifice?" asked Obi. "I have no money."

"If you are serious, you'll find a way," said Orunlá. "This is what you have to do. Take a can of corojo butter, two chickens, two roosters, and the clothing you have on. Sacrifice the birds and bundle them in your clothing. Take the bundle to the ruined palace that's in the forest and place it in the roots of a dead tree you'll find there. Then, pour the can of corojo butter on the roots."

"And then my luck will change?" asked Obi.

"First you will be very frightened," said Orunlá. "You have to go see what frightened you."

Obi went and borrowed, begged and stole everything he needed for the ebó. He killed the chickens and the roosters and let the blood soak into his clothes. He bundled up the birds and tied a piece of rag around his waist for modesty's sake. He put the can of corojo butter under his arm and headed into the forest.

Soon, he came to the ruined palace. Old trees grew in and around the walls. In the middle of the courtyard, there was a dead iroko, a kapok tree.

"This must be the tree Orunlá told me about," thought Obi.

He laid down his bundle on the gnarled roots and poured the can of corojo butter over it. The old tree creaked, swayed, and came down with a crash, almost flattening poor Obi.

"Solavaya," screamed Obi and ran away.

As he ran, his thumping heart began to repeat Orunlá's words, "You will be very frightened. You have to go see what frightened you."

Obi stopped running and turned back. "The tree can't fall down twice," he thought. "It's not going to chase me, so I don't have to run."

Obi went back to the fallen tree. He looked at the branches. He looked at the tangle of roots sticking up into the sky.

"I'm looking at what frightened me," thought Obi, "but I don't see anything."

Then he looked inside a crack in the tree trunk. It was filled with an enormous quantity of cowry shells.

"I'm rich! I'm rich," shouted Obi.

He gathered up all the shells and took them back to the village. He paid Orunlá his fee and lived the life of a rich man for a while. He lost all his money later, though, because he had forgotten to make ebó to give thanks to the Orishás.

5. OSHÉ
Blood runs through the veins.

The world was still young. Olofín, the Supreme Being, enjoyed taking walks through the jungle. Most of all, he enjoyed the sight of birds filling the air like bright musical jewels.

"How beautiful they are," he said. "I have to reward them for all the pleasure they give me."

Olofín summoned all the birds and told them, "You ease my days and take my cares away."

The birds preened and ruffled their feathers pleased with his compliment.

"I will hold a contest," said Olofín. "Tomorrow, all of you will pass before me. I will give a rich reward to the bird that pleases me most."

All the birds were terribly excited. Imagine being Olofín's favorite bird! What an honor that would be! They rushed off to prepare for the contest.

They took dust baths. They splashed in the small pools by the river. They practiced strutting and flapping their wings.

Odidé, the parrot, said, "You are all wasting your time. I will win the contest."

"What a braggart," said the peacock, spreading its tail. "How can you compete with my beauty?"

"You are gaudy and vulgar," said Odidé. "Olofín is refined and will appreciate my feathers' restrained colors."

Odidé had a right to brag. A parrot's feathers have marvelous colors. Their quality is very fine. But he should have kept his opinion to himself.

The hawk said, "I have courage."

"I can talk like the humans," Odidé told him. "Olofín loves the humans."

The eagle said, "I can reach the sky."

"You eat carrion," Odidé replied. "I eat fruits and my breath is sweet."

The macaw said, "My colors are as pretty as yours. I have a chance to win."

"You have a big nose," said Odidé. "Mine is just right."

Odidé kept on bragging. Finally, he said, "I have to go rest now. I want to look my best tomorrow."

A finch asked a sparrow, "Do you think he'll win?"

"Maybe," said the sparrow.

"He won't win," said the eagle. "I think."

"Maybe I am a little too showy," said the peacock. Odidé's bragging had taken away his confidence.

The bird's conversation took a nasty turn. They started to talk against Odidé.

"That braggart doesn't deserve to win," said one bird.

"He's just a puffed-up fool," said another.

"He's going to make us look bad before Olofín," said a third.

The more they squawked and chirped and trilled, the more upset they became. Odidé's bragging had made them hate him.

The peacock said, "I don't care who wins, as long as it isn't Odidé."

The macaw said, "We have to get him out of the way."

The hawk said, "If we get rid of him, Olofín might get upset."

The eagle said, "I live high up on the mountain. A powerful magician lives there. He might help us get rid of Odidé quietly. Olofín will never know."

All the birds flew to the top of the mountain and landed on the magician's house.

The magician was astonished when he saw all the birds flapping and hopping on his house. "Get off my roof before my house falls down," he shouted. "What do you want?"

"We want you to get rid of someone," said the eagle.

"Quietly," added the buzzard, who knew he wasn't going to win, but certainly didn't want Odidé to be the winner.

"I have what you need," said the magician. He gave them a small bag of afoché (magic powder). "Sprinkle this afoché on your enemy. He will be so confused and turned around that you will never see him again."

The day of the contest, Odidé flew through the jungle suspecting nothing. "I am sure to win the contest," he thought. "Look how the sun shines off my wings!"

He strutted back and forth on branches, puffing out his breast. "I'm the best," he squawked. "I'm the best."

Odidé was so busy with his strutting and squawking that he didn't see the birds waiting for him on the branches above.

The eagle screamed, "Now!" and the hawk blew the afoché on the parrot's head.

Odidé was covered in a cloud of dust. He screeched, "What? What?"

He sneezed and fell to the ground. When Odidé tried to stand up, he wobbled, and began to spin faster and faster until he looked like a small green tornado. He could not stop. He was out of control. Then he spun head first into a big tree and knocked himself out.

When Odidé woke up, his head was still spinning. "Oooo," he moaned. "The contest, I have to get to the contest."

He couldn't fly, so he had to walk. He was so dizzy, he took the wrong path. He weaved and stumbled away from where Olofín was holding the contest.

Elegguá was sitting comfortably on a rock where two paths crossed. He heard a whimper, "The contest, the contest." Elegguá shaded his eyes with his straw hat and saw Odidé staggering down the path.

"Someone has blown afoché on that parrot," said Elegguá. He picked Odidé up and carried him to a stream.

Elegguá washed and groomed Odidé until he had gotten the last speck of magic powder off his feathers. He did a thorough job. When he finished Odidé shone like a parrot made of rubies and emeralds.

"What happened," asked Odidé. "Where is the contest?"

"What contest?" asked Elegguá. Odidé told him all about it.

"You have envious enemies, parrot. Come with me," said Elegguá. "I will take you to Olofín through secret paths in the jungle. Your enemies won't know you are coming."

Meanwhile, the contest was almost over. All day long, Olofín had delighted in the bird's beautiful songs and bright feathers as they flew and soared through the jungle clearing.

"This is going to be a difficult decision," said Olofín to himself. "They are all so beautiful."

Elegguá came into the clearing with the parrot on his shoulder. Odidé took off and soared over the clearing. He was more beautiful and regal than any of the other birds.

Eleggua went to Olofín and said, "Let me tell you a story." He told Olofín about the attack upon Odidé, about the birds' envy and about the afoché.

Olofín said in a loud voice, "I am old and tired. I don't have much pleasure. Now I find that my source of delight is also a source of jealousy and hatred." All the birds in the clearing hid their heads under their wings in shame.

"I declare Odidé the winner of this contest," said Olofín. "I also declare that, in the future, this parrot's beautiful feathers will be the remedy that will brush off afoché when used for evil purposes."

So it was that Odidé's feathers have been used to do despojos and other great things. They are very important to the followers of Osha.

Another story related to this oddun is:

The world was new. The Orishás walked the earth. Olofín had three sons. The eldest was called Acham. The second son was called Acharuma. The youngest son was Eyoquile.

They grew up and, when they became men, Olofín told them, "It is time you began to work."

Olofín gave each of his sons a machete.

"What are we to do with these?" asked Acham.

"You can build houses," said Olofín.

"We don't know how to build houses," said Acham.

"You can make fences," said Olofín.

"We don't know how to make fences," said Acharuma.

"What do you know?" asked Olofín.

"We know how to gather palm fronds," said Eyoquile.

"Well, go do that," said Olofín.

The next morning, the three brothers went to the fields to start work.

Acham told Eyoquile, "If you had kept quiet, we'd still be home taking our ease."

"We were happy before," said Acharuma. "Why did you have to go along with our father's crazy idea?"

Eyoquile was troubled by his brother's words. Perhaps he had done wrong. "I will go to Orunlá's house and seek his advice," he told his brothers. "He will know if I did right in speaking up."

Acham said, "Oh, so now that you have made us go to work, you're trying to get out of it?"

"I want to know if I did the right thing," said Eyoquile. He went to Orunlá's house and told him what had happened.

"Now my brothers are angry with me," said Eyoquile. "Did I do the right thing?"

"It is right for children to become men and for men to work," said Orunlá. "But you must make a sacrifice."

"What must I do?" asked Eyoquile.

Orunlá told him everything that he had to get and how to make the ebó at the foot of Iroko, the kapok tree.

It took a long time for Eyoquile to gather all the ingredients for the ebó. He had to go to the market and get corojo butter. He had to go to the blacksmith and get a nail. He had to find a spotted rooster. He had to get many things.

Acham and Acharuma returned home from the fields. Olofín asked them, "Where is Eyoquile?"

The two brothers were still angry with Eyoquile, so they lied to their father. "He did not do any work," they said. "He is very lazy. He spent the day sleeping under a palm tree. We left him there."

Eyoquile arrived home after dark. "Where have you been Eyoquile?" asked Olofín. "Why do you come home in the night?"

"Orunlá told me to make ebó," said Eyoquile. "I am sorry to be late, but it took a long time to make the sacrifice."

"You're a liar," said Olofín. "Your brothers told me you spent the day sleeping. You will get no food until you work."

Eyoquile was very upset, but he respected his father and did not talk back.

That night, he asked his brothers, "Why did you say I slept through the day? You know I went to Orunlá to see if I'd done the right thing."

His brothers laughed at him. "You are a fool," they said. "We don't care what you do as long as we get your share of the food." Eyoquile was sad and angry and very confused.

The next morning, the brothers went to work. "I am going to visit Orunlá again today," said Eyoquile. "Our father has treated me unjustly and you do not behave as brothers to me."

"Do as you will," said Acharuma. "We don't care."

"Be sure that we will have what is yours," said Acham.

Eyoquile went to Orunlá's house. "My father is not my father and my brothers are not my brothers," he told Orunlá.

Orunlá consulted the oracle and said, "You must make ebó today." He told Eyoquile what to get and what to do.

Eyoquile spent most of that day getting what he needed and doing what Orunlá had told him to do. He did manage to get to work after his brothers had quit for the day.

When Acham and Acharuma got home that evening, Olofín asked them, "Where is Eyoquile?"

"He spent the day eating and sleeping under the palms," said Acharuma.

"But we worked hard," said Acham. "Look at the cart full of palm fronds we brought!"

Eyoquile came in after dark. He only brought an armful of palm fronds.

"You are lazy and good for nothing," shouted Olofín. "Your brothers spent the day working hard while you slept and made a pig of yourself."

"I spent the day following Orunlá's advice," Eyoquile told him. "This is all I had time to do."

"You will not sleep in my house tonight," said Olofín. "And you will not get any food."

"Father, you should give us his clothes," said Acham. "He does not deserve them."

"You're right, my son," said Olofín. "If he does not work, he should not have clothes."

Eyoquile fell asleep under a bush, hungry and cold. His brothers laughed at him inside the house.

The next morning. Eyoquile did not wait for his brothers to get up. He hurried to Orunlá's house.

"Your advice has hurt me and humiliated me." he told Orunlá. "Look at me. I don't even have clothes to wear."

"Make an ebó with your machete." said Orunlá. "Everything will come out right for you."

"My machete?" asked Eyoquile. "That's the only thing I have left."

"If you want your troubles to go away." said Orunlá. "you must give it up."

Eyoquile sighed and went away to make ebó with his machete.

"Now what am I going to do?" he thought. "I don't have anything. I might as well go and try to do a little work. Maybe I'll get a bite to eat tonight."

He went to the palm grove as the sun was setting. His brothers were gone.

"What am I going to do?" he said. "I don't have a machete. How am I going to get palm fronds?"

Eyoquile had no choice but to climb a palm tree and tear the fronds off by hand. Soon his hands were cut and bleeding. but he kept at his work. Then. when he tore a frond off the palm. he found a treasure. He found a precious parrot feather.

"This is a rare feather!" cried Eyoquile. "My father has wanted one of these for a very long time. He says that without them. he can't brush away evil influences." He scurried down the palm and hurried home.

Meanwhile. his brothers had arrived at the house.

"Did Eyoquile work today?" asked Olofín.

"Do you see him here with us?" said Acham.

"He spent the day stealing yams and sleeping again." said Acharuma.

"Don't you know that he is a lazy bum?" said Acham.

"I am not a lazy bum." said Eyoquile. standing in the doorway.

"Why are you late again?" said Olofín. "And how dare you come into this house after I have forbidden it?"

"I am late because Orunlá told me to make ebó with my machete," said Eyoquile.

"Hah," laughed Acham. "He probably traded it for some beer."

"You have lost your machete?" cried Olofín.

"I went ahead and tore off the fronds with my bare hands. I found this," said Eyoquile, holding up the rare and beautiful parrot feather.

"Oh, bless you, my son," said Olofín. "I have searched so long for one of those." Olofín embraced Eyoquile and went out into the street yelling, "Tani lea laguna, with my own hands I have made myself king." He waved the parrot's feather over his head and the people marveled and praised him.

Eyoquile became Olofín's favorite son. He regained everything he had lost and more. He was victorious thanks to his effort and perseverance. His brother's envy, malice, and resentment had to give way. Nothing could stand before Eyoquile and his gift to Olofín.

6. OBARA

The truth comes from legend. The king does not lie.

Obara, the son of King Obalube, spent his days hunting. When Obara went into the jungle, the people of the village knew that they could expect a feast that night. But Obara's luck turned. The only animals he could find were thin monkeys, small birds, or stringy gazelles. The buffaloes and the fat antelopes he was used to hunting did not cross his path.

Obara decided to visit Orunlá. Perhaps the oracle could tell him how to change his luck.

Orunlá threw his ekuele, peered at the pattern made by the necklace, and said, "The animals will not present themselves to you unless you make ebó."

"What kind of sacrifice do I have to make?" asked Obara.

Orunlá told him, "You must bring me a rooster, eight parrot feathers, and your bow before you can hunt again."

"Eight parrot feathers!" exclaimed Obara. "That is a lot of money." People still used feathers and shells for money at that time. They didn't use paper like they do now.

"You are a king's son," said Orunlá. "You can afford it."

"Very well," said Obara. "I will bring you what you ask."

On his way home, Obara met Eshú on the path.

"Where are you going in such a hurry?" asked Eshú.

"Orunlá told me I must bring him a rooster, eight parrot feathers, and my bow so that my luck in hunting will change," said Obara.

Eshú laughed and laughed.

"What are you laughing at?" asked Obara.

"Orunlá has fooled you," said Eshú. "He's going to take your money and throw a big party with it."

"Is this true?" Obara asked.

"Of course it is," said Eshú. "Aren't you already a great and famous hunter?"

"I am," said Obara, swelling with pride.

"So why should you throw money away to be what you already are?" said Eshú.

"What you say is true," said Obara. "Why should I give money to Orunlá? I am already a mighty hunter. I have no need to make ebó."

"Now you are showing sense," said Eshú. "Go into the jungle and hunt."

Obara took Eshú's advice. He did not make ebó. He went deep into the jungle.

Obara was carefully putting poison on his arrow points when an elephant came crashing and trumpeting through the trees.

Obara did not flinch. He took careful aim and shot an arrow into the elephant's right eye. The elephant fell at Obara's feet.

"I have killed the largest animal in the jungle!" shouted Obara.

He ran back to the village. "Come and celebrate!" shouted Obara at the king's door.

"What is all this noise, my son?" asked Obalube.

"I am a mighty hunter," boasted Obara. "I have killed a gigantic elephant, the largest animal in the jungle."

"Ring the bell!" shouted King Obalube. "Have the women sharpen their knives. Let the whole village come with baskets to carry the meat. We will feast for days."

Obara led the villagers to the place where he had killed the elephant. There was nothing there but a big pile of logs.

"Where is the elephant?" asked the king.

"I killed the elephant right here," said Obara.

"Obara has lied to us," yelled the villagers. "There is no elephant. There is no meat."

"The elephant must have turned into these logs," said Obara.

The people were indignant. "Do you think we will believe that? You made us leave our houses so you could laugh at us."

The king was furious. "Is this true, Obara?" he asked his son. "Is this some kind of a joke?"

"Father, I swear that I killed the elephant right here," said Obara.

"You are a fool," said the king. "There is no elephant here. You have made me lose face before my people."

"But father," pleaded Obara.

"Leave my presence," said King Obalube. "I have no son. I never want to see you again."

Everyone said, "Good riddance."

Obara and his wife had to leave the village and travel to a distant province where no one had heard about the elephant.

They had a hard life in their new home. Everything Obara tried turned to dust. He could not hunt because all the animals avoided him. He could not fish because the fish would not bite his line. He could not farm because his crops rotted in the ground.

"Everything will be all right," he said to his wife every day. But things went from bad to worse.

One day his wife said, "You fail at everything you try."

"Things will get better," said Obara.

"They will not," sobbed his wife. "We can't go on like this. We don't have any food to eat. We don't have any clothes to wear. We have nothing. If you had made ebó and followed Orunlá's advice none of this would have happened."

"What do you want me to do, wife?" said Obara.

"Go back to see Orunlá," said his wife. "Beg his forgiveness and do anything that he says."

Obara went to see Orunlá.

When Orunlá saw Obara at his door, he cried out, "Oho! Here is the mighty hunter that doesn't keep promises. Here is the great liar that fools his people. What does the prince that goes back on his word want?"

"I come to beg your pardon," said Obara meekly.

"What will you do for your pardon?" asked Orunlá.

"Anything you say," said Obara.

Orunlá consulted the oracles and said, "Know that the price of your sacrifice has gone up. You must bring me two roosters, sixteen parrot feathers, sixteen bundles of firewood, two bottles of aguardiente, and the clothes on your back. Then you can make ebó."

"How am I going to get those things?" asked Obara. "My wife and I don't even have food to eat."

"If you are sincere, you will find a way," said Orunlá.

Obara went back home and found that what Orunlá had said was true. He was able to find animals in the jungle. He was able to catch fish. His crops prospered. It took a long time and a lot of hard work, but he was able to get the things he needed for the ebó.

Obara returned to Orunlá's house and said, "I have brought the things you asked for."

"Leave the roosters and the feathers with me," said Orunlá. "Take the firewood and the aguardiente into the middle of the jungle. Make a large bonfire and throw your clothes into it."

"I will do these things," said Obara.

"That's not all," added Orunlá. "Watch and see what direction the smoke takes. Do not be afraid of what comes from that direction. Offer the aguardiente to whatever comes."

Obara went deep into the jungle until he came to a small clearing. He did as Orunlá told him. He took off his clothes and burned them and stood waiting naked for whatever destiny brought.

A party of warriors came out of the jungle. When they saw Obara, naked and covered in soot from the fire, they raised their weapons to kill him.

Obara raised the bottle of aguardiente and said, "Would you like a drink?"

One of the warriors said, "Be careful. He may be a spirit."

The other warriors said, "We can always kill him after we have a drink."

The captain of the warriors asked Obara, "Who are you?"

"I am Obara and I am a man, not a spirit," said Obara.

"We are part of a prince's escort," said the captain. "Our prince saw the fire and sent us to find someone who can lead us out of the jungle. Will you come with us?"

"I, too, am a prince," said Obara. "It would not be proper for me to meet your prince naked as I am."

"We have clothes you can wear," said the captain.

Obara dressed and followed the warriors. He was astonished to see size of the prince's party. It was an army with hundreds of warriors and dozens of drummers. There were horses and a long line of mules carrying bundles covered in costly tapestries.

The prince greeted him and said, "I am Prince Alade. Who are you and where do you live?"

"I am Prince Obara," Obara answered. "I am the son of King Obalube, the ruler of this land."

"King Obalube?" cried the prince. "That is just who I came to find. We have brought great riches to pay him tribute."

Prince Alade ordered Obara dressed in a robe of honor and gave him a horse to ride.

Obara said, "Follow me. I will take you to King Obalube's palace."

The warriors lined up. The drummers played a marching rhythm and the whole party followed Obara out of the jungle.

When King Obalube heard the drums approaching, he sent his warriors to see what was going on.

The warriors returned and told him, "It is Prince Obara at the head of a large army."

The king said, "He may be coming to punish me because I sent him away."

The warriors said, "They are too many for us to fight."

"Then I will have to receive my son," said the king.

Obara led Prince Alade's party to the palace doors. King Obalube asked him, "Is this your army?"

"No father," said Obara. "These people are with Prince Alade. They have come to pay you tribute."

"How is it that you lead them?" asked the king.

"They were lost in the jungle," said Obara. "That's where I met them. I offered to bring them here to meet you."

"I do not believe you," said the king. "First you fooled me with a disappearing elephant. Now you arrive dressed in a robe of honor and riding a horse at the head of an army. Do you expect me to believe that you met them by accident?"

"Your son speaks the truth," said Prince Alade. "I gave him the horse and the robe he wears."

"A likely story," said the king.

Prince Alade was offended. "If you do not believe me or your son, we shall go away."

"Do that," said King Obalube. He took a small ivory ball out of his sleeve and gave it to Obara.

"Throw this ball and let it roll," said the king. "You can stay wherever it stops with whatever wealth these people may or may not bring."

"Your father has very strange ways," said Prince Alade. "Do as he says. We will stay with you. Whatever wealth was destined for him will belong to you."

Obara threw the ball. It bounded and rolled and bounced, but the magic in it would not let it stop until it had gone a long, long way from King Obalube's lands. There, Obara founded a great city. Many people from his father's kingdom joined him and he became a powerful king, much to his wife's surprise and pleasure.

Another story related to this oddun is:

Sometimes people find themselves in a dangerous situation without a clear idea of how to get out of it. Sometimes they save themselves because they work on the part of the problem that they are able to understand. That is what happened to a pig.

The pig lived in a farm with many others of his kind. The farmer took very good care of them.

Every morning, the farmer came to the clean and comfortable sties and called out, "Here piggy, piggy, piggy! Come and get it!"

All the pigs rushed to the trough, oinking and grunting. The farmer gave them fresh yam puree, corn and greens which the pigs gobbled up.

Every afternoon, the farmer came back and called out, "Here piggy, piggy, piggy! Come and get it!"

The pigs rushed back to their trough and ate while the farmer said, "Who is Mr. Fatty today? Who is the plumpest pig on the farm?"

Then the farmer picked out the fattest, pinkest pig and took it away. The farmer made a very good living by butchering his fat pigs and selling the meat.

One of the pigs in the sty used to come and root and eat with his friends, just like all the other pigs. One day he saw a pig's head fall out of the basket the farmer carried. The pig recognized it. It was the "fatty pig" of the day before!

"The farmer feeds us and treats us well just so that he can kill us!" thought the pig. "I have to save myself."

The next morning, when the farmer called out, "Here piggy, piggy, piggy!" and all the other pigs rushed to the trough, the pig stayed away. He didn't want to be fat and get his head chopped off.

The other pigs asked him, "Aren't you going to eat?"

"Food is dangerous," said the pig. "I'm staying away from it."

The other pigs laughed. "Food dangerous?" they said. "You're crazy." They went ahead and gobbled up everything in their trough.

That afternoon, the farmer took a fat pig away. The wise pig said to his fellows, "You see? He is being taken away to die."

"How do you know?" asked the other pigs. "We think that he is going to be rewarded for being so nice and plump. Eat up!"

The pig did not eat. When the farmer came to feed them, the pig went to a corner of the fence and nibbled at a few banana shoots and garlic greens that grew there.

He rooted in that spot to keep his mind away from the hunger in his belly. The hole he made with his snout kept getting bigger every day.

One afternoon, the pigs were eating and the farmer was picking a nice fat one to take to market. The wise pig went to his usual place to root for banana shoots. He fell into the hole he had dug with his snout.

The surprised pig said, "Where did this hole come from?" He had been too hungry to notice what his snout had been doing.

"This hole almost goes all the way under the fence," he thought. "With a little digging with my snout, I can get under the fence and out of here!"

The pig rooted in the hole. Soon it was large enough that he was able to get under the fence. He was skinny because he had not been eating, so he had no problem getting through.

The wise pig ran away from the farm and into the forest. He spent the rest of his life happily digging up roots and mushrooms.

What happened to the other pigs? Some found the hole under the fence. But they were too fat to squeeze their way to freedom.

7. ODDI
Where the first grave was dug.

Aruma and Odima were lifelong friends.

As children they often played the stone game. Little Aruma would yell, "I have three stones left."

And little Odima would shout, "I have five stones left. I win!"

Little Odima also won the races and the war games. He never got caught stealing fruit from the neighbor's trees. Aruma was always caught and whipped when he tried to steal anything, even a banana.

When they became young men, Aruma and Odima chased the girls together. They went after the most beautiful girl in the village.

"Come with me to the bembé," pleaded Aruma.

"I'm going with Odima," said the girl. "He's the best dancer in the village."

Young Odima won all the girls' hearts with his dancing. He also became a skilled hunter and won the admiration of the men. Aruma had to settle for the ugly girls. All he ever brought home from the hunt were monkeys and birds.

When Aruma and Odima became men, their fields were next to each other's. They sold their produce in the market.

"Yams, yams!" shouted Aruma in his stall. "Who will buy my yams!"

"Who would want your yams?" a housewife asked him. "Yours are all spotty and small. I buy mine from Odima. He sells yams of the best quality."

It was true. Odima took baskets of large yams and bananas to market. Aruma was lucky if he was able to fill a single basket with little spotty yams.

This was the friends' condition in life. Odima had luck. He was able to get what he wished. He became well off. Aruma had to struggle for what little he had. As the years passed, Aruma became envious of Odima's luck.

One afternoon, Aruma went to Odima's market stall. "Come by my house this evening," said Aruma. "We'll have a drink."

"I'm sorry, I can't," said Odima. "I have an errand to run this evening."

Aruma walked away thinking, "So, now he's too good to have a drink with me."

A few days later, Aruma went to visit Odima and said, "My friend, I need to borrow a few coins from you."

"I'm sorry, I can't help you today," said Odima. It was true. He didn't have any money in the house that day.

Aruma went away in a black mood. "He's too greedy to lend money to his friend," he growled.

Odima liked to visit Orunlá regularly. The oracle gave him good advice and kept him out of trouble. One morning, Odima went to Orunlá's house to ask about a business deal.

While Odima consulted the oracle, Aruma was drinking with some friends who were as envious of Odima as he was.

"I asked Odima for a few coins and he turned me down," said Aruma.

"His head is swollen with his own importance," said one of the men.

"He thinks that he's too good for his old friends," said another.

"Let's get him to gamble," said a third. "We can get his money that way, even if he won't lend us any."

Meanwhile, in Orunlá's house, Orunlá threw the cowry shells and told Odima, "Don't lend your money and don't waste it. But also beware of greed."

"I will try to do as you say," said Odima.

On the way from Orunlá's house, Odima ran into Aruma and his friends.

Aruma asked him, "How about a game of dice this afternoon?"

"That will be fun," said Odima. He thought, "A little gambling is not wasting my money."

Odima's luck was with him. No matter what Aruma and his friends tried and no matter what game they played, Odima won all their money.

"You have wiped me out," said Aruma. "Lend me a few coins so I can buy dinner tonight."

"Well, Orunlá told me not to be greedy," said Odima, "and I can certainly afford it." He poured a few coins into Aruma's hand.

After that, Odima's luck changed for the worse. Locusts came and ate his crops. His house burned down. He was robbed of his money and his hair began to fall out.

He went to visit Aruma. "I'm in great difficulty, my friend," he said. "Could you lend me a few coins until I can get back on my feet?"

"Get out of here, you moocher," said Aruma and slammed the door in Odima's face. He was glad of Odima's misfortune. "That will teach him not to be so uppity," he thought.

Odima said, "Things can't get worse. Not even my friend will help me. "I might as well leave the village and seek my fortune somewhere else."

He walked all day and all night until he arrived at a neighboring village.

Odima asked everyone he met, "Do you have any work for me?"

A merchant said, "Carry these baskets for me and I will give you a coin."

A farmer said, "Clean my chicken coop and I will give you a coin."

Odima felt better when the two coins were in his pocket. But that was all the work he could find that day.

"I might as well go on to the next village," he thought. "There is nothing here for me."

He walked all night and got lost in the jungle. He fell into a thorn bush. As he struggled to get free, his clothes were torn to ribbons and he was left naked. Odima put the two coins in his mouth so he wouldn't lose them and kept walking until he came to a river. When he bent down to drink, the two coins fell out of his mouth and were swept away by the current.

"My coins!" cried Odima. "That is all I have left in the world! I must get them back."

Odima followed the river until it reached the sea.

He was looking for his coins under rocks and in the shallow pools when a voice said, "Who are you and what are you'd doing here?"

Odima looked up and saw a tall muscular man standing where the water of the river met the water of the sea. He had a large double-headed ax over his shoulder and was leaning on a cane.

Odima said, "My name is Odima. I have lost all I have in the world except for two coins that the river washed away."

"You can't go any farther without the permission of the Mistress of the Sea," said Aggayú. That's who the man was.

"When is she coming?" asked Odima.

"She will not return until tomorrow morning," said Aggayú. "Wait for her on the shore. You can have fish to eat if you like."

Odima ate a little bit of fish and spent the night shivering in the damp sand.

He awoke at dawn and saw a beautiful woman coming towards the shore on a silver boat rowed by seven silver oars. She stepped daintily out of the boat and walked on the white sea foam to where Odima stood.

"I am Olokún," she said. "What is it that you wish of the sea?"

"The river washed my two coins into the sea," said Odima. "I have nothing else left in the world, so I want them back."

"There is uncountable treasure beneath the sea," said Olokún. She reached into the water and brought up a handful of gold coins and jewels. "Which are your coins?"

Odima gaped at the gold and jewels. The treasure in Olokún's hands could buy everything in his village seven times over. Then he remembered Orunlá's words, "Beware of greed."

Odima looked through the gold coins until he found two small copper coins with his teeth marks on them. "These are mine," he said.

"You are an honest man and honesty should be rewarded," said Olokún. She began to dance. Her movements were as rhythmical and graceful as the surf. She danced faster and faster until Odima could not tell if he was looking at a woman dancing or at waves breaking on the shore. There was the tinkling of a small bell. A wave washed ashore a silver basket full of solid gold starfish and chunks of red coral.

Odima heard Olokún's voice, "You may take this away with you as a gift from the ocean."

Odima returned to his village a rich man. He bought fields and animals. He built a large house, larger than the king's.

Aruma came to visit. "How is it that you leave the village with empty hands and return rich?" he cried, full of envy. "You must have robbed a rich merchant."

"I don't need to explain myself to you," said Odima and turned away.

"Robber! You're not going to get away with it!" shouted Aruma. He jumped on Odima's back and began to punch and bite him.

The fight went on for a long time. It was all the fights they should have had as children. It was all the fights they should have had as boys and men rolled up into one.

When Aruma and Odima were too tired to fight any more, Aruma was still bitter and consumed by envy. Odima was still rich. The two never spoke to each other as long as they lived.

Another story related to this oddun is:

A long time ago, corpses were not buried as they are now. The custom people followed was this: When a person died, the body was taken to Iroko, the baobab tree. It was left at the base of the tree. That way, the person's spirit could live in Iroko's shade for all eternity.

Back in those ancient times, there lived a man called Mofa. Every day, his wife hugged and kissed him and said, "My darling husband, I love you so much!"

Every afternoon, when Mofa was at work in his fields, his wife went to her lover and said, "I can't stand that man! His sweat stinks and he doesn't know how to make sweet love to me like you do, my darling." What a lying, two-faced woman she was!

Mofa and his wife had a son. When Mofa was in the house, his wife stroked her son's hair and said, "I am so lucky to have the world's best son!"

The minute Mofa left, she would cuff the child and scream, "You worthless brat! Haven't you finished your chores yet?"

She made the poor boy do all the house work. She made him walk the stony path to the river and fill the heavy clay jars with water. The child's feet were always cut and bruised.

If he tried to take a bit of food out of the pot during the day, his mother burned him with live coals and said, "You greedy pig! That food is for me." What a cruel woman she was!

Mofa was a good husband. He kept their house's palm thatch roof in good repair. He worked hard in his fields. There was always food on the table. If there was a little something left over at the end of the month, he went to the market and bought his wife and son a present.

His wife took all Mofa gave and her lying mouth said, "Mofa, you are the best husband a woman ever had!"

To her lover, she complained, "I can't stand to live with Mofa and that squalling kid. I wish I could get rid of them!" She said this to a man who never gave her anything, not even food!

One afternoon, after making love, her lover said, "You complain all the time."

"I don't complain," said Mofa's wife.

"Shut up," said her lover. "I told you that if you argue with me, I'll give you a beating."

"Yes dear," said Mofa's wife meekly, for she loved the fool.

"I have an idea," he said. "Do you really and truly want to get rid of the kid?"

"You know that I do," said Mofa's wife. "I want to leave them and come live with you more than anything in the world."

"It's easy," said her lover. "This is what you are going to do. Pretend that you are dead. When they carry you out of Mofa's house and lay you under Iroko, I will come at night and take you to my house."

"That sounds like a good idea to me," said Mofa's wife. She thought her lover was a genius.

When she returned to her house, she told her son, "Go and get water."

"But mother, there are already three jars full in the house," said the son.

She hit him with a stick of firewood and screamed, "Don't you talk back to me! Go get more water."

When the boy was out of the house, Mofa's wife went to the yard and dug up a nest of red ants. She picked up a handful of ants and let them bite her under the arms and in her groin. She ran back into the house and rubbed flour on her face and smeared a bit of soot under her eyes. The she laid down on her mat and began to groan.

Her son returned with the water and cried out, "Mother, what's the matter?"

"I'm sick," she moaned. "Go get your father and have him bring the doctor."

Mofa rushed back with the doctor. "She is pale and her armpits and groin are swollen," said the doctor. "Babalú-Ayé must have brought the plague to her."

Mofa and his son spent the night outside the house, crying and praying for the evil woman. She waited until they were exhausted with grief. Then she went to the fire and smeared ashes all over her body until she was as pale as a corpse. She laid back on her mat and gave a loud cry.

Mofa and the boy rushed into the house. "Look at her," cried Mofa. "All the blood has left her body. My darling wife is dead!" They bundled her up and laid her to rest under Iroko after making the proper sacrifices.

That night, the lover came and unwound the sheet from her body. "Get up before anyone sees us," he whispered. "Run through the bushes until you get to my house."

Mofa's wife and her lover spent two weeks making love, drinking, eating, and telling each other how smart they were.

Then Mofa's wife said, "There is no more food in the house."

"Go gather okra and sell it in the market," said her lover. "Don't bother me with household details."

"I'll wear this shawl over my head so no one recognizes me," said Mofa's wife.

"Do what you want," said her lover, dismissing her with a wave of his hand. He had more important things to do, like smoking his pipe and looking at the lizards fighting up and down the walls. He was a very lazy man.

Meanwhile, Mofa had to work twice as hard since he no longer had a woman.

He told his son, "Go to the market and buy okra. I have to go to the fields and take care of the house when I get back. I don't have time to run errands."

The boy didn't mind. As a matter of fact, he had less work to do now that his mother was gone.

Mofa's son searched the market for a stall that sold okra. Imagine his surprise when he saw his mother with a basket of okra on her head.

"Mother," he cried. "This is a miracle! I am so happy I found you."

His mother shoved him away. "Get away from me. kid," she growled. "I'm not your mother."

"But you are my mother," said the child. "I recognize your eyes."

She picked up a stone and threw it at the boy. "Leave me alone, you pest."

Mofa's son ran home. "I saw mother at the market," he told his father. "She threw a stone at me. She didn't recognize me."

Mofa hugged the boy. "My poor son," he said. "You have to realize your mother is dead. She is under Iroko."

"But father, I saw her," whimpered the boy.

"Hush," said Mofa. "Eat a little bit and go to sleep. You'll feel better in the morning."

The next day, the boy waited until Mofa went to work in the fields. Then he ran to the market. He looked and he searched until he found the okra seller.

"That is my mother," said the boy. "I'm sure of it!"

He was careful not to let the woman see him, but he followed her around all day long. A gust of wind blew away the woman's shawl. The boy got a good look at her face.

"It is her," said the boy. He ran home as fast as he could.

"Father, father," he shouted. "It is her. I saw her face."

"Son, your mother is dead," said Mofa. "That woman is somebody else that looks like your mother."

"It is her," said the boy and he cried himself to sleep.

The next day, Mofa said to his son. "I'm going to the market to look at this woman. It's the only thing that will ease your mind."

Mofa went to the market and asked if anyone had seen the okra seller.

"There she is over there," said a man.

The woman had her back to them, but Mofa saw her hips and the way she stood and the way she held her head.

"That's my wife," he shouted. He ran to her and grabbed her arm.

"Let go of me," she shouted. "What are you doing? Help, robber!"

People gathered around the pair.

"What are you doing to that woman," they said. "Let go of her."

"You know me," said Mofa. "I am Mofa."

"We know you," they said. "Has your wife's death made you crazy?"

He tore the shawl from his wife's head. "You tell me if I'm crazy," he shouted. "Is this my wife or not?"

There was a great commotion.

Some people said, "It's her. That's Mofa's wife."

Other people said, "Mofa's wife is dead. That must be someone else."

A person of importance was called. When he saw the woman, he shouted, "What treachery is this? This woman is Mofa's wife even though she was laid under Iroko."

Mofa's wife broke down and told the whole story.

"Kill her," yelled the crowd. "She must be punished."

Mofa said, "She has died once already and here she is, walking around."

"Then how are you going to punish her?" asked the man of importance.

"I am going to dig a hole and put her in it," said Mofa. "That way, alive or dead, she will stay where she belongs."

Mofa's wife was buried alive with her lover next to her. Since that time, the dead have been buried to make sure they stay put.

8. EYEUNLE

The head rules the body. Use yours.

A very long time ago, there lived a highly respected man named Unle.

The elders of the village sought him out and asked, "Should we plant yams or corn this season?"

"Plant corn," said Unle. "The sky shows no sign of clouds."

The villagers did as Unle said. The corn crop kept everyone fed and happy that season.

Unle boasted, "The weather is no mystery to me."

The doctors came to Unle and said, "People have been getting sick. We don't know what to do."

"Tell everyone to relieve themselves farther away from the village," said Unle.

The villagers regained their health and praised Unle.

Unle boasted, "Sickness and health are no mystery to me."

The king himself came to visit Unle. He said, "Raiders have come into our land and are stealing cattle. What should I do?"

"Say to their king that we will block the river with large stones and leave them without water if they do not stop their raids," said Unle.

The king followed Unle's advice and the raids stopped.

Unle boasted, "Ruling a kingdom has no mystery for me."

Each success brought Unle more land, wealth, and wives. His reputation and power grew to be equal to, if not greater than, the king's. Unfortunately, his pride grew to match his position and wealth. Unle's head was filled with thoughts of his own importance.

There was another man who lived in the village. His name was Mora. He was not rich and powerful like Unle, but he was respected in his own way.

One day Mora visited Unle and said, "I have come to ask a favor from you."

Unle was full of pride that Mora had come to him. "Ask whatever advice you seek," he said. "My words have more wisdom than the oracles."

"It is not advice I need," said Mora.

"What is it then?" asked Unle, annoyed. Everyone sought his advice and here was Mora, casually turning it down.

Mora said, "I have a nephew who is skilled at working with stone and wood. I ask that you give him a position in your household. He would be useful to you."

347

"I have no need of someone with such common skills," said Unle.

"You are getting old," said Mora. "Don't you need someone to help you with your work?"

"My work is very high and sublime," sniffed Unle. "I work with my head, not my hands."

Mora insisted. "Even so. "Don't you want your palace to outlast you? Don't you want a monument to keep your memory alive after you are gone?"

Unle's pride went to his head. "Away!" he shouted at Mora. "Get off my property! Don't I know the mysteries of the sky, the water, and the land? There is no death for such a man as I. I will never die."

A parrot happened to hear Unle's words. It went flying through the jungle screeching, "I will never die! I will never die!"

Olofín heard the parrot and caught it. "How dare you say you will never die?" Olofín asked the parrot. "Will you go against what I have commanded?"

"I repeat what men say," said the scared parrot. "I heard a man say those words."

"What man?" asked Olofín.

The parrot told him who Unle was and where he lived.

"That man is wise in his own way," said Olofín. "I should tell him to change his ways before I take steps to punish him."

Olofín sent a message to Orunlá. When Orunlá read the oddun, the message in the cowry shells, he went to visit Unle.

"Welcome, Orunlá," said Unle. "So even you now come for my advice."

"You think too highly of yourself," Orunlá told him. "Your pride and self-importance grow daily. That is what I come to talk to you about."

Unle was indignant. "You dare to talk to me that way?" he asked.

"I talk to everyone, high or low," said Orunlá. "I tell them what they have to hear."

Unle shrugged and said, "Say what you have to say."

"Olofín sends word that you must change your ways," said Orunlá. "Your head is betraying you."

"My head is just fine," laughed Unle. "Just ask anyone in this village. I well know that if my head does not sell me, there is no one to buy me." What he meant was that, as long as he thought clearly, no one could take advantage of him. "Tell that to Olofín."

Olofín, of course, was furious. He sent a terrible storm to destroy half of Unle's palace. Winds howled and knocked down the walls. Lightning crashed down and split the foundation. Rain washed away Unle's treasures. When the storm was over, Unle found himself in rags in the middle of the ruins of that which had fed his pride.

"What am I to do?" wailed Unle. "I am old and weak. How am I to rebuild my palace? I will ask Orunlá's advice" He thought a moment, then said, "I better go at night. If people find out I sought out the oracle, my reputation will be ruined." That night, Unle made sure there was no one about and went to visit Orunlá.

Orunlá said, "You must make a sacrifice, an ebó. That is the only way you can restore your fortune. But your pride is still too great, otherwise, you would have come seeking my advice during the day, not at night."

Unle made ebó. He kept his visit to Orunlá a secret. His pride still ruled his head.

A few days later, the elders of the village gathered in what was left of Unle's palace and told him, "You have given great service to the village. Now it is time for us to do something for you."

Unfortunately, these were men who knew a great deal with their heads, but they knew nothing of practical matters.

They raised a wall. A light wind came and knocked it down.

They built a roof. A bird built a nest on it and the roof came down.

The posts they cut were too long or too short. The trenches for the foundations soon filled with water. The mortar crumbled under the weight of a single stone.

Finally, the elders said, "We cannot do this job. We need a carpenter. We need a mason. We need someone who can do things, not just think about them."

While the elders had been trying to rebuild Unle's palace, Mora's nephew had gone to Orunlá for advice.

He told Orunlá, "I am skilled, but I have no work. How am I going to feed my family?"

Orunlá didn't even have to consult the oracle. He said, "Make a small ebó of thanksgiving. After you do that, go visit Unle. He has lots of work for you."

Mora's nephew did as he was told. The next day he walked to the ruined palace.

He saw the ruined walls and said, "I am a mason. I can rebuild these walls so that they are never knocked down."

He saw the fallen roof and said, "I am a carpenter. I can raise a roof that no storm can blow off."

He saw Unle and said, "I can rebuild your palace so that it will outlast the ages. It will remind people of your name after you are long gone."

All thoughts of living forever had been driven out of Unle's head by the disaster. He told Mora's nephew, "You will not only rebuild my palace. You will be my heir." His pride was gone. He thought clearly again.

They both kept their promises, which is why we know their story.

Another story related to this oddun is:

Eyeunle was the king of a small but prosperous country by the sea. He was gentle and kind.

A man was brought before him accused of theft. Eyeunle said, "Let him pay back what he stole and work for the family for a year." He didn't cut off the man's hands as the previous king would have done.

A woman was brought before him accused of adultery. Eyeunle said, "Let her apologize to her husband and walk naked for a year, her body smeared with ashes." He didn't have her nose cut off, as was the custom.

A man was brought to him accused of murder. Eyeunle said, "Let him give all his property to the family and become their slave for the rest of his life." He didn't have the murderer crushed to death with heavy stones.

Eyeunle's subjects became restless and unhappy.

"What kind of a king do we have that does not follow the laws of our ancestors?" they said.

"We want a strong man to lead us, not a weakling," they said.

Some even said, "We want a new king."

The people dared to say these things because they knew the king was tolerant, the very thing they complained about. When he was told what the people were saying, the king only said, "My people have a right to their opinions."

There was a wicked and ambitious man named Omo Locum who wanted Eyeunle's throne. He was in the middle of all discussions. His voice was the loudest, his opinions the most radical.

Omo Locum shouted, "We are men. We don't want to be ruled by a woman. I will lead the people to greatness."

When word reached Eyeunle that even his warriors were paying attention to Omo Locum's ravings, he said, "The situation has grown from mutterings to open rebellion. I must consult Orunlá's oracle."

Eyeunle went to Orunlá's house. "My kingdom is in disarray," he told the old Orishá. "What am I to do?"

Orunlá consulted his Ifá board and threw the ekuele. "This is a serious problem that requires a serious sacrifice," he said. "You must make ebó with a goat and hide its head in a secret place."

Eyeunle sacrificed a goat under Iroko, the baobab and hid the goat's head in a boat.

But while Eyeunle was visiting Orunlá and making sacrifice, Omo Locum stirred up the people, shouting, "The time is now! Let us march to the palace and get rid of Eyeunle!"

The mob shouted, "Down with Eyeunle!" and followed Omo Locum to the palace. When they got there, they found the throne empty.

"This is a great victory," shouted Omo Locum. "The coward has fled. Let us celebrate."

The people shouted, "Long live Omo Locum."

Omo Locum held a great feast by the seashore. He hired drummers, singers, and dancers. He killed a goat, butchered it, and threw the head into the sea.

The people were impressed and said, "This is the way a king should act, with feasts and important acts."

They drummed and shouted and got drunk. They made so much noise that it reached Olofín's castle in the sky.

Olofín came down and asked, "What is wrong? Why is there so much noise?"

"There is nothing wrong," they told Olofín. "We are having a feast because Eyeunle is gone and we have a new king. Long live Omo Locum!"

Olofín went to Omo Locum and asked him, "Where is the animal you have killed for the feast?"

"It's already cut into pieces," said Omo Locum. "See? Here are the rear legs. Here are the front legs. There are the ribs."

"And where is the head?" asked Olofín.

"We threw it in the sea," replied Omo Locum.

Then Olofín addressed the people, "Have you ever seen a body that could walk without a head?"

"No," said the people.

"The head is what moves the body," Olofín told them. "You have thrown away Eyeunle, your head, at the very moment you needed it to govern yourselves. Instead, you have listened to this fool," he said, pointing at Omo Locum.

Omo Locum was angry. "I am the new king," he said.

At that moment. Eyeunle came walking along the beach. "You are nothing," he told Omo Locum. "I never left my people. I am still the king."

Olofín told the people. "Here is Eyeunle, the head that navigates the ship of state."

Omo Locum shouted. "The people have spoken. They say that I am their king."

Olofín raised his arms and announced. "Let whoever can bring back this goat's head be your king."

"That's impossible," said Omo Locum. "The ocean has carried it away."

Eyeunle went to the boat where he had hidden the goat's head and brought it to Olofín.

The people were astonished. "Long live King Eyeunle!" they shouted.

They threw stones at Omo Locum. "Death to the traitor!" they screamed. People have very short memories.

Eyeunle said. "I will be your king again. The first thing I will do is to follow Orunlá's and Olofín's advice. We will never throw away the heads of the animals we sacrifice. I now understand that we see, talk, and hear through the eyes, the mouth, and the ears. Without these things, which are the head, the body is nothing."

Omo Locum was frightened. "And what will you do with me?" he asked.

"I will apply the lesson you taught me," said Eyeunle. "I will cut off your head."

9. OSÁ
Your friend is your worst enemy.

Oggún. Oyá and Eshú are warriors. They are also friends. When the need arises, they fight together against their enemies. United, they are invincible since each one brings to a battle powers and gifts that the others do not have.

A very long time ago Oggún, Oyá, and Eshú went to war against the kingdom of Elegebo.

Oggún said, "I will make our weapons out of sharp iron. They will cut through our enemies like a machete slices through weeds."

He set up his forge and began to work. He made spears and swords for the whole army. Oggún's skill was such that no shield could protect an enemy warrior against the weapons he made. Nothing could turn them aside.

When Oggún finished his work, he said, "Enough of this boring stuff! I want to chop off some heads. I want to hack off some arms. I want to see some blood spilled!" He picked up a large sword and headed towards Elegebo's army.

Oyá held him back and said, "Not so fast. This is not the time to attack. I have laid out a cunning plan that will give us victory tomorrow."

Oggún grumbled about, "Not having any fun," but he followed Oyá's advice. Oyá had as much courage in battle as Oggún. However, she did not fight in Oggún's wild, uncontrolled manner. She studied a situation and planned her actions carefully. Then, when Oyá struck, it was with the force of a hurricane. No enemy could stand in her way.

Eshú said, "Oyá is right. The enemy is shouting, 'Victory, victory!' but what they are really saying is 'Fear, defeat!'"

Eshú knew this because he had Osá. With Osá, he could see the truth behind anyone's words. He could also change a situation or a thing through the power of the words that described it. He turned words into action. That was the power of Osá.

Oyá had a lieutenant. He was a mighty warrior who behaved in an honorable manner. Oyá trusted the man completely.

Oyá went to her lieutenant and said, "Tomorrow, we will attack Elegebo's army. Oggún will lead with the wild attack he loves so much. While our enemies are busy defending themselves, Eshú will attack from the left. Elegebo's king will think that his army outnumbers ours and will send all his men against

Oggún and Eshú. I will take my army behind the hills and attack from the rear. Do you understand the plan?"

Her lieutenant said, "Yes, it is a brilliant plan. It will work perfectly. What an honor to fight besides such a great warrior!"

Oyá said, "The honor is mine that I have a warrior like you fighting next to me."

"I would lay down my life for you," said her lieutenant. But when Oyá was gone, he said, "Who does that woman think she is? She takes the honor of battle away from the men who deserve it."

Envy ate at the lieutenant's heart. Secretly, he hated Oyá.

He muttered, "Oyá thinks that she is a better warrior than the men in her army. I'll put a stop to that." What he really resented was that Oyá, a woman, had more courage and was a better warrior than he was.

"I can't kill that woman by myself," he thought. "She fights like a demon. But if Elegebo's warriors kill her, I could take her place. Then I would be the mightiest warrior in the army. I would be greater than Oyá and fight alongside Oggún and Eshú!"

The lieutenant's lust after power and glory made him crazy. Ambition blackened his heart. He decided to betray Oyá to her enemies.

That night, the lieutenant waited for the moon to set. Then he crept through the sleeping camp and made his way to Elegebó's army.

"Halt, who goes there?" shouted a guard.

"It's a friend with important information for your king," said Oyá's lieutenant.

When he was taken to the king of Elegebo, the lieutenant said, "Oh, mighty king, tomorrow your army will be attacked."

"That I know," said the king.

"Know also," continued the lieutenant, "that Oyá's army will circle behind the hills and attack you from the rear."

"That, I did not know," said the king. "What else is she going to do?"

Oyá's lieutenant told him all of Oyá's battle plan. He made sure that the king knew where Oyá was going to fight and what she was going to wear. He wanted to be sure the king knew who to kill.

"Thank you for your information," said the king of Elegebo. "You will be richly rewarded for your services."

The lieutenant thought, "Seeing Oyá dead and out of my way will be enough reward." He went back to his camp and went to sleep as if nothing had happened.

The next day, the lieutenant said to Oyá, "I, myself, will be your honor guard. I do not trust anyone else to watch your back."

Of course, what he wanted was to make sure that no one could help Oyá when she was attacked.

The battle began. Oggún led his troops shouting, "I want blood. I want heads to roll!" but Elegebo's forces melted before him. There was no one to fight.

Eshú led his warriors from the left, but Elegebo's forces came at him from both sides and pinned him down.
"Treachery," cried Eshú. "There is treachery here!"

He knew Oyá was in danger, but he could do nothing. He had to fight desperately against the enemy.

Meanwhile, the largest part of Elegebo's army attacked Oyá.

"Move to the heights," she shouted, but Elegebo's warriors blocked the way.

"Move into the valley," she cried, but she found the passes full of enemy warriors.

Every move she made was countered by Elegebo's king. Her lieutenant had told him everything Oyá had planned.

Oyá fought a desperate battle against overwhelming odds. Her warriors were slaughtered. There was no place for her to retreat. She hacked with her sword to the right and to the left and led her remaining warriors to a hill top. There was no hope of victory or rescue. She was completely surrounded, but her courage did not fail her. She fought on.

"Surrender!" yelled the king of Elegebo.

"Never!" shouted Oyá, turning aside a shower of spears and arrows with her sword. "To me lieutenant, to me!" she cried out. But the treacherous man had disappeared. Oyá stood alone, with no one to defend her. She had been betrayed by her closest friend.

"Surrender or die!" yelled the king of Elegebo.

"I will fight!" shouted Oyá.

Wounds covered her body. Blood dripped from her arms and legs. She could no longer stand and fell to the ground.

The king of Elegebo walked up to Oyá. "Surrender or die!" he told her. Oyá's lieutenant stood next to the king, grinning from ear to ear. He saw Oyá defeated. He saw his dream of glory about to come true.

"I will fight," whispered Oyá, trying to raise her sword.

"Then die," said the king, bringing his ax down upon her head.

"I will fight," thought Oyá.

Ikú (death) came for Oyá. To her surprise, she found that Oyá was still breathing.

"Your time on earth is done," said Ikú. "You must come to my kingdom."

Oyá was not afraid of Ikú. She was not afraid of anyone. "I will not die," she said. "It is not my time. I have many more battles to fight and many things to do."

"Everybody says the same thing," said Ikú. "It does not matter what you want. You must come with me."

"I will not die," said Oyá. "I will fight."

"I'm not going to return to my kingdom empty handed," said Ikú, beginning to get upset.

Oyá said, "You can come or go as you like, but I'm not dying."

Ikú didn't know what to do. No one had ever had the courage to refuse her commands.

Ikú thought, "Oyá may not be dead now, but as soon as she sees the horrors in my kingdom, she will die of fright. That will solve the problem." She then said to Oyá in a stern voice, "Come with me. Dead or not, you have to come if I say so."

"I will go with you if I must," said Oyá. "But I will not die."

Ikú took Oyá to her kingdom. "Look at what is coming for you," said Ikú.

Rotting corpses walked up to Oyá. "This is what you are," they said.

Oyá told them, "You may be rotting, but I don't have time for such silly games. I will not die."

"Oyá has courage," thought Ikú. "But it's only a matter of time before she dies of fright."

Ikú took Oyá to her torture rooms. Screaming men and women cooked in boiling oil. Wild animals ate corpses. The dead bodies felt every bite.

"This is what awaits you," said Ikú.

Oyá shrugged, "Only if I die and I will not die." She was not afraid of Ikú or her horrible tortures.

"Then you have to make your own way around here," said Ikú. "I'm busy." She left Oyá alone in a long dark tunnel.

Hands came crawling out of holes in the walls. They were like huge bloody spiders. Oyá picked up a rock and calmly smashed every single one of them.

"You're still alive?" exclaimed Ikú when she came back. She had been sure that the crawling hands would scare Oyá to death.

Oyá looked straight into the dark holes in Ikú's skull and said, "Yes, I am and I plan to stay that way. I have wars to fight and things to do."

"I give up," said Ikú. "You won't cooperate by dying of fright and I don't have the right to keep a living person in my kingdom."

"Then you must take me back to the world," said Oyá.

"I will take you back," said Ikú. "I will also honor your courage. When you return, you will be the Queen of the Cemeteries."

Ikú took Oyá back to the world. When Oyá opened her eyes, she found Oggún and Eshú at her side. Her victory over Ikú had given her tremendous personal power. It surrounded her body with a blinding radiance.

"I came to rip your killer's head off," said Oggún. "But you are still alive. I never get to have any fun."

Eshú said, "You have grown, Oyá. You are more alive now than you ever were. Your courage deserves a reward."

Osá, the power over words, was attracted to Oyá's personal power. It flowed out of Eshú and became part of Oyá.

When Eshú saw what had happened, he was glad. Osá was a gift worthy of Oyá's courage.

The power of Osá flowed through Oyá.
She said, "Victory," and Elegebo's warriors were destroyed. She said, "Vengeance," and the king of Elegebo and her treacherous lieutenant appeared before her.

To the king, she said, "You and I are enemies, but in our hate, we spoke truthfully to each other. Do you surrender?"

"I surrender," said the king.

"May your life be long so you can taste your bitter defeat," said Oyá. She turned to her lieutenant and told him, "Your lying words deceived me and they deceived you. Let Ikú appear before us."

Oyá's words were now events. Ikú appeared before her. Oyá said, "Since my lieutenant's greatest wish is to be as I was, I grant it to him. He is now yours, Ikú. Take him and show him all the things in your kingdom that you were so kind to show me."

Ikú dragged the screaming lieutenant away. "Oyá is so nice," she told him. "It's so important to keep things balanced and tidy." She smiled a horrible smile. "We're going to have such fun together!"

This was the way a friend's words became a double edged blade. This was the way a trusted friend tried to bring destruction. This is how a friend can become one's worst enemy.

10. OFUN
When a curse is born.

Ofun reached middle age without marrying and without having any children. This did not mean he did not like children. He did.

When he walked to the store, all the neighborhood children shouted, "Here comes Ofun!" They trailed behind him, laughing and shouting, for he always bought everyone candy and treats. Ofun was a kind man.

One day he was buying candy for the children when he heard a young woman say to the storekeeper, "Please give us credit for just another week. My husband is sure to get a job. Then we can pay what we owe and get a little place to live somewhere."

"I'm not a charity," said the storekeeper severely. "I am a businessman and must feed my family too. I can't give you any more credit."

The woman began to cry. Ofun asked, "What is the matter that you cry on such a beautiful day?"

"My husband lost his job last month," said the woman. "We have no money for rent, so we were thrown out of our room. Now my husband, my daughter, and I have no place to stay. We have no food to eat."

"Give her what she needs," Ofun told the storekeeper. "I will pay for it."

"The Orishás will repay you for your kindness," said the woman.

"My name is Ofun," he told her. "I'm well known in the neighborhood. If there's anything else I can do to help, let me know."

"There is one thing," said the woman, but I'm ashamed to ask."

"Don't be ashamed," said Ofun. "Hard times come to everyone. The poor have to help each other."

The woman blurted out, "Is there a little corner of your house where we can live? Just for a little while, until we can get back on our feet?"

Ofun hesitated, but then a young man came into the store holding a little girl by the hand.

"This is my husband," said the woman, "and this is my little daughter, Ananagu."

Ofun fell in love with the little girl. "If she lives in my house," he thought, "it will be as if I had a child of my own."

He told the couple, "I have a small storage room where you can stay."

The family followed Ofun to his house. He had a corner of the front room curtained off with a sheet. Behind the sheet, he kept his secrets, his mysteries.

"My house is yours," he told the family. "But what is behind the sheet is private and not to be looked at."

"We will do as you ask," said the woman.

"We will respect your things," said the man.

"I wonder what's back there," thought Ananagu, the little girl.

Ofun was happy to have the family living with him. He didn't feel alone any more. The little girl's laughter tinkled through the house and made Ofun happy.

The next day, Ofun told the little family, "I have to go out of town. Take good care of my house for me."

"We will," said the couple. "Don't worry."

Ofun bent down and said to Ananagu, "I know you are a curious little monkey. I want you to promise me you will not look behind the sheet. My secrets will lose their power if someone looks at them."

"I promise, Uncle Ofun," lisped the little girl.

They kissed Ofun and wished him a safe trip.

After Ofun left, the young man went out to look for work. The mother went to the yard to do laundry. Little Ananagu stayed in the house by herself.

She looked at the sheet and said, "I won't look, I promised."
She spent the morning playing with an old pot. She spent the
afternoon playing with a bird. Every time she passed the sheet,
she said, "I won't look. I swore I wouldn't." But every time she
passed that corner of the house, her curiosity grew.

Dinner time came. Ananagu couldn't eat.

"What's the matter, daughter?" asked her mother.

"I have a little tummy ache," said Ananagu, but it was the torture of wanting to know what was behind the sheet that didn't
let her eat.

That night, Ananagu couldn't sleep. She tossed and turned.
"Maybe there's a treasure behind the sheet," she thought. "Maybe
there are baskets full of good things to eat." She stuck her head
under the blankets. "It doesn't matter. I promised I wouldn't
look."

The long night passed and the little girl's head whirled and
turned until a new thought came, "I promised I wouldn't look
behind the sheet. I never promised that I wouldn't look over
the sheet."

When the sun came up, Ananagu crept out of bed. She went
out into the yard and got a ladder that rested against a banana
tree. Quietly, slowly, so as not to wake her parents, Ananagu
dragged the ladder into the house and leaned it against the wall
next to the sheet.

Ananagu climbed the ladder and peered over the sheet. Her
eyes widened. A little cry escaped her throat. She lost all the
strength in her hands. Ananagu fainted and fell to the floor just
as Ofun came through the door.

Ofun saw the ladder. He saw the little girl on the floor.

"My secrets has been profaned," yelled Ofun. "Their power
is gone."

The frightened couple ran into the room and knelt by the
little girl.

"My baby, my baby. What's happened?" cried the mother.

"What have you done to my child?" said the husband.

"Your daughter has broken her promise," shouted Ofun. "Your daughter has ruined my life."

"Everything is as it was," said the husband. "Nothing has been broken. Nothing has been touched."

"She looked," said Ofun grimly. "That is enough. Get out of my house. Go out into the street where you and your daughter belong. May you never know peace or happiness for the rest of your lives."

So it happened. The family lived out their lives in the street in pain and misery.

11. OJUANI

Bailing water with a basket. There is no gratitude.

The Orishás were new at their job. They were still defining their powers and responsibilities. One day they were gathered together when the conversation turned to Orunlá.

"What does that old man do?" asked Shangó. "He always has plenty to eat, but I never see him do anything."

Osaín said, "He never leaves his house or does a bit of work."

Oggún grumbled, "I spend my days at the forge. I cut back the forest but I get fewer sacrifices than Orunlá does."

"I have to throw thunder and lightning in order to eat," said Shangó. "That's harder work than banging on a piece of iron."

Oggún shouted at him, "Oh, you think so, you blowhard?"

"I know so, you good for nothing," Shangó yelled back.

A big fight started, as usually happens when these two Orishás get together.

Yemayá said, "Don't argue. It's easy to get the answer to our question. We'll visit Orunmilá and see how he lives and what kind of work he does to make such a good living."

All the Orishás agreed to this. They went to Orunlá's house.

"Look how big his house is," said Inlé.

"Look how many animals he has outside," said Orishá Okó.

"Look at all the baskets of yams and fruits," said Oyá.

All the Orishás said, "Orunlá is greedy. He never shares any of this with us."

"We've never visited his house before," Yemayá reminded them.

Orunlá opened the door and greeted them, "Welcome my friends. How nice of you to visit."

After a little polite conversation, Oggún couldn't hold still any longer and he asked Orunlá, "What is it that you do and how is it that you have all these good things when we never see you do anything?"

"What I do is this," said Orunlá. "I wait here for people to come visit me. They bring me their problems and their questions. I then look at my Ifá board and throw the cowry shells. I tell the people what the oracle says and they pay me. That's how I live."

"You mean people pay you to stare at a piece of wood?" asked Oggún.

"And to throw a few seashells around?" asked Shangó.

"It's not so easy," said Orunlá. "You have to know what these things mean."

The Orishás looked at each other. They did not believe a word of what Orunlá said. How could such an easy job pay so much?"

"He doesn't even have to leave his house," exclaimed Obbá.

"We have to test him," Osaín muttered.

The Orishás smiled at Orunlá, all the while racking their brains on how to prove whether what Orunlá had said was true or false.

Babalú-Ayé had an idea. "If what you say is true, Orunlá," he said, "Perhaps you can help us with a difficult case."

"Tell me and I'll see what I can do," said Orunlá.

Babalú-Ayé said, "Not far from here, there lives a king who has suffered for a long time from a terrible disease."

"That's awful," said Orunlá, for he is full of compassion.

"Yes it is," continued Babalú-Ayé. "His doctors have given up on him. It's a shame that he is ill because he is a good ruler."

"Why haven't you healed him?" asked Orunlá.

"His illness is a mystery to me," said Babalú-Ayé.

This was not true. The Orishás knew that the king was ill because his palace was too close to the river. The humidity had paralyzed the king.

Oggún said, "If you can heal this king we will believe what you say about the seashells."

"I will be glad to ask the oracle how to heal him," said Orunlá. "From what you say, he is a worthy man."

"But what if Orunlá finds a cure?" whispered Oyá. "We'll look like fools."

Osaín whispered back, "Don't worry. I did a working on his wood board. If it talked before, it won't talk now."

Eshú, who is everywhere and hears everything, was hidden behind the door post and overheard Osaín.

"I don't really care if that king gets well," he thought. "But I sure would like to trick these fools. How dare they think that they are tricksters? That's my job."

The Orishás said goodby to Orunlá. He went to his Ifá board immediately and asked its advice. But no matter what he did, he could not get an answer.

Eshú knocked three times and came into Orunlá's house.

"A working has been put on your board by Osaín," he told Orunlá. "There is no way that you can get an answer out of it." He also told him everything that the Orishás had said and done.

"What am I to do?" said Orunlá. "I need an answer to help the king. Also, I don't want to look like a charlatan."

"Tell the king to move his palace away from the river," said Eshú. "He is to sacrifice a rooster to me. Then he has to say a mass for the dead and give them, the Eggun, food to eat."

Orunlá sent this message to the king. To his subjects' delight, the king was up and about in a few days, as if he had never been sick.

The king declared, "Let Orunlá have what I receive as tribute during a month."

He sent an army of porters to Orunlá's house with everything that is good to eat and drink. He also sent precious pieces of cloth and many wonderful pieces of jewelry.

When the other Orishás heard of this, they rushed to Orunlá's house.

"Share your good fortune with us," they demanded. "If it hadn't been for us, you would have never even heard of the king. Part of your reward should be ours."

"You came to my house to mock and trick me," said Orunlá. "You get nothing."

Eshú told them, "You tried to lie and twist. That's my job. That's my right. You get nothing."

And so, one hand in front and one hand in back, the Orishás had to leave Orunlá's house with nothing.

12. EYILA CHEBORA
When there's war, the soldier never sleeps.

Moderiko was the king's son and it had gone to his head.

When he walked down the street, he pushed people aside and said, "Out of the way, fool. Make way for the king's son."

If he saw a good looking woman, he ran his hands over her body and said, "Such a treasure is wasted on your man. Come with me."

If the husband said, "Hey, wait a second there, that's my wife," Moderiko said, "You all belong to the king and I'm his son. She's mine."

Moderiko took all the best animals, the best food, the best beer and clothes. In short, he took the best of anything in the kingdom. He took these things as his right. He never thanked anyone.

The people hated Moderiko.

"I hate that arrogant fool," said the wronged husbands.

"He's a bully and a thief," said the farmers.

"He's not even a good lover," said the women.

The king knew about Moderiko's abuses, but there didn't seem to be anything he could do about them.

If he said anything to Moderiko, the prince replied, "What does it matter what people think? I am a prince and everything will soon be mine anyway."

The king called his counselors and told them, "It saddens me to say it, but my son is not a good man."

"That is so, our king," said the counselors.

The king went on, "I am worried. The people hate Moderiko. When I die, he will not be a good king. The people will revolt and my kingdom will be destroyed because of my son."

"You are right, o king," said the counselors. "What if we were to hold an election and let the people decide who will succeed you?"

"No," said the king. "An election will set man against man and family against family."

One of the counselors said, "I have an idea. Let whoever kills an elephant be your heir. The people will recognize and respect that man's courage and strength. There will be no disagreements."

The king liked the idea. "People won't say that I have played favorites," he said. "I decree that the man who kills an elephant with a single arrow will be my heir."

Meanwhile, Moderiko had gone to Orunlá's house to consult the oracle.

"I am a great and mighty prince," he told Orunlá. "But I want to make sure that I am the greatest and mightiest. Look and see how this can be done. And do it quick, I don't want to sit around this hut all day."

Orunlá threw the cowry shell oracle and told Moderiko, "Bring me three roosters, a goat, a bottle of aguardiente, and twelve arrows. After you make ebó with those things, I will tell you."

Moderiko left Orunlá's house and went home. He took his quiver and counted out his arrows. There were thirteen. He made a bundle with the twelve, but kept the extra arrow.

"Maybe I will find game on the way," he thought. "You never know."

He went out to the courtyard to get the animals Orunlá wanted, but then he said, "Why should I suffer loss when it's my subject's duty to pay me tribute?"

He went to his neighbor's house and took the roosters, the aguardiente, and the goat.

"Be glad that you can serve your prince," Moderiko told his neighbor.

"Thief," thought the man. He didn't dare say anything, though. After all, Moderiko was the prince.

Moderiko was on the way back to Orunlá's house with the ingredients for the ebó when a huge elephant crashed through the bushes and came trumpeting down the path at him. Moderiko took the remaining arrow from his quiver and shot the elephant dead.

Moderiko shouted, "I am great. I am the best. I am magnificent."

He left the dead elephant on the path and went on to Orunlá's house to make ebó. He wanted to make sure he was not only great, but the greatest.

Not much later, one of the villagers came walking down the path. He had heard about the king's decree and was looking for an elephant. He saw the dead elephant, took out Moderiko's arrow, and went to the king.

"I have slain the largest elephant in the jungle with this arrow," said the man. "I claim the right to be your heir."

The king said to his counselors, "Go with this man and see if he is telling the truth."

The counselors returned and told the king, "This man has indeed killed a large elephant with a single arrow."

"Let it be known far and wide that he is now my heir," said the king. "Prepare for the ceremonies."

Moderiko was making ebó at Orunlá's house while all this was going on. In the middle of the sacrifice, Obatalá appeared to him, told him of the king's decree and said, "What is yours is being claimed by another. Return to the palace."

The prince arrived at the palace just as the parrot feather crown was being placed on the liar's head.

"Stop the ceremony," shouted Moderiko. "I was the one who killed the elephant."

"No one here believes you, Moderiko," said the man. "I say that I killed the elephant."

"Moderiko is jealous," said the people.

"He's a thief," said his neighbor.

"The arrogant fool is trying to keep the kingdom," said the counselors.

"Quiet!" shouted the king. Then he said, "My son, you are making a grave accusation. I must agree with my people as to your character. Your word is not enough. We must have proof."

A counselor said, "Let the arrow that killed the elephant be placed in the middle of a hundred arrows. If Moderiko can pick out the correct arrow, we will listen to what he has to say."

"You old fool," said Moderiko. "Of course I can recognize the arrow. Get on with your test before I burn off your beard."

The hundred and one arrows were placed before Moderiko. In a second he picked his arrow out of the pile.

"This is mine," said Moderiko. "Is that proof enough for you?"

But everyone, including the king, thought, "Moderiko has managed to cheat somehow."

The counselor said, "If this is indeed your arrow, you must have some others that are just like it. Bring them."

"I will do it and make you bow before me," said Moderiko.

He went to Orunlá's house. "I need the bundle of arrows I brought you for the ebó," said Moderiko.

"They are here waiting for you," said Orunlá. "That is why I had you bring them."

Moderiko took the arrows back to the palace. "Here is a whole bundle of my arrows," he said. "They are all like the arrow that killed the elephant, as even fools like you can see."

"My son speaks the truth," sighed the king.

"The arrows are alike," grumbled the counselor. "He is the one that killed the elephant."

Even though Moderiko was still disliked by everyone, they had to agree. "He is the heir."

They cut the lying man's head off. They had to put up with Moderiko's insufferable ways.

THE ORISHÁS

The following is a list of the Orishás (divine beings) that appear in these stories. The name of the Orishá is followed by the Lukumí phrase most commonly associated with him or her.

The Orishá's qualities, fetishes, ornaments, and other qualities pertaining to the Orishá when he or she "comes down," that is, becomes physically manifest in a participant, are then discussed.

OLODUMARÉ, OLORÚN, OLOFÍN
(The Supreme Being)

> Olorún a che e (Olorún does as he wills)
> Olorún wa (Olorún is everywhere and sees everything)
> Olorún oba tobi tobi (Olorún is the greatest king on earth)
> Olofín egua wo (May Olofín help us get up)
>   [morning prayer]
> Olodumaré egbeo (May Olodumaré grant us a good day)
>   [morning prayer]

Olodumaré created the universe and the Orishás. He is tired and one should not appeal to him for help. If a person has a problem, he or she should call on the Orishás. Olodumaré does not want to be called. He is retired. All he wants is to be respected and left alone.

ELEGGUÁ, ESHÚ

Elegba (He who hits with a stick)
Eshú ota Orishá (Eshú is the adversary of the Orishás)
Ikú lori Osha (The dead give birth to the Orishás)
Laroyé! (Honor the opener of the way)

Elegguá butts in the affairs of all Orishás and humans. He is the Trickster. Elegguá is first among the Orishás. He is the first to be called and offered sacrifices in any ceremony. He is invoked first because he opens the way. He is also the last to be bid farewell.

Elegguá is the guardian of doorways and crossroads. He holds the keys of destiny. He opens and closes the door to luck or misfortune.

Eshú is the mischievous, malevolent aspect of fate. He is the incarnation of humanity's problems. Elegguá/Eshú represent the inevitable duality of good and evil.

He is the first in the group of warrior Orishás (Elegguá, Oggún, Oshosi and Osún).

SAINT: The Holy Child of Atocha.
HOLIDAY: January 1.
FETISH: Elegguá resides in a head-shaped stone (they are now made of cement) with three cowry shells making up the eyes and the mouth. The stone should be placed on the floor behind the front door. He may also be represented by a coconut.
ORNAMENTS: Elegguá likes anything used by children in their games: kites, whistles, balls, dolls, etc.

Other ornaments that surround his fetish are: Keys, a machete, a straw hat, lianas, deer antlers, hunting and fishing equipment, gold nuggets and silver coins, sticks collected in a wild place, decorated dry coconuts, large beer bottles, and goat horns.
POWER OBJECT: The garabato stick, a shepherd's crook. Sometimes it's only a crooked stick or cane.
NECKLACE: Red and black beads.

Repeat pattern: Three red beads followed by three black beads, then a red bead alternates with a black bead three times.

CLOTHING: Elegguá dresses in a frock coat and knickers with a big red chef's hat on his head. The costume is all in red and black. Sometimes, the colors alternate in stripes. The whole costume, especially the hat, is liberally ornamented with small bells and cowry shells.

OFFERINGS: Elegguá likes strong colorless liquors (vodka, aguardiente, white rum), cigars, toasted corn, smoked fish, corojo butter, and sweets. Goats, roosters and mice are sacrificed to him.

DANCE: When Elegguá "comes down," he will run and stand behind a door. He will leap and shake, making childish faces and playing children's games. Some of his movements may be quite erotic. Elegguá will joke with the participants and may disappear from sight only to return when least expected.

One of his characteristic dance steps is to stand on one foot and to twirl rapidly.

Elegguá is always handed a garabato stick. He will use it to mime opening a path through heavy bush.

The other dancers imitate Elegguá's movements, either individually or as a group, moving counter clockwise.

OGGÚN

Oggún kabu kabu (Oggún is very great)
Oggún yééé! (Welcome Oggún)

Oggún is a powerful warrior, a lover of adventure and the hunt. He is the patron of blacksmiths, mechanics, engineers, chemists, and soldiers. He has power over keys, locks, chains, and jails. Oggún is the Orishá of iron, metals, and tools as well as the owner of the forest.

SAINT: St. Peter.
HOLIDAY: June 29.
FETISH: Oggún resides in a small three-legged iron cauldron.
ORNAMENTS: Models of a machete, a shovel, a pick, a hammer, an anvil, a hoe, a knife, etc. are placed inside and around his cauldron. Oggún is also accompanied by a black dog and a snake.
POWER OBJECTS: A machete.
NECKLACE: Green and black.

Repeat pattern: Seven green beads followed by seven black beads. Then a green bead alternates with a black bead seven times.
CLOTHING: On his shoulder, Oggún wears a tiger-skin bag ornamented with cowry shells. His coat and pants are purple. The hat is flattened out. He wears a belt festooned with long fringes of palm-leaf fibers.
OFFERINGS: Oggún likes roasted yam, kola nuts, and aguardiente. Goats and roosters are sacrificed to him.
DANCES: When Oggún "comes down," he is known by two characteristic dances: In the warrior dance, he strikes the air with his machete while squatting down, advancing with one foot and dragging the other. In the laborer's dance, he harvests plants with his machete or mimes beating on the machete, using his fist like a blacksmith's hammer.

The other dancers imitate Oggún's movements, dancing around him in a circle.

OSHOSI

Oké aró! (Great hunter)

Oshosi is the hunter. He hunts with Oggún and is the only one who can get along with him.

Oshosi is the patron of those in trouble with the law. Along with Oggún, he has power over jails. He is a great magician and seer; as well as a warrior, hunter, and fisherman.

SAINT: St. Norbert.

HOLIDAY: June 6.

FETISH: Oshosi resides in a clay frying pan. It is always next to the fetishes belonging to Elegguá and Oggún.

ORNAMENTS: Oshosi owns all things associated with hunting and fishing. Next to these, there should be: Deer antlers, three arrows, three dog figurines, and a small mirror.

POWER OBJECT: A bow and arrow.

NECKLACE: Green beads. Amber or brown beads. Also common are collars made up of dark blue beads alternating with coral beads.

CLOTHING: Oshosi's clothing is a combination of Elegguá's and Oggún's. The color is lilac or light purple. His hat and his shoulder bag are made of tiger skin. Oshosi always carries his bow and arrow.

OFFERINGS: Smoked fish, deer and all game birds are sacrificed to him.

DANCES: When Oshosi "comes down," he shouts as if driving animals, "EEE," while mimicking the movements of a hunter looking for game. As Oshosi dances, he raises his left leg and mimes shooting an arrow. He dances with Oshún quite often.

OBBÁLOKE

Obbáloke is the King of the Mountain. He is Obatalá's defender.

Obbáloke is the patron of anything that is high. He is the strength of all the Orishás. His cult is not very widely spread.

SAINT: St. Robert, St. Santiago.

HOLIDAY: July 25.

INLÉ

Inlé is a male river Orishá. He is the healer of the Orishás and owns, with Oshún, the rivers and fresh water fishes.

Inlé is the patron of doctors and fishermen. He is the personification of the world as provider of human sustenance.

SAINT: The Archangel Raphael.
HOLIDAY: October 24 or September 29.
FETISH: Inlé resides in a soup toureen covered with a plate. His ornaments are placed on the plate. Next to the toureen is a little pot in which his companion Orishá's secret is kept.
ORNAMENTS: Inlé has a pedestal in the shape of a cross. Snakes and small fishes hang from each arm. Two snakes coil around the shaft of the cross, similar to a doctor's caduceus. Inlé also owns two rings and a fishing hook made out of silver or white base metal.
POWER OBJECTS: Fishing line and a net.
NECKLACE: Dark green.
CLOTHING: Inlé dresses in blue, yellow and white. His costume is heavily decorated with cowry shells. He may also dress in dark green.
OFFERINGS: Inlé likes sweet wine and cake as well as almond oil. White rams and white roosters are sacrificed to him.
DANCES: Inlé seldom "comes down." Dances are held in his honor. The dancers gather in a circle, bent over and moving the right hand from side to side, as if peering through shrubbery. They take zigzag steps.

The dancers also imitate the movements of fishermen rowing in a canoe or pulling in nets.

BABALÚ-AYÉ, CHAPONÓ, CHAKUANA, OLODÉ

Oba lou aye (The king of the world)
Baba lou aye (The father of the world)
Konfieddeno kofidenu (Compassion and clemency)
Atotó! (Silence)

Babalú-Ayé has become the Orishá of miraculous healing and compassion in the Caribbean, but he was greatly feared in Africa since he owns smallpox, leprosy, and now, AIDS. He punishes evil with disease. He's a very hot Orishá and hard to work with.

SAINT: St. Lazarus.
HOLIDAY: December 17.
FETISH: Babalú-Ayé resides in a large clay frying pan, with another turned upside down on top as a cover. A gourd, in which guinea hen feathers from a sacrifice are inserted, is placed on top.
ORNAMENTS: Babalú-Ayé has two crutches and a rattle such as lepers used in the middle ages to warn passerbys. Two figurines of white dogs with yellow spots made out of any type of material accompany him.
POWER OBJECTS: Babalú-Ayé carries an ajá, a corojo palm or coconut palm frond broom held together by a piece of sackcloth. The broom is trimmed with cowry shells and beads.
NECKLACE: White beads with blue streaks.
CLOTHING: Babalú-Ayé wears the typical dress of St. Lazarus as depicted in devotional images. It is made out of sackcloth and covered with cowry shells.
OFFERINGS: Babalú-Ayé likes fermented corn meal, stale bread and water. A mottled rooster is his sacrifice.
DANCES: Babalú-Ayé always "comes down" as a sick person, with a bent back and gnarled hands. He limps and is very weak, falling down at times. His nose is full of mucus and his voice is congested and nasal.

His movements are those of a feverish person, shooing away flies that land on his open sores with the ajá. Babalú-Ayé also makes sweeping gestures through the air to clean it of evil influences. Whoever is possessed will want to lick any pustules or wounds on those participating in the ceremony.

While bakini bakini bakini is being performed, water is poured on the floor. Everyone wets their fingers and pass them over their foreheads and the back of the neck. Later, the hand is kissed to protect against illnesses.

Babalú-Ayé is followed by a circle of dancers who dance bent over and limping.

OSAÍN

Ewé aró! (Great herbs)

"Without Osaín, there is no remedy."

Osaín owns all herbs, medicinal plants, and any vegetation with magical powers, ashé.

He only has one hand, one leg, and one eye. One of his ears is large and the other, the one that receives petitions, is small.

Since all ceremonies involve some sort of herbal preparation, Osaín must participate in them all. He is reputed to be very selfish.

SAINT: St. Silvester.
HOLIDAY: December 31.
FETISH: Osaín resides in a hanging gourd with four feathers above clay pots containing an amazing amount of items, according to which path of the Orishá is being worshipped. A turtle shell should also be nearby.
NECKLACE: White, red and yellow.

Repeat pattern: One white bead, followed by nine red beads and eight yellow beads.
OFFERINGS: Osaín likes tree sap and herbs. Goats, turtles, and red roosters are sacrificed to him.

OSÚN

Osún is Obatalá's messenger. He owns the power of witchcraft and secret ceremonies. Osún watches over the eledá, the spirit that resides in the heads of human beings.

SAINT: St. John the Baptist.
HOLIDAY: June 24.
FETISH: Osún resides in a metal cup topped by a rooster (It could also be a dove, a dog, or a lizard, according to his path) and placed on a pedestal. The base is very heavy. Its perpendicular axis is threaded through a covered receptacle.
NECKLACE: Blue, red, brown, green, yellow, black, and white beads.
DANCE: Very private and secret ceremonies.
OFFERINGS: Osún receives all the food offerings given to the other warriors. White doves are sacrificed to him.

OBATALÁ, ODDUDUÁ

Oba a ti ala (The king who dresses in white)
Alamo Rere (He who works with the best clay)
Ki oricha ya na re ko ni o (May Orichanla make us a work
    of art) [prayer of pregnant women]
Adimula (The assured one)
Obata Arugbo (The ancient father king)
Ibikeji Edumare (Olodumaré's deputy)
Odu dawa (The king who stands alone)
Epa baba! (Here's the father)

Some consider the oldest Obatalá to be Odduduá, who, with his wife Odduaremu created the other sixteen Obatalás.

"Olofín made the head, but only put in one eye. Obatalá Iba Ibo was he who put in the other eye, the mouth, gave voice and word. Then Olodumaré blew and the heart went, 'FUQUE FUQUE.'"

379

Obatalá is the Orishá of creation. He is the head of all the Orishás and Olodumaré's deputy.

Obatalá created the earth and made humanity. His purity gives him power over all that is white. He also has power over the head, its thoughts and dreams.

Obatalá is respected by all the Orishás. They seek him out to negotiate arguments. He does not like nudity or crude phrases.

Odduduá took part in the creation of the world side by side with God (Olofín), which makes him the oldest of Obatalá's avatars, the one who created Obatalá himself. Odduduá is the creator and administrator of justice. He represents the mystery and secrets of death, and has power over solitude.

SAINT: Our Lacy of Mercy.

As Odduduá, St. Manuel or Jesus Christ.

HOLIDAY: September 24.

FETISH: Obatalá resides in a white toureen.

As Odduduá, he resides in a silver coffin containing a metal skeleton. It is covered with cotton and a sheet and placed in a high place.

ORNAMENTS: Obatalá owns everything white, including silver and white metals. He has a crown with four parrot feathers, a sun, a moon, a snake and six bracelets; all made out of silver. A silver hand holds up a white scepter. He also owns two ivory eggs.

Odduduá owns two ivory balls and a white horse. He also owns an almond oil lamp which is lit every Thursday. He is surrounded by a sword or machete, a globe, two identical dolls, and a rod made of white metal supported by a round base with a white metal dove on top. Jet, coral, amber, mother of pearl and ivory also belong to Odduduá.

POWER OBJECTS: Obatalá has an iruké, a white horse tail whisk. It has a handle made of eight rings of white, black, red, and yellow beads.

As Odduduá, he carries an opá, a scepter of power, and a silver bracelet.

NECKLACE: White beads. Also 21 white beads followed by a coral bead repeated to the desired length.

As Oddudúa: Mother of pearl and coral.

Repeat pattern: sixteen mother of pearl beads followed by one coral bead.

CLOTHING: Obatalá always dresses in white. His warrior aspects have a red sash across their chest. Suns and moons are embroidered on his costume. Eight ribbons go around his waist.

As Oddudúa: White clothing with a red girdle. When the girdle is tied, the right end should be longer than the left. A hat or a kerchief covers the head.

OFFERINGS: Obatalá likes white rice and all white foods. White chickens are sacrificed to him.

As Oddudúa: White animals, although some say that no animals should be sacrificed and that only food and flowers should be offered.

DANCES: When Obatalá "comes down," he does not dance. To honor him, the dancers imitate the cautious, slow movements of the very old. If the dance is in honor of a warrior avatar, they mime a rider brandishing a sword. He speaks very softly and makes predictions, brushing clean those present with his iruké.

DADÁ

Dadá is Shangó's sister. She raised him.

She is the patron of the newborn, especially those with curly hair. She is also known as the Orishá of vegetables.

SAINT: Our Lady of the Rosary St. Raymond Nonnatus.
HOLIDAY: August 31.
FETISH: Dadá resides in a pumpkin decorated with cowry shells. A ball of indigo is placed on top of the pumpkin.
DANCE: A group dance with no particular choreography.

OGGUÉ

Oggué is Shangó's companion, the patron of all horned animals.

SAINT: St. Blas.
FETISH: Oggué resides in a small calf's horn placed inside Shangó's fetish. He is the horns of the bull that live with Shangó.
ORNAMENTS: Two calf horns painted with red and white stripes.
OFFERINGS: Doves and horned animals are sacrificed to him.
DANCE: Oggué does not "come down." During a circular dance in his honor, the dancers put their forefingers up to their foreheads, simulating horns.

AGGAYÚ

Aggayú sola dale koyu (Aggayú must be paid what is offered)

Aggayú is Shangó's father, the volcano.

Aggayú is the patron of walkers, travelers, stevedores and porters. He also protects all forms of transportation on land or air.

He owns those rivers that serve as frontiers as well as lava and earthquakes.

SAINT: St. Christopher.
Holiday: July 25.
FETISH: Aggayú resides in a wooden or clay basin painted in seven colors (black, white, red, blue, yellow, green, and brown).
ORNAMENTS: He has an oshé, a double-headed ax painted red and white with hanging decorations in yellow, green, and blue. Two calf horns and a cane should be nearby.
POWER OBJECTS: A double-headed ax and a cane.
NECKLACE: White, red and yellow.

Repeat pattern: A big white bead followed by nine red beads and eight yellow beads.

CLOTHING: Aggayú's coat and pants are dark red. Multicolored kerchiefs hang from his belt.

OFFERINGS: Aggayú likes seven big crackers with corojo butter. He accepts all fruits. Roosters and doves are sacrificed to him.

DANCES: Aggayú takes very long steps and lifts his feet extremely high, as if stepping over obstacles. At the same time, he strikes out with his oshé. He likes to lift children to his shoulders. The other dancers imitate his steps in a circle.

ORUNMILÁ, ORUNLÁ, IFÁ

Orun mila (Heaven knows who will be saved)

Orunmilá is the Orishá of wisdom and oracles. He is Obatalá's counselor.

Orunmilá is a great benefactor of humanity and its principal adviser. He reveals the future through the secret of Ifá, the supreme oracle.

He is also a great healer. Whoever ignores his advice may suffer the curse of Eshú.

SAINT: St. Francis.

HOLIDAY: October 4.

FETISH: Both of Orunlá's fetishes are consulted to obtain oracles. The ekuele, is a chain about 16 inches long threaded through charms and talismans. The talismans are made of metal, coconut shells, seeds and pieces of tortoise shell.

The até, or Ifá board, is a round piece of wood about 14 inches across. It is engraved with the four cardinal points and other symbols necessary for the babalawó's reading of the oracle.

ORNAMENTS: Kola nuts, a scale and deer antlers surround Orunmilá's fetish.

POWER OBJECTS: The Ifá board, which is used as a percussive instrument in some ceremonies. He also carries a horse hair whisk used to drive away evil.

NECKLACE: Alternating yellow and green beads.

OFFERINGS: Orunmilá likes yam puree. Black chickens are sacrificed to him.

DANCES: He has no specific dance, since he does not "come down." Dances are held in his honor.

ORISHÁ OKÓ

Orishá Okó is the Orishá of cultivated earth, agriculture, and crops. He is the patron of agricultural workers.

Orishá Okó settles disputes among the Orishás. On earth, he's an arbiter in arguments, especially among women.

He assures the prosperity of the earth and is responsible for all food. Sterile women turn to him for help.

SAINT: St. Isidore.

HOLIDAY: March 22 or May 15.

FETISH:

Orishá Okó resides in a flat porcelain tray with a little pot placed on top.

ORNAMENTS: He owns all farming tools. There should be a horizontal tile and a model of a plow with an umbrella pulled by two oxen next to his fetish.

POWER OBJECTS: An ashere, or large gourd covered in beads is shaken to call Orishá Okó. It is painted in dark red and white longitudinal stripes.

NECKLACE: Pink and turquoise.

Repeat pattern: Seven lilac or pink beads alternating with seven turquoise beads.

OFFERINGS: Orishá Okó likes everything that is cultivated. Goats and red roosters are sacrificed to him.

DANCES: Orishá Okó does not "come down." There are dances in his honor, but they do not have a set choreography.

THE IBEDYÍ (TAEBÓ AND KAINDÉ)

Be! Be! Be! (Like a child babbling)

The Ibedyí are male and female twins. Playful, gluttonous, mischievous, they receive the love of all the Orishás and are considered the patrons of all children. They are the result of the union of Shangó and Oshún.

SAINT: St. Cosme and St. Damian.
HOLIDAY: September 27.
FETISH: The Ibedyí reside in two little pots. One is painted red and white; the other, blue and white.
ORNAMENTS: The are represented by two small wooden dolls seated on miniature stools, tied together by a cord. The male doll wears Shangó's necklace. The female doll wears Oshún's necklace.

POWER OBJECTS: The Ibedyí own two rattles, two small drums, two sets of bells and two white gourds with crosses painted on the sides.
NECKLACE: The same as Shangó's and Oshún's.
CLOTHING: The twins do not "come down." There is no prescribed clothing.
OFFERINGS: They like sweets, popcorn and the treats children crave. Men suffering from impotency offer ram and goat testicles.
DANCES: The circle of dancers imitate the small skipping steps of children at play, giving little hops forwards and back.

SHANGÓ, OBAKOSO, ALAFÍN, JAKUTA

Oba ko so (The king did not hang himself)
Alafi Ilé Lodi (The castle above the clouds)
Kawó kebie sile!

Shangó owns fire, thunder, and lightning. He also controls war and the bata drums. Shangó is the patron of masculine beauty as well as music and dance.

He represents a great number of human virtues and imperfections. A hard worker, courageous, a good friend, a soothsayer and a healer, Shangó is also a liar, a womanizer, likes to provoke fights, is a braggart and a gambler.

SAINT: St. Barbara.

HOLIDAY: December 4.

FETISH: Shangó resides in a wooden tub with a cover, preferably made out of cedar wood. It is painted red and white and may have the shape of a castle.

ORNAMENTS: Shangó's image, an Indian warrior, carries a cedar and palm wood scepter. It ends in a sharp point or in the shape of a double hatchet as a symbol of divinity. He also owns a shekere made out of a turtle shell. His fetish is also surrounded by a black horse, a tambourine, a bright red flag, three hatchets a club, and a scimitar.

POWER OBJECTS: Shangó carries a double-headed hatchet, a cup, and a sword.

NECKLACE: Red and white.

Repeat pattern: Six red beads follow six white beads. Then, red and white alternate six times.

CLOTHING: Shangó wears a loose shirt and pants with red and white stripes. Sometimes, he wears cut off pants with the legs cut in points. His chest is bare. He might also wear a short jacket with red and white stripes and a crown in the shape of a castle.

OFFERINGS: Shangó likes plantains, corn meal and okra. Rams and red roosters are sacrificed to him.

DANCE: Shangó will butt with his head and do three forward rolls towards the drums. He opens his eyes extremely wide and sticks out his tongue. Characteristic movements are waving his hatchet and grabbing his testicles. No other Orishá jumps higher, dances more violently or makes stranger gestures. He commonly eats fire.

Shangó's dances are either warlike or erotic. As a warrior, he waves his hatchet and makes threatening gestures. As a lover, he tries to demonstrate the size of his penis, bumps and grinds and acts very lasciviously with the women present.

The circle of dancers imitate his movements and join in his sexual exhibitionism.

YEGGUÁ

Yirró!

Yegguá is the Queen of the Cemetery, a title she shares with Oyá. She lives among the tombs and the remnants of the corpses, which she turns over to Oyá.

Yegguá is old, a virgin and extremely chaste. Her oracles have great prestige.

Yegguá demands that her "children" remain lifelong virgins, avoiding any contact with men. Her cult is not very popular.

SAINT: Virgin of Mt. Serrat.
FETISH: Yegguá resides in a small doll house placed on a high shelf in an inner room of the house. It can also be nailed on the wall. Her house should be placed far from Oshún's fetish.
ORNAMENTS: Her belongings are a doll, and a basket or a small pot.
NECKLACE: Pink beads.
CLOTHING: Yegguá wears a pink dress. The wide skirt is bound at the waist by a sash of the same material. She wears a crown heavily decorated with cowry shells.
OFFERINGS: Female goats are sacrificed to her.
DANCES: Yegguá seldom "comes down." When she does, she mimes tying a bundle with twine. Her demeanor is somber. She is very shy with men, since she is a virgin, and she does not dance.

OYÁ, YANSÁN

Obirin t' o t' ori ogun da rungbon si (The woman who grew
  a beard due to war)
Efuele ti da gi l'oke l'oke (The wind that uproots the trees
  from on high)
Ilé Yansán (Yansa's house, the cemetery)
Okwo chon chon ilé Yansa (He died. He went to Yansa's
  house)
Epa hei! (Praise the wind)

Oyá "owns" shooting stars and the wind, whether breeze or hurricane. One of Shangó's wives, she is violent and impetuous, loves war and accompanies Shangó on his campaigns.

Oyá also "owns" the cemetery and lives at its door, being the gate of death.

SAINT: Our Lady of Candlemas.
HOLIDAY: February 2.
FETISH: Oyá resides in a porcelain toureen painted in nine colors.
ORNAMENTS: Her image has a crown with nine points from which hang nine ornaments: A pick, a hoe, an Oshosi fetish, a lightning bolt, a scythe, a stick, a mattock, a rake, and a hatchet. She also owns a rainbow and a shooting star.
POWER OBJECTS: Oyá carries a black horsetail whisk, an iruké, and nine copper bracelets.
NECKLACE: Black and white.
  Repeat order: Nine black beads followed by nine white beads. Then, black and white beads alternate nine times.
CLOTHING: Oyá dresses in skirts made of the dried fibrous tissue found on the upper part of the royal palm frond, yagua, and the fan palm. She also wears an over skirt made of hanging kerchiefs in nine colors. The remainder of her costume is flowered crinoline. A strip of the same material, or multi-colored ribbons, is wound around her head.

OFFERINGS: Oyá likes white rice with eggplant and black eyed peas. Black female goats and black chickens are sacrificed to her.

DANCES: When Oyá dances, she shakes the black horsetail whisk to clean bad influences from the air. Her dance is very frenetic, very fast, delirious. She carries a flaming torch in her right hand, making a fiery whirlwind as she spins to the left.

OSHÚN, YALODÉ

> Oshún Gbó (Oshún is ripe)
> Oshún sekese ofigueremo (The beauty of the rivers, protect us)
> Yeye kari, yeyeo (The sweet, the adorable)

Oshún is the Orishá of love, femininity and sweet water. She embodies coquetry, grace and female sexuality. She helps women give birth. Oshún is Shangó's favorite mistress/wife.

SAINT: Our Lady of Charity.

HOLIDAY: September 8.

FETISH: Oshún lives in a multicolored soup toureen full of river water. Yellow predominates.

ORNAMENTS: Oshún's image has a halo with five sharp points. She is also surrounded by small gold fishes, shrimp, conch shells, small boats, mirrors, jewels, coral, embroidered sheets and kerchiefs rattles, shekeres and cowbells. Oshún owns all objects associated with female beauty: Brushes, make up, etc.

POWER OBJECTS: Oshún fans herself with a yellow sandalwood or peacock feather fan. She jingles five gold bracelets. A half moon, two oars, a star, a sun, and five little bells are embroidered on her dress. These objects change according to which of her paths is manifested.

NECKLACE: Amber beads, also coral and amber beads.

Repeat pattern: Five coral beads followed by five amber beads. Then, amber and coral alternate five times.

CLOTHING: Oshún wears a yellow dress cinched by a girdle with a rhomboid stomacher. The dress is hemmed in points with hanging jingle bells.

OFFERINGS: Oshún likes spinach and shrimp, honey and any type of sweets. Turtles, neutered goats and white chickens are sacrificed to her.

DANCES: Oshún's dance is very sensual. She laughs like Yemayá and shakes her arms to make her bracelets jingle. Oshún runs her hands over her body to emphasize her charms. As she dances, she makes very voluptuous movements and asks men for sex with extended hands and thrusts of her hips. She asks for oñi, honey, craving the sweetness of sex and life.

She mimics rowing a small boat and grinding in a large pestle.

When she combs her hair, admiring herself in a mirror, she is very haughty and looks down her nose at those around her.

YEMAYÁ, OLOKÚN

Yeye omo eja (The mother of fishes)
Obiri adu adu (The woman with very black skin)

Yemayá is the Orishá of the oceans. She is the epitome of motherhood. From her comes all life and all the Orishás. She also personifies the destructive aspects of the sea.

She has a huge amount of paths, each one with its own rhythm and characteristics.

SAINT: The Virgin of Regla.
HOLIDAY: September 7.
FETISH: Yemayá resides in a blue and white soup toureen painted with large flowers.
ORNAMENTS: Her fetish is surrounded by a sun, a full moon, an anchor, a life preserver, a boat, seven oars, seven silver rings, a key, and a star. All of these objects are made out of silver or white base metal. Her altar is decorated with nets, sea shells, sea horses, starfish, and anything to do with the sea.

POWER OBJECTS: Yemayá carries an agbegbe, a peacock or duck feather fan decorated with mother of pearl and cowry shells. She also has a horsetail whisk with blue and white beads. A bell is rung when her worshippers call.

NECKLACE: Crystal and blue.

Repeat pattern: Seven crystal beads followed by seven blue beads. Then, crystal and blue alternate seven times.

CLOTHING: Yemayá wears an embroidered crepe mantle. She waves her agbegbe. Her dress is navy blue and has blue and white streamers, with little tinkling bell sewn all over it. A wide cloth belt with a rhomboid stomacher goes around her waist.

OFFERINGS: She likes watermelons, banana chips and pork cracklings. Lambs, ducks and fish are sacrificed to her.

DANCES: When Yemayá "comes down," she gives loud peals of laughter. Her body moves like the waves of the ocean, first gently, then, as if agitated by a storm. She proceeds to turn like a waterspout. She may mime swimming and diving into the ocean and bringing up treasures for her "children." She also mimes rowing.

The other dancers circle around her. They make wavelike movements that grow faster and faster until they begin to twirl.

OBBÁ

Shangó obá o mangue alado yina (Obá is the first wife of the prince, Shangó)
Obá ishi!

Obbá represents conjugal fidelity and sacrifice.

She is a matronly Orishá with power over lakes and ponds. She shares ownership of the cemetery with Yegguá and Oyá.

SAINT: St. Rita, St. Catalina of Palermino.

HOLIDAY: November 25.

FETISH: Obbá resides in a white toureen painted with flowers.

ORNAMENTS: She owns a wooden anvil, two keys, a shield, a mask, a toothed wheel, a book, armor, and ears. All items are made out of wood and copper.

POWER OBJECTS: Obbá has five golden bracelets like Oshún's.

NECKLACE: Alternating yellow and pink beads.

OFFERINGS: Doves are sacrificed to her.

DANCES: Obbá cannot dance. Dances are performed in her honor She does not "come down." A designated "slave" in the center of the dancers' circle is whipped while the chorus sings. The face of the "slave" is covered with a mask.

BIBLIOGRAPHY

Arostegui, Natalia Bolivar. LOS ORISHÁS EN CUBA (Havana, 1990).

Cabrera, Lydia. ANAGO; VOCABULARIO LUCUMI (Miami, 1970).

Cortez, Julio Garcia. PATAKI (Miami, 1980).

——. EL SANTO (LA OCHA) (Miami, 1971).

Sandoval, Mercedes Cros. LA RELIGION AFROCUBANA (Madrid, 1975).

ACKNOWLEDGMENTS

I would like to thank Oggún Onira and Oshún Olobá who made this possible along with mãe Suelen de Oxum and pai Chico de Ogum.

I would also like to thank the many followers of the religion who had the patience to tell me these stories and put up with my endless questions.

GLOSSARY

BEMBÉ
In Cuba, bembé is a generic term that refers to drumming cer-emonies where the rhythms related to the Orishás are played. The rhythms, songs, and dances are derived from the Yorùbá tribe in present-day Nigeria and probably influenced by other cultures in Africa.

EBÓ
An ebó is any sacrifice or offering to the Orishás. In the case of an initiation, the ebós are the sacrifices the novice must make to appease the Orishás offended by his or her past faults or evil actions.

GÜEMILERE
It is the most unstructured part of traditional batá (a trio of hourglass shaped double-headed drums played during religious rituals to the Orishás) drumming ceremonies. The güemilere follows the oru seco (drumming only) and the oru cantado (drumming accompanied by singing). The drumming during the güemilere goes on for much longer and uses more insistent rhythms than those used in other parts of the oru. The acceler-ated repetitions are meant to cause a trance state in which the Orishá "comes down," takes possession, of the participants.

IFE-ILÉ

Located in south-western Nigeria, in the Osun state, it is the spiritual center of the Yorùbá people.

LUKUMÍ

Lukumí is the Yorùbá word for "friend." It was used in Cuba, and to a lesser extent is still used, to designate group identity. Since the Yorùbás in Cuba went around saying "Lukumí" to each other, the word became a generic term for the Yorùbás and their language. So, you can say, "she's Lukumí (a descendent from the Yorùbás) and practices Santería." You can't say, "she practices Lukumí." You could, however, say, "she practices the Lukumí religion."

OMIERO

A purifying liquid made from a a mixture of rain water, river water, sea water, and holy water, aguardiente, honey, corojo or cocoa butter, powdered eggshell, pepper, and various other herbs and ingredients particular to the mixture's purpose. It is brewed by immersing a live coal wrapped in a fresh taro (Malanga) leaf into the mixture, which has been steeping since the the previous day.

SANTERÍA (OSHA, LA REGLA)

Santería orginated in Cuba as a combination of the Western African Yorùbá religion and Catholicism. It was developed out of necessity by the African slaves so that they could continue to practice their native religion in the New World. The Catholic saints became the new guises of the African deities, the Orishás. With the abolition of slavery in 1880, Eulógio Gutiérrez, an ex-slave from Matanzas, decided to return to Africa. The Orishás demanded that he return to Cuba and found the Rule of Ifá, the sacred order of the babalawós. Around 1900, a babalawó in Matanzas, Lorenzo Samá, became worried about the lack of unification among the Yorùbá cults. Along with a "daughter" of Shangó, Latuan, he worked to unify the different cults into a single liturgical body, which he named the Rule of Ocha (La Regla de Ocha). His ideas gained general acceptance and modern Santería was born.

YORÙBÁ

The Yorùbá are a large ethno-linguistic group or nation in West Africa. The Yorùbá constitute approximately thirty percent of Nigeria's total population, and number upward of forty million individuals throughout the region of West Africa. Yorùbá is the first language of West Africa and is spoken by populations in Southwestern Nigeria, Togo, Benin, and Sierra Leone.

ABOUT THE AUTHOR

Although LUIS MANUEL NÚÑEZ lived in Cuba until age ten, "the American educational system proved to be very effective." He found his parents' beliefs merely quaint. Marriage to a Cuban woman revived his heritage, leading to his first book, SANTERÍA: A PRACTICAL GUIDE TO AFRO-CARIBBEAN MAGIC (Spring Publications, 1992). He is currently conducting research in Brazil on the Afro-Brazilian religious traditions.